At Home on the Range

other cookbooks from Gibbs Smith, Publisher

COWBOY POETRY COOKBOOK
Menus and Verse for Western Celebrations
Cyd McMullen and Ann Wallace McMullen

PAT OPLER

PEREGRINE SMITH BOOKS

First edition
96 95 94 93 92 8 7 6 5 4 3 2 1

This is a Peregrine Smith Book, published by
Gibbs Smith, Publisher
P.O. Box 667
Layton, Utah 84041

Design by J. Scott Knudsen
Manufactured in the United States of America

Many of the pictures are from *Food and Drink: A Pictorial Archive from Nineteenth Century Sources* by Dover publications.

Library of Congress Cataloging-in-Publication Data

Opler, Pat.
At home on the range cooking school cookbook / Pat Opler.
p. cm.
Includes index.
ISBN 0-87905-466-2 (hb) — ISBN 0-87905-465-4 (pbk.)
1. Cookery. I. Title.

TX714.065 1992
641.5—dc20 92-5924
CIP

In recent years, the small Wyoming community of Jackson Hole rallied around the effort to preserve a portion of a beautiful and traditional Hereford ranch—the Hardeman Meadows. The community raised hundreds of thousands of dollars through events and gifts, large and small. In a partnership with the Jackson Hole Land Trust, Teton County made the unprecedented commitment of funds for the preservation of this critical scenic corridor.

The stunning red Hardeman barns, at the base of Teton Pass, are to come alive again. Their restoration will benefit the community while retaining the traditional character of a Jackson Hole ranch. Ed and Pat Opler have personally undertaken this restoration. All proceeds from *At Home on the Range* will contribute to this project.

CONTENTS

FOREWORD 9
ACKNOWLEDGMENTS 11
INTRODUCTION 13

SPRING 18

Strawberry Time 20
Finnish Bread Bakers Do Hapanleipä Right 23
En Papillote Cooking Keeps Food Under Wraps 26
Pain d'Hier: Yesterday's Bread 28
Pasta, No? Pasta Si! 32
Real People Do Eat Quiche 40
Too Much Parsley? Read This 43
Lemons, Lemons and More Lemons 46
Cheesecake: The Ultimate Indulgence 50
Swedish Church-Social Delights 56

SUMMER 60

Just Help Yourself to the Flowers 62
Raspberry Season 67
Summer's Highlight: Homemade Ice Cream 72
The Glorified Meat Loaf: Pâtés and Terrines 76
The Survival of the "Hostess Cupcake" 82
A Half-Empty, or Half-Full Coffeepot 85
Blue-Ribbon Sourdough 89
Tians Meld Last Flavors of Summer 94
Stamp Out Brown Lettuce 98
Tarts Are Really Just Fancy Pies 102
A Vegetable Tart from Provençe 105
Sundried Tomatoes Are Easily Made at Home 110

AUTUMN 114

The Pulchritudinous Pear 116

"Don't Shoot, Miss Pat...Them's Tweeties 121

Polenta: A Garnish for Garden Warblers 126

Chocolate: A Way of Life for the Oplers 129

Pumpkin Delights 133

Idaho Potatoes: A Culinary Treasure 138

Dried Wild Mushrooms 144

Hazelnuts: America's Culinary Outcast 150

Raisins Are Something to Dance About 154

Italian Sweets to Tempt Even the Hardhearted 158

Making the Most of Our Freshwater Trout 162

WINTER 168

A Lust for Rice: Creamy Risotto 170

Bread Baking Can Be Fun! 176

Croissaant...Kwa-Sawn...Crescent 182

In Search of Better Christmas Cookies 184

Making Brioche: A Heady Effort 188

Tea & Scones: A Civilized Indulgence 190

Soup: The Whole Is the Sum of Its Parts 192

Turn Over a New Turnover 198

Seeds: The Gift of the Opium Poppy 202

INDEX 205

Foreword

Seasoning by seasons is but one of the reasons that you will be entranced by this striking departure from conventional cookbookery. Another is that its heritage is in a class by itself—the classes at Pat Opler's At Home on the Range Cooking School.

This book speaks for itself. I speak for its author from my background years in the world of food.

As a frequent diner at my Baker Restaurant in Chicago, Pat was always interested and articulate in culinary matters. She has been a voluntary assistant at many of my food demonstrations for charity. And I, in turn, have been fortunate to provide catering service for major international events she conducts as a socialite—sophisticated and with impeccable and innovative taste. It has been a joy to hear her recipe and menu suggestions and pursue them to perfection.

I shall always relish the hospitality as a guest at Pat's home. I have been an observer and learner at her classes.

It must, and can only, be said that At Home on the Range is a necessity for all who cook, or even for those who get pleasure just from reading.

Louis Szathmáry
Chef Laureate
Johnson & Wales University
Providence, Rhode Island

Acknowledgments

cookbook reflecting a life devoted to the cooking and sharing of wonderful foods could be compared to a long simmering kettle of soup. Subtle flavorings convey a quality that deeply influences the overall taste and satisfaction, hard to identify but undeniably important. Many names and occasions, specifics no longer within my memory, have left an indelible impression on my kitchen. Every person, place and taste has exerted a special influence reflected in the overall flavor of these pages.

Other seasonings and ingredients are more pronounced and dominant in a soup. Such are the lessons, encouragement, sharing and enthusiasm of Julia Child, Simone Beck, Chef Louis Szathmáry, Dottore Enrïco Massimo Carle, Bernard Clayton, Richard Nelson, Nelly Dancer, Nina Bégué, Lydie Marshall, Mary James Lawrence, Signora Irene Sanna, Signore Lino Morganti, Joan Campbell, Diane Holuigue, Robert Hülsmann, Doris Hülsmann, At Home on the Range students, and my dear friend and colleague Madelaine Bullwinkel. I thank you all.

My parents' love of good food and the pleasures of cooking brought me to the stove.

My husband, Ed Opler, Jr., and our family have endured and enjoyed my years of marathon cooking. I thank them for sharing in my fun.

To my friends and colleagues, who shared their words in praise of food and friendship, my encouraging and food-loving editor, Madge Baird, and my publisher, Gibbs M. Smith, I say thank you for bringing the *At Home on the Range Cooking School Cookbook* to the table.

Pat Opler
March 1992

COOKING DEPT.
GIRLS NORMAL SCHOOL

INTRODUCTION

Throughout years of teaching and writing about food I have come to realize that kitchen confidence is the essential ingredient in successful cooking. In my At Home on the Range cooking classes, students express a renewed excitement for cooking as they master basic culinary techniques, encounter new ingredients, and learn about what really happens when foods are combined and cooked. Eight students participating together to complete each day's menus generate a wide variety of questions and problems from which students *and* teacher learn. Confidence is built by experience, and in At Home on the Range cooking classes students of all levels of experience work together, "hands-on," as they discover their own new understandings and skills. Happy reports from students returned home make it clear that their newly found kitchen confidence has energized the entire approach to their cooking.

Today's busy lifestyles necessitate that the goodness of food not be directly proportional to the number of hours spent at the stove. Not all pasta sauces are the traditional long-simmered ones of my youthful spaghetti days. Quick skillet-cooked sauces bring a pasta dish to the table easily within thirty minutes. No time, you think, to make bread? I've whipped up a chewy Focaccia in one hour and topped it with bits of leftover cheeses and salad vegetables as a bonus. A hankering to serve a homemade dessert can be satisfied in less than thirty minutes: make NZ's 15-minute Cheesecake first thing in the morning and leave it to complete its baking in the cooling oven. It will be ready to serve when you return to the kitchen to complete dinner preparations.

The real keys to "control cookery" are feeling comfortable with basic culinary techniques and choosing recipes and menus which respect the demands of your lifestyle. No matter how much you may love to cook, you must assess your schedule honestly. What are your goals for the day, for the week, for the dinner? Make certain your menus allow you to enjoy the creative opportunities cooking and serving your meals offer. Don't crowd menus with too much challenge. You'll be glad when you've learned to bone a trout or to make Italian sausage. You will also be happy that you decided to reserve a bit of last night's Chocolate Cream Pie filling to serve tonight as Chocolate Mousse.

Even complex-looking recipes such as Brioche and Croissants can be reorganized to respect scheduling demands. Recipes throughout *At Home on the Range* respect time. Tips are highlighted throughout. In each cookbook section, certain culinary topics are explained in depth. Basics are listed in the tables of contents and the index. Knowing HOW to control one's culinary projects generates confidence and an eagerness to try new ideas. Dishes we read about, see in our travels and confront on menus, become less mysterious and intimidating.

Organization is critical to successful and stress-free cooking. While soups and sauces are gently bubbling to marry their seasonings, and yeast breads are patiently rising as they develop flavor and texture, the well-organized cook is free to play tennis, to look after some paper work or perhaps to approach another recipe needing closer attention. By overlapping cooking tasks which need less policing with recipes that are more challenging, the well-planned menu will allow the cook more flexibility in her schedule. I often use this flexibility to investigate a new technique, ingredient or recipe.

Many steps can be accelerated or slowed with only the positive results that the cook's scheduling needs *and* culinary expectations are met. *Acceleration*, to my At Home on the Range students, often means literally turning up the heat. An attempt to reduce necessary cooking time, this technique demands stove-side attention and, usually, continuous stirring. For example, classic Italian Risottos were traditionally started, cooked and served in one rather tedious and lengthy process. In my directives for risotto-making, after an earlier precooking of the Arborio rice (done up to twelve hours in advance) the cooking is completed in two final high-speed evaporations taking only five to ten minutes just before serving.

Evaporation of liquids is a fast way to intensify flavors for sauces and soups. Pasta sauces may be combined in a large skillet and cooked rapidly to meld flavors and reduce liquids just to the correct pasta-coating consistency. Quick Provençal Tomato Sauce can be made in half the specified time, but beware: vigilance and constant stirring are required to prevent scorching or sticking.

In the case of more time-consuming recipes one might be tempted to accelerate, such as Croissants, Brioche, Crème Fraîche and Sourdough Bread, I recommend manipulating the timing in the recipes to meet scheduling difficulties. It is not necessary to complete these tasks without interruption. Life simply won't permit this! Recipes like these encourage flavor and texture development by the gentle nurturing of yeast and dairy culture micro-organisms. Acceleration of this process will either kill the organisms or sacrifice results.

Planning ahead will allow for the easy and leisurely incorporation of bread-making into your schedule. Yeast doughs may be covered and successfully refrigerated to retard rising time with the added advantage that the chilled, risen dough will rise more slowly when a second rise is required. When a recipe, such as for Limpa Bread, instructs the baker to let bread rise several hours, I assume this can also mean all afternoon or all night. I have yet to be unhappily surprised. Sourdough bread depends upon flavor and texture for its reputation. Drag this process out to suit yourself. Give it an extra rise if you need to. Crème fraîche needs to mature, too. This is a task requiring advance planning. However, as it keeps, refrigerated, for two to three weeks, why not make it whenever you have time. Keep some on hand. It's a great substitute for sour cream, whipped cream and buttermilk in most recipes.

Many recipes may be made quickly without sacrificing quality. Some may even use commercially prepared ingredients. Such recipes are meant to meet scheduling demands. Busy First Lady's Soup and Roquefort Soup are two quick and easy foundations for light luncheon or supper menus. I'd serve First Lady's Soup with a crunchy salad of mixed greens tossed with toasted walnut pieces, a cheese board of aged domestic white cheddar, a nutty blue-veined Stilton and a creamy St. André or Camembert, and my French Whole-Wheat Baguettes. Dessert could be fresh fruit and Poppy Seed Cookies or a hunk of Texas Sheet Cake (with or without Vanilla Nutmeg Ice Cream).

The richer Roquefort Soup is a bit more refined and could nicely precede a slice of savory Provençal tart. One-rise Italian Bread would be interesting spiked with coarsely ground mixed peppercorns and a savory Herbed Rice Salad alongside a bouquet of springy watercress to round out the meal. How about a Pear Mousse for dessert?

Intelligent menu planning is a must! What is "intelligent menu planning"? In my "On the Range" newspaper column, At Home on the Range cooking classes, and in my undocumented culinary activities, I think carefully as I approach every day, every week and every meal. My goals are to lessen the burdens of everyday cooking, provide healthy, interesting and delicious meals and to enjoy it all while carrying on a busy and demanding lifestyle. When I make breakfast for family or houseguests, I assess what I need to use, what needs to be reserved for later use, and how I can be efficient as I feed the forces. For example, consider bacon. Why cook it for breakfast and then cook more later to toss in a salad? I admit to being a fast starter in the morning. If you aren't, think such things out the evening before as you put away dinner's leftovers.

Leftovers are a culinary opportunity that makes good sense. Look for chances to complete two tasks in one. Make my Pork and Veal Pâté as a hot meatloaf for dinner, and serve it with mustard and pickled onions the next day as a chilled pâté. Cook extra pasta or rice to redesign as salads for another meal. Reserve a little of the unfrozen ice cream mixture to serve as a sauce beneath a tart, cake or fruit.

Divide the tasks required in a recipe. Quiche is definitely best when it is hot from the oven. But by making, forming and freezing the pastry shell (why not make more than one?) well in advance, you have already made the task simpler. The quiche custard mixture can be made, covered and refrigerated the day before, as well. Only assembling and baking the quiche will be required at mealtime.

Intelligent cooking means assessing our tasks and lives realistically. What amount of time do we really have? What do we want to accomplish by our cooking? Our goals will vary from day to day. How can recipes we wish to cook be accomplished in ways that respect our scheduling needs? Intelligent cooking means taking control. Control cookery is the right approach for the economic, physical and psychological demands for health in the 1990s. Use my tips to guide you to control your own cooking. Before you realize it, you will be applying control cookery attitudes all by yourself. I did!

At Home on the Range is the culmination of my many years as a food professional. An increasingly demanding lifestyle and a desire to continue investigating and sharing my interest in the world of food naturally evolved into a culinary survival technique I call "control cookery." As *At Home on the Range* demonstrates, busy lives and wonderful home cooking need not be mutually exclusive.

PAT OPLER

All in all, I admit that Alice is, in her own way, a pretty good eater herself. The last time she failed to order dessert, for instance, was in the spring of 1965, in a Chinese restaurant that offered only canned kumquats. I have been with her in restaurants when she exulted over the purity and simplicity of the perfectly broiled fresh sea bass she had ordered, and then finished off the meal with the house specialty of toasted pound cake covered with ice cream and chocolate sauce. I suppose her only serious weakness as an eater—other than these seemingly uncontrollable attacks of moderation—is that she sometimes lets her mind wander between meals…There are times when in a foreign country, she will linger in a museum in front of some legendary piece of art as the morning grows late and I become haunted by the possibility that the restaurant I have chosen for lunch will run out of garlic sausage before we get there…I say on these occasions, in a stage whisper…"Alice, Alice, let's eat!"

CALVIN TRILLIN

Alice, Let's Eat: Further Adventures of a Happy Eater, (Random House, 1978). Used by permission of the author.

SPRING

Whether it is an acceleration of pace, the softening of the soil, or the return of migrating warblers, there is definitely something exciting about the return of spring. Days get longer and life is invigorated by warmed afternoons. Attitudes green up with renewed life in the garden. Outdoor activities beckon windows open. We renew acquaintance with our old friends fresh herbs, rhubarb and strawberries.

Easier and lighter fare comes to mind. Steamed foods and pastas benefit from the vigorous fresh produce blossoming on grocers' displays. Nature re-energizes our kitchens with its lively freshness. Schedules speed up, outdoor activities vie for time, and it becomes tricky to get everything done. Good planning and efficiency come naturally with the bounty of spring.

APPETIZERS, FIRST COURSES, SALADS, AND SOUPS

Basic Pasta 33
Crispy Brie or Camembert Wedges 30
Easy Crustless Quiche 41
Gnocchi 36
Panzanella 31
Pasta with Garlic and Chilies 37
Pasta with Ham and Cognac 38
Pasta with Tomatoes, Olives and Capers 39
Peas Potage 44
Pretty Herby Pasta 35
Quiche Lorraine 41
Russian Garden Soup 45
Spinach Pasta 34

FISH AND MEATS

Chicken *en Papillote* 27
Parslied Cube Steaks 44
Salmon *en Papillote* 27
Trout *en Papillote* 27

BREADS

Finnish Sour Rye Flat Bread 24
Scandinavian Limpa Bread 25
Swedish Cardamom Rolls 57

SWEETS

Almond Coffeecake 59
Apples or Pears *en Papillote* 27
Cheese Strudel 53
Cheesecake 51
Danish Butter Cookies 58
Fifteen-Minute Cheesecake 52
Frozen *Kolackys* 54
Fruit Quiche 42
Gratinéed Berries 21
Lemon Madeleine Cakes 47
Lemon Tart 49
Strawberries Romanoff 21
Strawberry Whipped-Cream Cake Roll 22
Torta di Ricotta 55

ACCOMPANIMENTS

Old-Fashioned Lemonade 48

BASICS

En Papillote Cooking 27
Leftover Bread 29
Pasta 33

Strawberry Time

They're fragole in Italy, fresas in Spain, fraises in France, erdbeeren in Germany, mansikoita in Finland, and strawberries in America.

In spring my fancy turns to strawberries. Memories of the perfect, fragrant, red ripe buds of fruit waft into my culinary memory. My mouth is watering!

Banners shout "Erdbeeren Zeit" (Strawberry Time) in Dusseldorf. Cascading berries gleam and roll from precariously abundant displays which garnish the Helsinki harbor. Teeny little fraises de bois lie in wait for the impecunious French housewife or impetuous American gourmande in Jarnac, France.

The world relishes the arrival of strawberry season. Bright red berries punctuate the table. Paint boxes spring open to capture their fleeting jewellike essence. Picnickers caress the treasures. Chocolate enrobes them. Hands get sticky. Lips are reddened. Taste buds sing.

Ed Opler's Strawberries Romanoff

Serves 12

Ingredients

4–5 pints fresh strawberries
2 tablespoons sugar
1 pint whipping cream
1 teaspoon confectioners' sugar
juice of 1/2 lemon
1 ounce dark rum
2 1/2 ounces Cointreau
1 1/2 quarts best-quality vanilla ice cream, slightly softened

Procedures

1. Wash and dry whole or halved berries.
2. Sprinkle sugar over the berries. Toss lightly.
3. Beat whipping cream with confectioners' sugar until almost stiff.
4. Fold in fresh lemon juice, rum and Cointreau.
5. Fold whipped cream mixture into softened ice cream.
6. Spoon ice cream mixture over berries in individual bowls.

Gratinéed Berries

Ingredients

Berries of your choice, frozen or fresh, to make a single layer in each heat-resistant serving dish, ramekin or cocotte.
1–2 teaspoons complementary liqueur per serving
1 pint whipping cream
2 egg yolks
3 tablespoons confectioners' sugar
granulated sugar for top of gratinéed dessert

Necessary Equipment:

ramekins, cocottes or custard dishes
broiler or propane torch

Procedures

1. Preheat oven to 500°F.
2. Spread desired amount of fruit in single layers in individual serving dishes. Sprinkle with liqueur.
3. Beat whipping cream until it begins to mound softly, and then continue to beat it with the yolks and sugar until stiff.
4. Spoon the cream mixture over the berries. Don't fill the entire dish because the cream is going to puff up in the oven and will spill over and burn.
5. Cook the berries and cream mixture in the hot oven until puffy and irregularly browned.
6. When desired look is achieved, remove from oven carefully and sprinkle with granulated sugar, if desired.
7. Caramelize this sugar with a hand torch or under a hot broiler.
8. Immediately serve on napkin-lined dessert dishes.

Strawberry Whipped-Cream Roll

I got this recipe from friend Nelly Dancer and have been using it for over 20 years.

Ingredients

For the cake roll

1 cup flour plus 2 tablespoons
1 1/2 teaspoons baking powder
1/2 teaspoon salt
4 eggs, separated
3/4 cup granulated sugar
1/2 teaspoon almond or vanilla extract
rind of 1 lemon, grated

For filling

1 pint whipping cream
2 teaspoons confectioners' sugar
1 teaspoon vanilla extract
1 1/2 pints strawberries (reserve 10 perfect berries and slice the rest in 1/8-inch slices)

Procedures

1. Sift flour, baking powder and salt together.

2. Preheat the oven to 350°F.

3. Beat egg whites until frothy. Keep beating while gradually adding 1/2 cup of the sugar. Beat until soft peaks form.

4. Beat egg yolks with remaining 1/4 cup sugar until thickened and lemon colored.

5. Add extract to lemon yolks.

6. Fold yolks into meringue.

7. Sift dry ingredients over egg mixture. Fold together.

8. Line a four-sided cake pan with two layers of kitchen parchment paper. Oil the top piece surface.

9. Bake the cake roll for 15 minutes at 350°F or until lightly golden and springy to the touch.

10. Turn the baked cake onto a sugar-coated linen-type tea towel. Remove parchment slowly.

11. Roll the hot cake and towel together from one long side to the opposite long side. Cool at room temperature.

12. When cake is cooled, whip the cream with sugar and vanilla until nearly stiff.

13. Unroll the cake and fill with 2/3 of the whipped cream and sliced strawberries. Reroll the cake carefully and transfer to a serving plate.

14. Mound remaining cream along the top of the roll.

15. Place strawberries along the roll top, one for each slice.

16. Chill until serving time.

Finnish Bakers Do Hapanleipa Right

With each visit to Helsinki, my excitement about the rustic rye breads of Finland grows.

A few years ago, my husband, Ed, and I combined company business with his participation in the IX World Flyfishing Championships held near Kuusamo, Finland—in central Finland, near the Russian border. While in Helsinki, I strolled and sketched early each morning in the harbor-side marketplace as I gnawed on hapanleipä, a particularly delicious Finnish sour rye bread.

Small vendors sell steamy cups of robust coffee. In June fresh, deep-red strawberries roll from their artfully displayed mounds. The smells of dill and smoked fish waft through the air. The market buzzes with activity in the shadows of an eighteenth-century domed Eastern Orthodox church and 200-year-old Russian buildings. The Helsinki market is a pleasing context in which to sample Finnish country breads.

On this visit I toured the huge bakeries of the Fazer Corporation, Finland's largest confectioner. Their bakery division preserves traditional rural recipes and distributes hundreds of loaf styles daily to stores, airports, hotels and Fazer coffee shops throughout southern Finland. For some loaves, a wood-burning oven is still used.

Country people of Finland are serious bakers. Baking ovens are constructed in tunnels inside walls behind wood stoves. Warmed by the red hot embers of a wood fire, oven temperatures are controlled by dampers. The lengthy time required to ready these traditional ovens encourages quantity baking.

A round loaf of hapanleipä has a hole in its center to permit its hanging on poles from farmhouse ceilings. Though it does dry out with storage, I am told that it can be revived to its proper chewy texture by being submerged in a barrel of grain kernels which harbor minute reservoirs of moisture. Happily, freezing tightly wrapped circles of this wonderful loaf is an equally sucessful storage method. I smile at the image of large hapanleipä "dough-nuts" hanging from my ceiling. Grain barrels, however,could become a family issue!

Finnish Sour Rye Flat Bread (Hapanleipä)

Requires 24 hours

Makes 2 loaves

Ingredients

2 cups potato cooking water
2 packages (2 tablespoons) dry yeast
1 teaspoon granulated sugar
2 1/2 cups medium rye flour
2 1/2 to 3 1/2 cups unbleached flour
1 teaspoon salt

Procedures

Two days ahead

1. Cook potatoes for dinner 2 nights before you want to make this bread. Reserve the water at room temperature, uncovered, for use the second day.

One day ahead

2. Stir yeast and sugar into 1 cup warmed (90°F to 100°F) potato water.
3. Allow yeast to foam for 12 minutes.
4. In a medium bowl, combine yeast mixture, remaining water, and the rye flour. Beat until a smooth batter forms.
5. Cover tightly. Allow to ferment 24 hours to develop a "sponge."

Next day

6. Transfer the sponge to a large bowl and add 2 1/2 cups white flour and the salt.
7. The dough will be fairly stiff. Allow it to rest, covered, 30 minutes.
8. Turn dough onto a lightly floured surface and knead, adding white flour, until dough is elastic, not sticky, and satiny on the surface.
9. Cover dough with a damp towel or plastic wrap and let rise until doubled in volume.
10. Punch down dough and divide into 2 portions.
11. Form into 2 flattened 12-inch rounds of uniform thickness.
12. Place rounds on a greased cookie sheet and cut a 2-inch hole from the center.
13. Prick the rounds all over with a fork. Prick the cutouts too.
14. Allow breads to rise until doubled.
15. In a preheated 375°F oven, bake the loaves for about 30 minutes.

Cutouts will bake more quickly. Bake them separately and enjoy them hot from the oven!

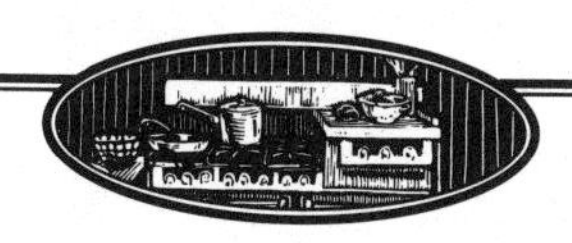

Scandinavian Limpa Bread

This bread needs 3 slow rises.

Makes 2 loaves

Ingredients

1 package (1 tablespoon) dry yeast
1/4 cup 95°F to 110°F water
1/2 cup brown sugar
1/3 cup dark molasses
1 tablespoon shortening
1 tablespoon salt
1/2 teaspoon anise seed
2 teaspoons caraway seeds
2 teaspoons orange peel (optional)
1 1/2 cups hot water
4 to 4 1/2 cups all-purpose flour
2 cups medium rye flour

Procedures

1. Dissolve yeast in 95°F to 110°F water. Allow it to develop for 12 minutes.

2. In a large bowl, combine sugar, molasses, shortening, salt, anise, caraway and optional orange peel. Pour hot water over and let stand until lukewarm.

3. Stir into the bowl 1 cup all-purpose flour, then the yeast mixture and 2 cups rye flour. Beat in enough of the remaining flour to make a soft dough.

4. Knead the dough until it is shiny, firm and elastic.

5. Put in a lightly greased bowl and cover tightly. Allow to rise until doubled (about 3 hours). (It rises more slowly than white or whole-wheat bread.)

6. Punch down the dough and allow it to rise again. (2 to 3 hours.)

7. Shape the risen dough into 2 loaves of desired shape. (I make round loaves.)

8. Allow the dough to rise again on a greased baking sheet until the loaves double. (1 1/2 to 2 hours.)

9. In a preheated 375°F oven, bake the loaves for about 30 minutes, until they are a dark medium brown.

En Papillote Cooking
Keep Foods Under Wraps

Here is a pretty, and healthy, French culinary technique with sister methods around the globe. It is called *en papillote* cooking and is worth trying, if not pronouncing. Try it . . . "on pap-ee-yote." Great! Now let me define it and explain why it is worth knowing.

Cooking en papillote means the preparation of delicate, quick-cooking, partially-cooked and sauced foods inside a pouch which inflates with steam as it exudes intriguing aromas.

The en papillote technique nicely suits fish and thin meat fillets or medallions as they gently steam in their own juices. Each portion is served in its individual package.

Historically, wrapping foods before exposing them to direct heat is a technique nearly as old as the process of cooking. Wrap-cooking evolved throughout the world to protect foods from the drying effects of heat. Primitive societies wrapped foods in available leaves and often further protected them with a layer of clay before cooking in pits or fires. Island cultures used leaves such as papaya, hollowed bamboo stalks and reed baskets. Leaves and seaweeds imparted their own subtle flavors. Early English kiln workers enclosed their lunches in clay. Later, the meat pie evolved and a lard pastry enrobed savory fillings. Mexican cooking uses corn husks around tamales. Greeks use their grape leaves. Cabbage leaves are used deliciously, and inventively, in Eastern Europe and Scandinavia.

American Girl Scouts use foil squares to build a memorable layered packet of hamburger and individually controlled veggies, which is tossed onto the campfire. The French use pastry *(en croûte)*, en papillote, and in the days of Nouvelle Cuisine, almost anything edible and/or pliable was drafted to protect delicate ingredients.

The attractive and tantalizing presentation of individually cooked packages is fun for guests. Additionally, en papillote cooking can be as lowFat and low-calorie as the cook's intentions.

The Technique of Cooking En Papillote

Foil or cooking parchment should be cut into heart shapes double the size necessary to cover the volume of the food being enclosed. Fold the heart in half. Brush the inside edges with cooking oil. Place 1/2- to 3/4-inch-thick pieces of meat or fish, along with precooked or quick-cooking vegetables, near the fold and in the center of one half of the wrapper. Don't place food close to the edge. Add a few tablespoons of chosen liquid (wine, stock, etc.), as well as complementary herbs and seasonings. Double-fold the edges together to enclose the food. Crimp and crease in between folds, overlapping the folds as you go. Twist the resulting pointy tip to seal the entire package. Place papillotes in a well-greased ovenproof baking dish and bake until packages puff and fish or meat should be cooked. Use a preheated 400°F oven and begin with 15 minutes of oven time. Cooking time will vary with ingredients and quantities.

A note about the choice between foil and kitchen parchment: Foil has good insulating qualities, but foods will take slightly longer to cook. Parchment makes a nicer table presentation. In either case, both will provide the fun of wrap-cooking and the satisfaction of healthful creativity.

A FEW SUGGESTIONS TO GET YOU STARTED

CHICKEN EN PAPILLOTE

Skinless, boneless chicken breast halves with pea pods, bean sprouts, spinach leaves, soy, ginger, sesame oil and wine.

SALMON EN PAPILLOTE

Salmon fillet with lemon slice, green onion slivers, zucchini slices, freshly ground black pepper and a splash of dry white vermouth.

TROUT EN PAPILLOTE

Rainbow trout, boned and stuffed with fresh herbs and capers, and slivers of fresh carrots and zucchini.

APPLES OR PEARS EN PAPILLOTE

Apple or pear slices sprinkled with cinnamon, nutmeg, lemon juice, toasted coconut and a splash of Cranapple juice.

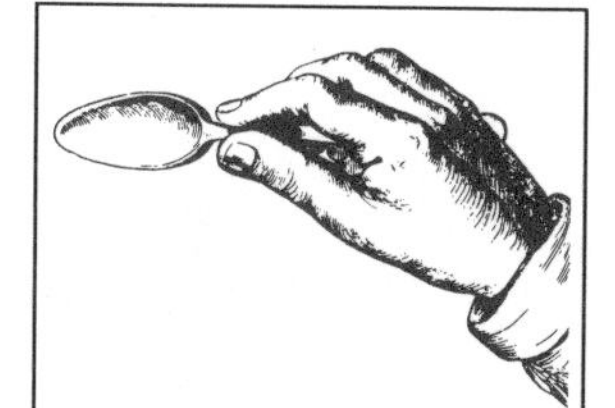

TO SERVE

1. Place packages on plates.
2. Snip along the folded edge.
3. Bring plates to the table for guests to uncover their own surprises.

Pain d'Hier: Yesterday's Bread

I rarely have fewer than five kinds of bread in my house at one time. I love bread, all kinds. I will drive across the city for a meaty brick of Baltic pumpernickel, a crusty heart-shaped baguette, a leathery Lithuanian rye, a real German-baked Kaiser roll or a warm, sweet loaf of orange-infused Limpa. I use my Visa card to order a special Wisconsin rye from the Clasen Bakery (608) 831-2032.

Chemical fluff is never seen in the Opler house. Homemade or bakery-produced, the joys of bread abound in our kitchen, but alas . . . what to do with the bits and pieces which succumb to old age or loss of attention.

Using day-old or stale bread successfully is a learning experience. Most cuisines have some type of staple bread. Research confirmed my suspicion that perking up "yesterday's bread" is a global affair. In many European countries, bread is eaten at all meals. As breads without preservatives stale quickly, frugality and thriftiness led to innovative solutions.

During my days as an inexperienced cook, I thought that creative cooking meant starting from scratch every day. I now know and enjoy the concept that real culinary creativity and fiscal responsibility are not mutually exclusive. In fact, they go hand in hand.

Using Sliceable Bread

In addition to French toast, croutons, cheese stratas, bread puddings, dumplings, toads-in-a-hole and Welsh rarebits, there are many other wonderfully resourceful uses for slightly staled bread in slices or hunks:

❦ Hollowed "breadboxes" can be oven-toasted and filled with chived scrambled eggs or rubbed with garlic and walnut oil as individual salad or dip containers. (Try toasting these on the grill.)

❦ Rolls can be hollowed and lined with cooked Canadian bacon and 1 or 2 eggs, then baked.

❦ Sweet breads can be scooped, buttered, sprinkled with cinnamon sugar and oven-toasted to hold poached fruits and ice creams.

❦ The trick to making Melba toast is to toast thick slices of bread, then immediately remove crusts and slice horizontally through the soft middle with a sawing motion.

❦ The traditional Italian *crostini* is simply a sautéed, baked or grilled slice (any shape or size) of bread served as an appetizer usually with a savory topping. Try blending 3 blanched and squeezed tomatoes with 1 red pepper, basil leaves, salt, freshly ground black pepper and 1 tablespoon olive oil. Serve on crisped breads and top with cheese, olives or anchovies. If the vegetable mixture is too watery, cook it slightly in a skillet to evaporate excess liquid before serving.

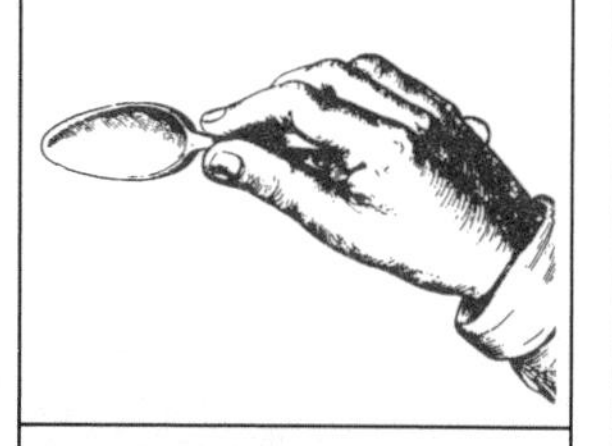

FRESHENING BREADS

❦ Freshening stale bread is a useful technique. Crusty French-style breads quickly lose their moisture and become stale. They get soft and rubbery if wrapped in plastic.

❦ Immediately before serving, quickly pass stale loaves under cold water and then crisp them in a preheated 400°F oven for 10 minutes.

❦ Madeleine Kamman (*The Making of a Cook*, Atheneum, 1971) tells us that frozen homemade breads should be reheated at their baking temperature.

Crispy Brie or Camembert Wedges

These cheese wedges fry most successfully if thoroughly chilled.

Serves 6

Ingredients

Small Brie or Camembert wheels, cut into 6 wedges (1 wedge per serving)
Dry white wine or chicken broth
All-purpose flour
2 large egg whites, beaten until frothy
Bread crumbs
Corn oil for cooking cheese wedges
Crusty French-style bread
Strawberry jam

Procedures

1. Dip wedge into wine or broth, then flour, then egg whites, then crumbs, coating evenly.

2. Chill cheese wedges thoroughly. Refrigerate up to 24 hours before proceeding.

3. Heat oil until a piece of bread turns deep golden almost immediately upon immersion.

4. Fry wedges and drain on paper towels while reheating oil and frying the remaining cheeses.

Serve immediately as a brunch or luncheon dish with jam and bread.

MAKING AND USING BREAD CRUMBS

❦ Breads of all kinds may be ground into crumbs in a food processor. Keep dark, light and sweet crumbs labeled separately and tightly sealed in the freezer for use in:

❦ Meatballs or meat loaf

❦ Fresh-seasoned bread crumbs

❦ Stuffings

❦ Lining buttered casseroles or soufflés

❦ Fresh fruit pies (as a thickening agent)

PANZANELLA

Stale moistened bread is transformed by the freshest ingredients into a traditional Tuscan salad.

PROCEDURES

1. Soak bread in cold water 15 minutes.

2. Squeeze out all liquid by hand.

3. Tear bread into chunks to combine with best-quality olive oil, red wine vinegar, salt, freshly ground black pepper and any combination of the following:

Tomatoes ❦ Onions ❦ Garlic ❦ Capers ❦ Olives ❦ Basil, Parsley ❦ Peppers ❦ Cucumbers ❦ Hard-cooked eggs ❦ Cheese chunks ❦ Sausage, Ham, Bologna, Prosciutto chunks

The perfect picnic dish! Use whatever you have on hand. Buono appetito!

How do I feel about food? I love everything but the calories. I love the colors, and the textures, flavors, and perfumes. I love the geographical and seasonal availability. But most of all, I love what Italians do with their ingredients, their strong sense of tradition, heart, and home-style cooking."

FAITH HELLER WILLINGER, ROVING FOOD WRITER (ITALY), AUTHOR *EATING IN ITALY.*

Pasta, No? Pasta Si!

Let's consider a question that I have asked myself for some time. Is pasta, the darling of foodies, haute cuisiniers, and hard bodies alike, nutritional? Can it contribute to my battle against bulge? Should I bother to make it myself? If so, why?

In the early eighties I was privileged to work in two exceptional Milanese restaurant kitchens. Osteria Francesco and L'Assassino are arrogantly untrendy and pride themselves in serving only fresh and authentic Northern Italian dishes. On the antipasti table, huge hunks of aged Reggiano Parmesan cheese and platters of freshly roasted red sweet peppers flank red snappers flaunting airplane tickets—proof of their daily arrival from Genoa.

My experiences in Italian kitchens introduced me to the wonders of pasta before it became the rage in the U.S. I discovered that real Italian restaurants traditionally do not make their own pasta unless a special shape or flavor is unavailable in a top-quality commercial product. This bit of information liberated me. I had been convinced that any table-worthy pasta had to be homemade.

Cooked inside a sieve, immersed in lightly oiled boiling water, slithery noodles are then drained, not rinsed, and tossed into a large skillet where sauce ingredients wait. High heat combines and intensifies sauce flavors while reducing excess liquids. Perfectly coated pasta is poured from the skillet onto prewarmed plates to be served simply and alone as a first or main course.

Quickly cooked pastas with more-quickly cooked sauces became my credo. Open box, cook pasta! Open refrigerator, create sauce! My previous spaghetti-with-meatball mind-set was easily replaced with the revelation of nearly instant and seemingly endless Northern Italian pasta sauce recipes.

Now, ten years later, I have joined the health conscious in the effort to look and feel good as I age. I believe that I have to get old, but I don't have to get fat. I read labels and eat more thoughtfully. I consider what I put in my mouth, how it will taste, and how my body will use it.

Pasta is nutritionally sound. Complex carbohydrates are found in pastas, breads, cereals and beans. They are an inexpensive and nutritional energy source. When using commercial pastas, one should remember that the nutritional value of wheat is reduced during processing. Even some whole-wheat flours are processed and therefore have fewer nutrients. Products made with enriched flours are the healthiest choice. When reading labels on pasta packages, look specifically for the word "enriched." However, when white flour is enriched, even though thiamine, niacin, riboflavin and iron are added back, fiber and other trace elements may no longer be present.

My case for homemade pasta emerges, but it is challenged by the reality of convenience. Time is a consideration. With knowledge, intelligent choices can be made. Traditionally, pasta was made by fork-beating the eggs inside a volcano of flour, while incorporating the flour, to achieve a medium-stiff dough—about 5 minutes' work. (The food processor reduces this time to about 30 seconds.) After a half-hour rest, the dough was rolled by hand or machine until nearly transparent in thickness and then cut or formed as desired.

Pastas and other starches, in reasonable amounts, are not excessively fattening. Minimizing fats while eating nutritious carbohydrates will help in weight loss and maintenance. A good source of quick energy, complex carbohydrates supply essential vitamins, minerals, fiber and protein and are a deliciously complete, intelligent and inexpensive way to continued good health.

Buono appetito!

Basic Pasta

Serves 4 to 6

Ingredients

For Pasta

1 3/4 cups enriched all-purpose flour
3 large eggs, room temperature
2 to 4 tablespoons bran or wheat germ may be optionally substituted for some white flour

For Cooking

6 quarts water
2 tablespoons olive oil
1 teaspoon salt

Procedures

For Pasta

1. Make a volcano with the dry ingredients.

2. Break eggs into crater.

3. Beat eggs with a fork, incorporating flour from inside edge.

4. Knead dough to moisten all flour and to form a medium-stiff dough (See tip.)

5. Wrap dough in plastic wrap and let rest 1/2 hour.

6. Roll on surface dusted with flour. (I use Wondra.) If using a pasta-rolling machine, cut dough into quarters. Press them into flat disc shapes. Dust them with flour (or Wondra) to prevent sticking.

7. Roll dough as thinly as possible either with a rolling pin or pasta machine.

8. Cut or form into desired pasta shapes. Cook immediately, or cover lightly with a tea towel to dry. Then store, tightly sealed or frozen, for later use.

For Cooking

9. Bring water with olive oil and salt to a boil.

10. Drop pasta into the boiling water and cook until nearly al dente.

11. Drain pasta and serve as desired.

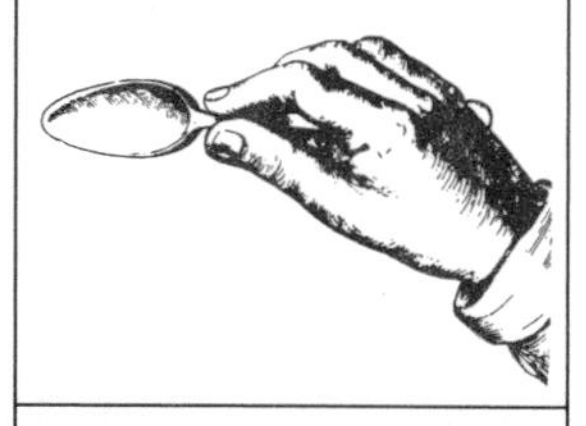

HOMEMADE PASTA TIP

❦ Additional teaspoons of water may be necessary to hold the dough together. Eggs vary in volume and flours vary in moisture content. Be confident enough to add small amounts of water until dough holds together.

❦ Press dough together with fingers to see if it masses.

❦ Wrap tightly in plastic film to prevent drying.

❦ Freeze in a flattened disc if not using within 12 hours.

"Our criteria is: serious work and passion, always first quality, and the greatest respect for our customers' tastes."

Ottavio Gori and Lino Morganti, Owners of Ristorante L'Assassino Milan, Italy

Spinach Pasta

Serves 4

Ingredients

For Pasta

1 1/2 cups all-purpose flour
1/2 teaspoon salt
1 large egg, room temperature
3 ounces cooked spinach, squeezed to remove excess liquid and then puréed
1 tablespoon water

For Cooking

6 quarts water
2 tablespoons olive oil
1 teaspoon salt

Procedures

For Pasta

1. Mix dry ingredients together on a flat work surface. Form into a volcano shape making a generous crater in the center of the flour mixture.

2. Add spinach, liquid and egg into this crater.

3. Mix liquids with a fork and incorporate dry ingredients from the inside edge of the volcano.

4. Continue until dough is moistened, and knead until the dough is a smooth mass.

5. Tightly wrap and refrigerate, or let rest 20 to 30 minutes.

6. Roll dough as thinly as possible either with a rolling pin or pasta machine. (I use Wondra flour to roll out pasta.)

7. Cut or form into desired pasta shapes. Cook immediately or cover lightly with a tea towel to dry. Then store, tightly sealed or frozen, for later use.

For Cooking

8. Bring water with olive oil and salt to a boil.

9. Drop pasta into the boiling water and cook until nearly al dente.

10. Drain pasta and serve as desired.

Pretty Herby Pasta

Serves 4 to 6

Ingredients

For Pasta

1 3/4 cups unbleached white flour
3 large eggs, beaten with 1 tablespoon olive oil
1 tablespoon fresh herbs (chives, parsley, sage, thyme, sorrel, basil or rosemary), minced

For Herbed Butter

4 to 6 tablespoons unsalted butter
2 to 3 tablespoons mixed herbs

Procedures

For Pasta

1. Make pasta as directed (see Basic Pasta recipe p. 33), incorporating herbs with dry ingredients.

2. Make pasta into fettucine noodles. Cook immediately or cover lightly with a tea towel to dry. Then store, tightly sealed or frozen, for later use.

3. Cook in lightly oiled and salted boiling water until pasta is al dente. Drain.

For Herbed Butter

4. Melt butter and stir in herbs.

5. Toss cooked pasta in a large serving bowl with herbed butter.

Edible herb flowers or nasturtiums are a nice garnish.

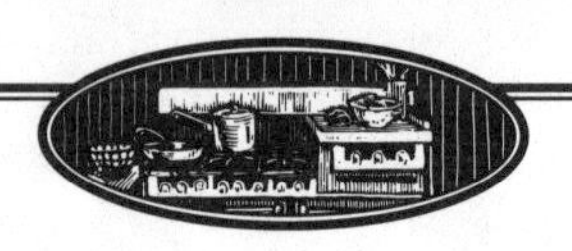

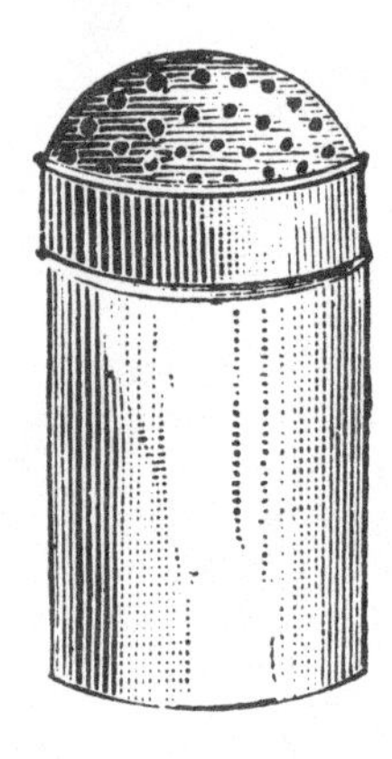

Gnocchi

Serves 4 to 6

Ingredients

4 baking potatoes
1 1/3 cups all-purpose flour
1 teaspoon salt
1 1/2 teaspoons nutmeg, freshly grated
1/4 cup Parmesan cheese, freshly grated
2 large eggs

Procedures

1. Boil potatoes until they drop from a fork when lifted.

2. Run under cold water. Peel.

3. Mash potatoes and sift flour and salt over them.

4. Grate nutmeg and Parmesan cheese over potato/flour mixture. Toss to blend.

5. Make a volcano with the potato mixture.

6. Break eggs into crater and beat with a fork.

7. With fingers or a pastry blending tool, mix eggs with potato mixture.

8. Knead gnocchi mixture on a lightly floured surface until smooth.

9. Roll dough into 1/2-inch-diameter sausage shapes.

10. Cut into 1-inch lengths. *Do not collect in a pile*—they will stick together.

11. Bring to boil a large pot of salted water. Reduce heat to a gentle boil.

12. Cook the gnocchi until they float.

Serve warm gnocchi tossed with melted butter and freshly grated Parmesan cheese, or combine gnocchi with your favorite pasta sauce. Serve hot on prewarmed plates.

HOW TO REHEAT GNOCCHI

❦ Gnocchi may be cooked in advance and tossed lightly with olive oil. Reheat them later that day by placing briefly into gently boiling salted water and then into a waiting sauce.

❦ Unsauced, cooked gnocchi may be frozen, unwrapped, in a single layer. When frozen, store in a tightly sealed plastic container. To use them, defrost gnocchi and heat in desired sauce.

Pasta with Garlic and Chilies

Serves 4 to 6

Ingredients

1 recipe pasta, cooked al dente and drained (see Basic Pasta recipe p. 33)
1/3 cup olive oil
2 cloves garlic, peeled and slivered
1/2 teaspoon crushed chilies
Fresh parsley, finely chopped and squeezed to remove moisture
Parmesan cheese, freshly grated

Procedures

1. Heat the oil in a skillet over medium heat.

2. Add garlic and chilies and cook in the oil until garlic is deep golden.

3. Remove chilies and garlic from the oil and reserve.

4. Combine pasta with oil and parsley, add chilies and garlic and toss thoroughly.

Serve on heated plates or in wide shallow bowls with freshly grated Parmesan cheese.

Cara Pat, Ristorante Francesco expresses the spirit, style, refined cuisine and friendly atmosphere of Italy's business capital with 'la buona cucina italiana.'
Grazie,
Di tutto amore"

IRENE SANNA, OWNER OF
RISTORANTE FRANCESCO
MILAN, ITALY

Pasta with Ham and Cognac

From Ristorante Francesco

Serves 4 to 6

Ingredients

1 recipe pasta, cooked until nearly al dente and drained (see Basic Pasta recipe p. 33)
4 tablespoons unsalted butter, room temperature
1/2 pound ham, sliced into 1/3-inch thick slices, then diced
5 ounces beef or chicken consommé
1 tablespoon Worcestershire sauce
1 tablespoon good-quality brandy or cognac
1 cup heavy cream, room temperature

Procedures

1. Place all ingredients, except pasta, in large skillet or shallow pan with at least a 12-inch opening, preferably 14 inches.

2. Pour drained pasta into skillet and toss to mix with sauce ingredients.

3. Over high heat, cook, stirring constantly, until ingredients concentrate and coat pasta evenly.

Serve immediately on heated plates or in shallow bowls.

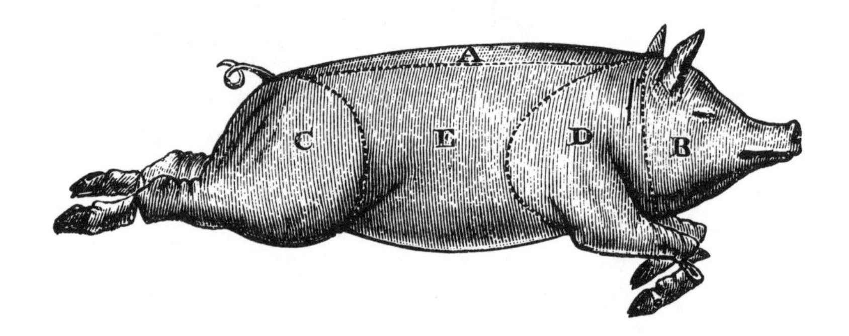

Pasta with Tomatoes, Olives and Capers

Serves 4 to 6

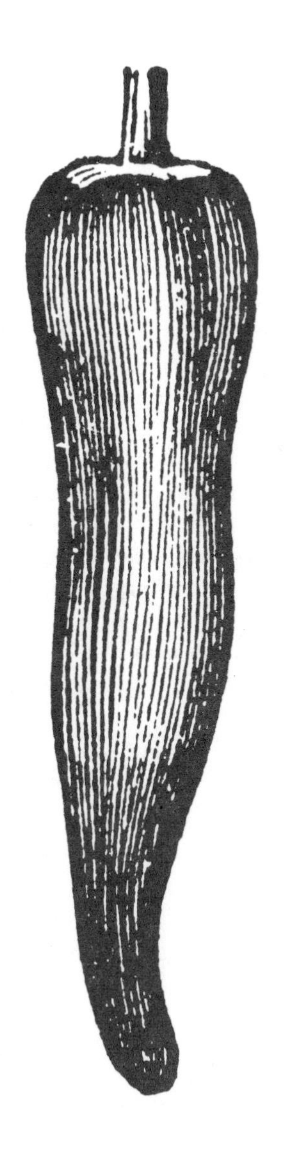

Ingredients

- 1 recipe pasta cooked al dente and drained (see Basic Pasta recipe p. 33)
- 2 tablespoons onion, minced
- 1 tablespoon butter
- 1 tablespoon olive oil
- 14 ounces Italian plum tomatoes, chopped
- 3 fresh basil leaves, chopped
- 5 tablespoons additional olive oil
- 1 clove garlic, pulverized
- 1 whole red chili pepper
- Salt to taste
- Pinch of sugar
- 1 tablespoon capers, coarsely chopped
- 2 tablespoons Mediterranean olives
- 2 teaspoons anchovy paste
- 2 tablespoons additional fresh basil, chopped

Procedures

1. Sauté onion in butter and 1 tablespoon olive oil until translucent.

2. Add tomatoes, basil, remaining olive oil, garlic and chili pepper and cook on low to medium heat, uncovered, until thickened (about 30 minutes).

3. Add salt to taste and a pinch of sugar.

4. Mix remaining ingredients with completed tomato sauce in a serving bowl.

5. Drain pasta and stir it immediately into sauce.

6. Garnish with fresh basil.

This dish may be served at room temperature.

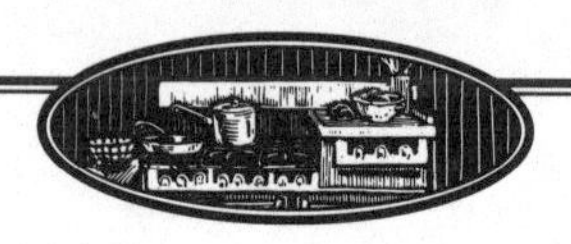

Real People Do Eat Quiche

I admit that quiche may have suffered from "overmenufication" and poor execution. But quiche is a delicious and intelligent use of both inexpensive and leftover ingredients. Culinary imaginations in French farmhouse kitchens saw leftover bits and pieces as opportunities. This pursuit of good value has produced many favored recipes, such as tetrazini, beef bourguignon and pâté.

A custardlike mixture of eggs, combined with anything, poured into a mold or pastry shell and baked until set, quiche is practically foolproof. The pastry can be partially baked in advance. Fillings may be prepared and refrigerated ahead. Assembled, and baked until a knife plunged into the center comes out nearly clean, this openFaced tart will remain puffed for 10 minutes in a turned-off oven. Though it will sink and not puff fully again, quiche may be reheated.

Uncomfortable making pastry? The crustless quiche will be a cinch. The fruit quiche is a sweet one which can be made with any fruit. Juiciness of different fruits may vary cooking times.

Quiche is no wimp. It can be prepared easily and in advance. It can be served for any course and at any temperature.

Easy Crustless Quiche

Serves 6 to 10

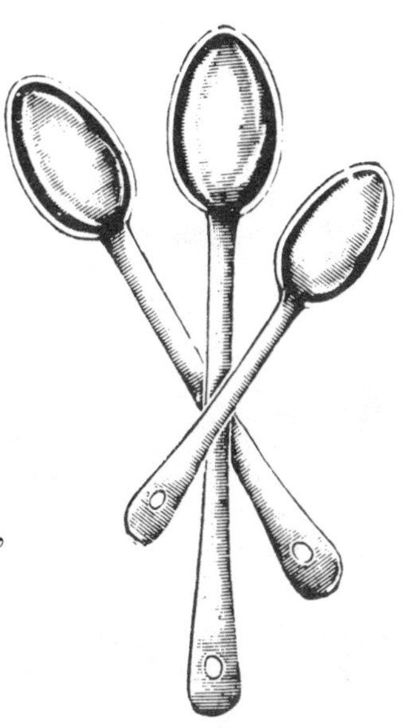

Ingredients

2 tablespoons butter, softened
1/3 to 1/2 cup coarse bread crumbs
3 large eggs, room temperature
1 pound cream cheese, softened
7 ounces sour cream
3 ounces blue cheese
1/4 cup parsley, chopped
2 teaspoons fresh basil, chopped
1 clove garlic, crushed

Procedures

1. Heavily butter a 9-inch pie or quiche dish.
2. Coat it thoroughly with crumbs. Chill the dish.
3. Mix remaining ingredients thoroughly.
4. Pour into prepared pan.
5. In a preheated 375°F oven, bake about 40 minutes, until knife inserted comes out clean.
6. Let stand at least 15 minutes before cutting.

Traditional Quiche Lorraine

Serves 4 to 6

Ingredients

1 8-inch partially baked pastry shell, made using 1/2 Basic Pastry recipe (see p.109)
6 to 8 slices bacon, cut into pieces, browned and drained
3 large eggs
1 1/2 cups heavy cream
1/4 teaspoon salt
1/8 teaspoon ground nutmeg
1 to 2 tablespoons very cold butter, thinly flaked

Procedures

1. Distribute bacon on pastry.
2. Mix remaining ingredients, except butter.
3. Pour mixture over bacon.
4. Dot surface of quiche with butter flakes.
5. In a preheated 350°F oven, bake 25 to 30 minutes, or until knife plunged into center comes out clean.
6. Allow to set at least 10 minutes before serving.

This basic recipe can be altered by the addition or substitution of other filling ingredients.

Fruit Quiche

Serves 6 to 8

Ingredients

1 9-inch baked pastry shell, made using 1/2 Basic Pastry recipe (see recipe on p. 109)
2 large eggs
2 large egg yolks
1 1/2 cups heavy cream (may substitute up to 3 tablespoons fruit juice or liqueur)
1/2 cup granulated sugar
1 teaspoon pure vanilla extract
1 teaspoon lemon rind (try orange rind for a change)
3 cups fresh berries, rhubarb or pitted cherries (or dried fruits plumped 2 minutes in microwave with liqueur or fruit juice, then drained)
2 tablespoons powdered sugar

Procedures

1. Combine eggs, egg yolks, cream, sugar, vanilla and lemon rind.
2. Place fruit, drained if necessary, into pastry shell.
3. Pour liquid mixture over fruit.
4. In a preheated 350°F oven, bake 30 to 40 minutes, or until set.
5. Cool tart, then sift powdered sugar on top.
6. Caramelize tart top under broiler.

TIPS FOR SUCCESSFUL QUICHE

❦ Quiche molds should be filled no more than 3/4 full. Determine mold capacity by filling 3/4 full with water. Measure volume.

❦ The correct proportion for quiche-making is 2 large eggs to 1 cup filling.

❦ An 8-inch pie plate will hold 3/4 pound filling and serves 4. A 10-inch pie plate will hold about 1 1/8 pounds filling and serves 8.

❦ Salts cannot be eliminated from a sweetened quiche recipe. They encourage diluted egg proteins to gel.

❦ It is not possible to make a thickened custard by replacing milk with water.

❦ Don't raise oven temperatures to speed setting of egg protein. The lower the rate of heating, the greater the margin of safety between setting and curdling.

❦ A knife plunged into the cooked quiche center should emerge relatively clean. When egg proteins set (gel, bond together) they are unlikely to stick to anything else.

Too Much Parsley? Read This . . .

For many years, as a homemaker and professional cook, I found that a bunch of grocery-store parsley was too much for my recipe. Parsley is difficult to weigh in recipe-sized quantities. My problem existed because I disliked parsley "trees" as dinner plate garnish.

At some point, my kitchen confidence level escalated and I tried using parsley, even when it was not specified in the recipe. Successes encouraged me to continue seeking new ways of using this tasty, healthy herb.

Perhaps you have never experienced the pressure of unrequited bunches of parsley languishing in your refrigerator. Even if you do know enough ways to use it all, sometimes schedules don't cooperate. You might have to leave town before the parsley is gone! Kitchen experience has taught me that adding parsley to almost anything will enhance its food value, appearance, texture and taste.

One of the parsley-related tips that I learned early, during work at The Bakery Restaurant in Chicago, was washing, chopping (including the non-woody stems) and squeezing parsley dry. A French chef's knife is the perfect tool for the task. A mini food processor can do a fair job, but a full-sized food processor will chew, mash and liquefy the parsley rather than chop it. After finely chopping the herb, place it in a damp, non-terry dish towel. Gather up the corners and, to remove excess liquid, squeeze the parsley over a sauce, salad dressing, vegetable purée or soup pot. This liquid contains vitamins and need not be wasted. The "dried" parsley can now be easily sprinkled without matting. Sprinkling it from 6 inches above the plate will ensure nice distribution over food. The resulting parsley mince can be frozen, tightly sealed, to be easily measured and used right from the freezer: healthful and frugal, too.

Finely chopped parsley may be added to biscuit, pasta, bread and pastry doughs with the dry ingredients. No adjustments need to be made in the recipe. Stir the tasty minced herb into eggs, gravies, cottage cheese or potato salad.

I once savored a delicious salad in La Jolla, California: Coarsely chopped parsley was combined in a nearly equal toss with those trendy and tangy sun-dried tomatoes. Leftover rice and pasta can be mixed with diced vegetables, vinaigrette salad dressing and a generous handful of parsley to make picnic-perfect rice and pasta salads. Cook a little extra rice or pasta next time and assemble the salad for the following day.

Northern Italians make an incredible mixture of parsley, garlic and lemon rind to serve on a traditional veal shank dish called ossobuco. This savory gremolata is made by mincing a handful of parsley with 1 large garlic clove and the rind of 5 lemons. Try it on trout, grilled chicken, lamb shanks or in tabbouleh or couscous.

Happy cooking!

Ed Opler's Parslied Cubed Steaks

Serves 3 to 4

Ingredients

1/4 pound unsalted butter
1/4 cup fresh parsley, chopped finely
2 tablespoons Worcestershire sauce
1 pound cubed steak, cut into 3 or 4 portions

Procedures

1. Melt butter in a large skillet until foamy.
2. Toss in parsley and stir.
3. Add Worcestershire sauce and steaks.
4. Cook over medium-high heat 1 minute per side.

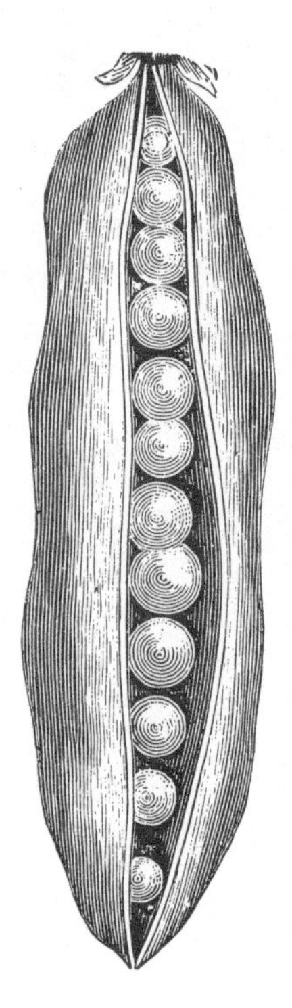

Margery Howe's Peas Potage

A wonderful spring soup

Serves 4 to 8

Ingredients

5 tablespoons salted butter
4 green onions, minced
1/2 small white onion, minced
1/2 head Boston lettuce, coarsely shredded
1 heaping tablespoon flour
1 teaspoon ground coriander
1/4 teaspoon ground white pepper
1 package frozen peas
4 cups chicken broth
1 heaping teaspoon sugar
1 cup medium cream
Salt to taste
1/4 cup parsley, finely chopped

Procedures

1. In a large saucepan, stew onions and lettuce in butter until wilted.
2. Add flour, stir to mix and cook 2 minutes over low flame.
3. Add coriander, pepper, peas, broth and sugar.
4. Simmer until peas are tender.
5. Purée. Return to heat and add cream and salt.
6. Heat but do not boil. Swirl in remaining butter and parsley.

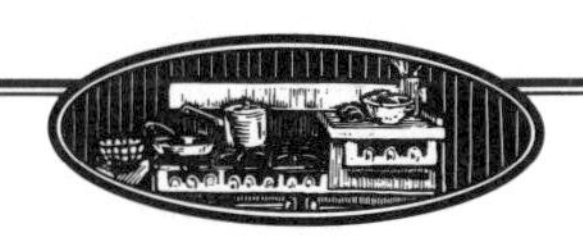

Kay Wauterlek's Russian Garden Soup

Serves 4

INGREDIENTS

1 bunch fresh red beets, peeled (about 6 average beets)
1 quart water
1 tablespoon sugar
1 bunch (about 6) green onions, cut into 1/2-inch pieces
2 tablespoons cider vinegar
1 cucumber
2 teaspoons salt
1/4 teaspoon ground white pepper
2 tablespoons fresh lemon juice
10 radishes, very thinly sliced
2 tablespoons parsley, chopped
Sour cream or crème fraîche (see recipe on p. 68)

PROCEDURES

1. Cook beets in water with sugar. Cool beets in water. Drain, reserving the liquid.

2. Mash green onions with the side of a French chef's knife to bruise and extract onion juices. Put onions and vinegar together and allow to stand at room temperature 10 minutes.

3. Grate 1/4 of the cucumber. Toss with the salt, pepper and lemon juice. Allow to stand while completing recipe.

4. To the reserved liquid, add enough water to make 1 quart.

5. Grate the beets. Dice the remaining cucumber.

6. Add all ingredients to the reserved beet-cooking liquid and stir.

Chill before serving with sour cream or crème fraîche.

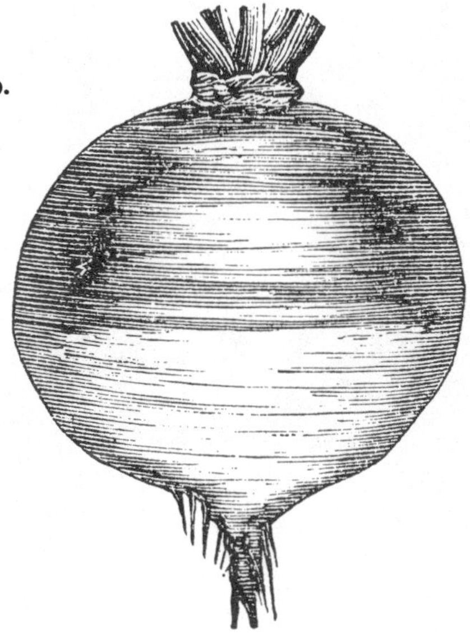

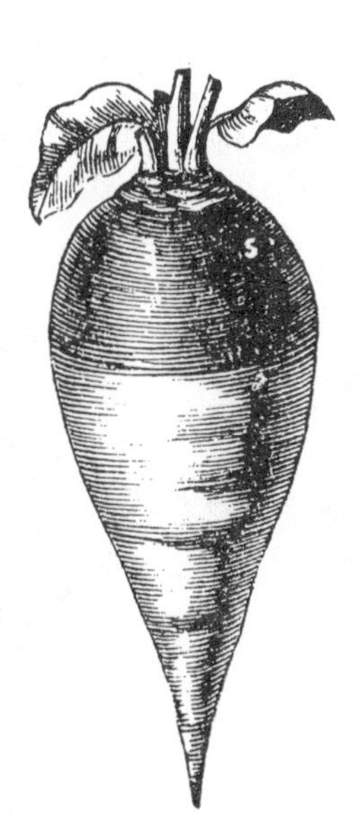

Lemons, Lemons and More Lemons

There are few ingredients in cooking more flavorful and health-contributing than the lemon. From the freshest lemonades of summer to the monotony of winter vegetables, the clean, sharp perfume of the Eureka lemon, common in supermarkets, with its tangy peel, is an inspiring addition to millions of dishes worldwide. It is hard to overstate the importance of fresh lemon as a kitchen staple.

My husband likes to add a squeeze of lemon to his orange juice and prefers to stir lemon juice into cocktail sauces rather than onto his oysters. Having given up salt, he uses lemon rind and juice liberally as a substitute. After filleting a fish, he uses a lemon half to get the fishy oils off his knife and hands.

My friend Madelaine Bullwinkel, owner/teacher of the Chez Madelaine cooking school, shared a "chilling" experience: In one of her beginner's "cooking camp" classes, a student revealed he had never squeezed a real lemon. Recovered from recalling this encounter, Madelaine described lemon as a "balancer" in the kitchen, used often to take the direct hit out of sweetness. She recommends lemon juice and peel (zest) for salad dressings, beverages, and marinades and as a finishing touch on grilled or sautéed meats, fish and vegetables.

When I queried my mother about her use of lemons, she revealed her dependence on frozen lemon juice. The discussion faded, but I vowed to do a little comparative research. I bought some lemons and a bottle of frozen "pure" lemon juice. The bottle yielded a reconstituted mixture of 7.5 fluid ounces of concentrate and water and, of course, no peel. I gently warmed my *fresh* lemons for 1 1/2 minutes, medium power in the microwave. Removing the yellow zest with grater, zester or stripper gave me 1 tablespoon of fragrant, chewy zest per lemon.

Using a hand-held lemon juicer, juice measured about 3/8 cup per average lemon. Three lemons yielded 3 tablespoons of reusable zest *and* 1 1/8 cups of vitamin-filled juice for under $1.15. The bottled frozen juice was $1.59. My suspicion was right: Why pay more for packaging, and get less?

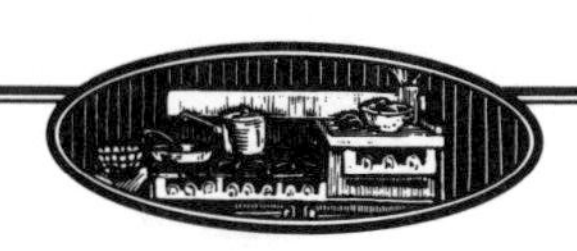

Lemon Madeleine Cakes

Yields 18–24

Ingredients

6 large egg yolks
1/2 cup granulated sugar
1 tablespoon lemon juice
2 tablespoons lemon zest, finely grated
1 cup cake flour
6 tablespoons warm, melted unsalted butter

Procedures

1. Beat yolks and sugar together until thickened and light yellow in color.

2. Stir in lemon juice and zest, then flour, just to blend.

3. Fold butter into batter just until blended.

4. Fill well-buttered and floured madelaine molds (or muffin tins) with 1 tablespoon of batter.

5. Bake in an accurate 375°F oven until firm to touch and edges are golden—about 12–15 minutes.

6. Allow to cool *in the pan* only about 10 minutes.

7. Remove from pan by inverting pan over your countertop and tapping the pan edge to jolt cakes out of their molds.

8. Cool on a cake rack and store airtight. Dust with powdered sugar to serve.

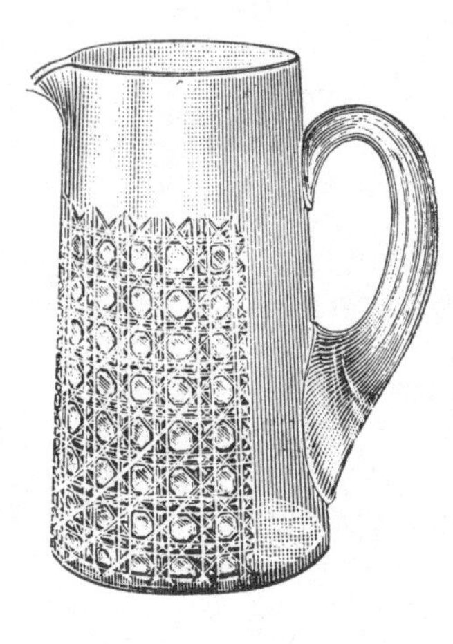

Old-Fashioned Lemonade

1 to 2 servings

Ingredients

2 cups water
4 1/2 to 6 tablespoons granulated sugar
3 tablespoons fresh lemon juice

Procedures

1. Stir or boil the water and sugar together until sugar is dissolved to make a syrup.
2. Mix lemon juice with this syrup.
3. Serve chilled over ice.

Garnish with mint sprig from herb garden or a fluted lemon disc.

WAYS TO USE LEMONS

In these days of changing eating habits, lemon is a year-round gift to the cook.

Add lemon juice:

- to water, in pastry or biscuit making
- as a flavor-sparking substitute for salt
- to lightly sugared berries and sliced fruits
- to a baked potato, instead of butter
- to soups and stews
- when sautéing mushrooms
- as a sprinkling over steamed vegetables, especially green ones.

Use lemon peel and zest:

- in your sugar bowl to give a fresh flavor
- in tomato sauces and soups
- in pies, salads, fruit compotes, muffins, pastries, and cheesecakes.

...N TART

6 to 8

...NGREDIENTS

pie pastry for 9-inch pan (see Basic Pastry recipe on p. 109)
Rind of 1 lemon
3/4 cup granulated sugar
3 large eggs
1/2 stick unsalted butter, room temperature
Juice of 4 lemons
3 teaspoons liquor (approximately) to taste—such as Grand Marnier, Cointreau, or rum
Powdered sugar for decoration

PROCEDURES

1. Preheat oven to 400°F.

2. Prepare desired amount of pastry crust and line a 9-inch pie pan or tart pan.

3. Chill thoroughly before baking "blind," weighted, at 425°F for 10–12 minutes and then, with weights removed, 5 minutes more.

4. Combine the rind, sugar and eggs in a stainless steel bowl. Place the bowl above a pan of simmering water and cook until thickened visibly.

5. Remove mixture from heat and stir in butter until incorporated.

6. Strain in lemon juice and liquor. Stir to blend.

7. Fill pastry 2/3 full and bake at 400°F until knife comes out clean. The tart should be quite dark golden.

8. After cooling, sift powdered sugar over the tart.

"Cooking is a thoughtful process, not a matter of simply doing what you are told. And students need to participate to experience the rhythm of kitchen work, to develop pride in their manual skills. It's not enough to buy some new appliance to do the work for you.

Building skills builds confidence. I want my students to leave here feeling they can tackle any recipe they choose."

MADELAINE BULLWINKLE, OWNER CHEZ MADELAINE COOKING SCHOOL, CHICAGO IL; PUBLISHER *MADELAINE'S KITCHEN SECRETS*; AUTHOR *GOURMET PRESERVES CHEZ MADELAINE*

CHEESECAKE: THE ULTIMATE INDULGENCE

Cheesecakes are distinctly outré among the health-minded these days. However, I know very few people who don't occasionally succumb to the desire for the lusciously rich flavor and velvety texture of these creamy delicacies.

Some years ago, I decided to listen to the protests of my bridge-playing friends: "Please, Pat, not such rich desserts next time. I never should have eaten it. It was wonderful, but . . ." So the next time it was my turn as hostess, I decided to respect their words. I served a perfectly ripened mango to each woman. Lovely pearl-handled fruit forks and knives, linen napkins and my best china did absolutely nothing to dull their dismay. They hadn't eaten all day, etc. I quit.

Cheesecake aficionados openly declare their favorite variety. There are the drier, lighter types, usually made with separately beaten egg whites. The Germans would embed plumped golden raisins or sour cherries. In my childhood, Zwieback (a baby teething biscuit) was used to make the crust. That was in the days before Nabisco made graham crackers so user-friendly in the form of boxed crumbs and pre-formed crusts. The delicate sweetness of the old-fashioned Zwieback crust still haunts my taste buds. But I admit I have been known to tip my tongue towards convenience, too.

Some cheesecakes are just plain cream cheese, sometimes "diluted" with sour cream. These are distinctly more solid and, consequently, are easier to cut in thin slivers. I find myself eating a two-inch slice publicly; and then *privately* thin-slivering with my sharpest fish filleting knife.

The cheesecake pie is frequently a more quickly baked type, *gateau de fromage*. No one needs a springform pan to bake it. If you buy the crumb crusts, you won't even need to own a pie plate!

Cheesecakes take on character with the addition of lemon or orange zest, chocolate chips, toasted nuts or nearly anything. I even made a savory cheese torte for a picnic by eliminating the sugar and crust from NZ's 15-Minute Cheesecake and by adding fresh herbs and ham slivers. The pan was heavily buttered and coated with homemade bread crumbs before being filled and baked.

As traditional cheesecakes go, I prefer my mother-in-law's recipe. But often my life demands that I bow to convenience. Whatever your cheesecake preference, these recipes will fit your need when the menu and moment are right.

As an extra temptation, I have included my friend Nelly Dancer's simple cheese strudel. My favorite kolacky recipe follows as another use for the strudel filling.

Alice Opler's Cheesecake

Serves 10 to 12

Ingredients

For Crust

1/2 box Zwieback biscuits, crushed into crumbs
1/8 cup sugar
1 stick unsalted butter, melted

For Filling

12 ounces cream cheese
1/3 cup sugar
1/4 teaspoon salt
6 large eggs, separated
2 tablespoons all-purpose flour
8 ounces sour cream
2 teaspoons vanilla extract
1 tablespoon grated lemon rind

Procedures

For Crust

1. Mix crumbs and sugar together. Blend in butter.
2. Push crumb mixture into 9-inch springform pan 3/4 inch up sides.
3. Blend cheese, sugar and salt.
4. Stir in yolks, one at a time.
5. Fold flour into cheese mixture.
6. Beat egg whites to soft peaks.
7. Stir in 1/3 of beaten whites.
8. Fold in remaining whites with sour cream, vanilla and rind.
9. Pour creamy mixture into crumb-lined pan.
10. Bake 30 minutes at 350°F.
11. Reduce heat to 325°F and bake 30 minutes more.
12. Cool cake in oven after turning heat off.

Serve chilled or at room temperature. Fresh berries or a sweetened sauce or purée of strawberries or raspberries *would* be sensational.

NZ's 15-Minute Cheesecake

The Easiest Cheesecake Imaginable!

Prepare and bake several hours before chilling and/or serving.

Serves 10 to 15

Ingredients

For Crust

1 1/2 cups graham cracker crumbs
1/2 cup unsalted butter, melted
3 tablespoons granulated sugar

For Filling

24 ounces cream cheese, room temperature
1 cup granulated sugar
3 large eggs
1/2 cup unsalted butter, melted and cooled
1/2 teaspoon orange peel (or lemon)

Procedures

For Crust

1. Combine crumbs, butter and sugar, and press into a 9-inch springform pan. Crumbs should come up 3/4 inch on the side of pan.

For Filling

2. Beat cheese with sugar until light.

3. Beat in eggs.

4. Add butter and the peel; blend.

5. Pour filling into waiting unbaked crumb crust.

6. In a preheated 450°F oven, bake 15 minutes. Turn off oven. Let sit all day (or night).

7. Chill or serve at room temperature.

Nelly Dancer's Cheese Strudel

Each strudel serves 8 to 10

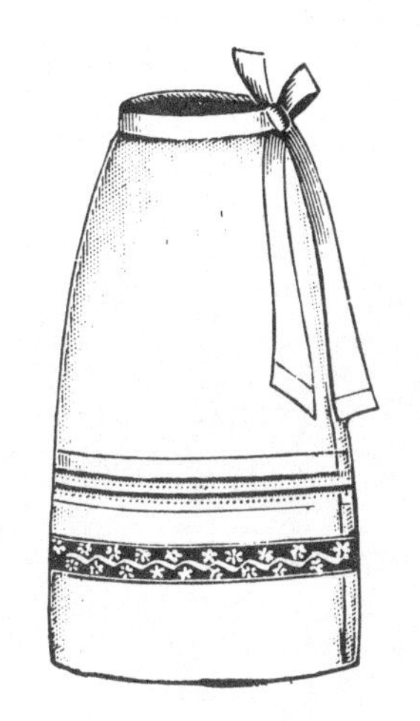

Ingredients

For Crust

1/2 cup unsalted butter, frozen
1 cup all-purpose flour
1 large egg yolk
1/4 cup cool water
Powdered sugar for dusting

For Cheese Filling

12 ounces cream cheese
1/2 cup sugar
3 large egg yolks
1/2 cup golden raisins, plumped (see tip on p. 155)
2 teaspoons lemon peel, freshly grated
1/2 cup butter, melted
1 cup Nilla Wafer or graham-cracker crumbs

Procedures

For Crust

1. In a food processor, cut butter into flour until a mealy consistency is present.

2. With machine running, gradually add a liquid mixture of yolk and water.

3. Process only until the dough begins to mass into a loose dough ball on the steel blade.

4. Refrigerate dough, flattened into a rectangular 1/2-inch-thick disc. Wrap in plastic, chill about 1 hour, until firm. Dough may be frozen for later use at this stage.

5. When chilled, on a lightly floured surface, roll dough gently into a large rectangle (about 10 inches by 16 inches); place on a jellyroll pan.

Proceed to filling recipe and continue as directed.

6. Bake about 20 to 25 minutes in a preheated 400°F oven.

7. Remove golden strudel to a serving plate and, when slightly cooled, dust with powdered sugar.

For Filling

1. Blend cream cheese, sugar and yolks until smooth.

2. Stir in raisins and lemon peel. Refrigerate until slightly firm and spreadable.

3. Brush pastry with melted butter on a central rectangular area about 6 inches wide and 10 inches long, reserving some for the top.

4. Sprinkle the buttered area with crumbs and top with filling mixture.

5. Overlap the long edges of pastry rectangle over filling, then turn up the short ends.

6. Brush the top with reserved butter. Chill for 1 hour minimum before baking.

Proceed with steps 6 and 7 of the Crust recipe.

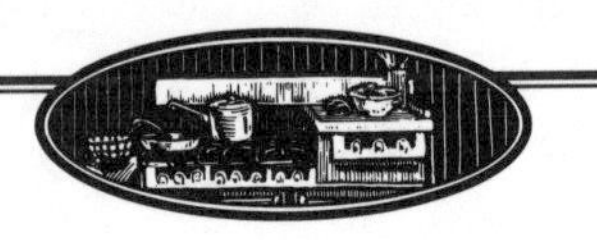

Frozen Kolackys

Makes 4 dozen

For me the greatest pleasure received through food is not in its consumption but rather in the enthusiasm that I as a teacher can create. It is the excitement of a student's mastery of a concept that allows them to deviate from my rules and ideas and their realization that food is a moment of creativity, a great equalizer and finally, a friendship"

Mary James Lawerence, owner/president Cook's Corner, Ltd., Greensboro, NC

Ingredients

1 cup unsalted butter, room temperature
2 cups flour
3 ounces cream cheese, room temperature
3 tablespoons powdered sugar
1 Recipe Cheese Strudel Filling (see recipe on p. 53), chilled
Additional powdered sugar for dusting

Procedures

1. Blend first 4 ingredients together just until mixed thoroughly. (I use a food processor.)
2. Form into 3-inch rolls, each 1 1/2 inches in diameter.
3. Wrap tightly in plastic.
4. Freeze 3 or more hours.
5. Cut 1/3- to 1/4-inch-thick circles from the rolls.
6. Top with fillings, leaving a 1/4-inch margin of dough free of filling.
7. In a preheated 350°F oven, bake 10 to 12 minutes on an ungreased baking sheet, until lightly golden on edges.
8. Cool slightly before removing from sheet.
9. Dust with powdered sugar when cooled.

Torta di Ricotta

Serves 8 to 10

Ingredients

For Pastry

1/3 cup granulated sugar
1 1/2 cups all-purpose flour
1 large egg plus 1 yolk
6 tablespoons unsalted butter, melted and cooled

For Filling

15 ounces low-fat ricotta cheese
4 egg yolks
2/3 cup granulated sugar
1/2 teaspoon cinnamon
1 ounce glacéed mixed fruit
2 ounces golden raisins
2 ounces pine nuts, toasted lightly

For Meringue

3 egg whites, room temperature
3 tablespoons granulated sugar

Procedures

For Pastry

1. In food processor, mix sugar with flour.

2. Add egg and butter, mixing just until a ball forms. Press into a 3/4-inch-thick disc.

3. Allow dough to rest, wrapped and refrigerated, while making filling.

For Filling

4. Blend ricotta with egg yolks, sugar and cinnamon.

5. Mix above with fruits and nuts and beat well.

6. Preheat oven to 375°F.

To Assemble and Bake

7. Butter a 9-inch cake pan with a removable bottom.

8. Roll dough out to 3/8 inch thickness, between waxed paper if necessary.

9. Fit the crust into the prepared pan and trim the edge carefully.

10. Distribute filling evenly and bake the torta 45 to 50 minutes. Let cool 15 minutes.

To Make Meringue

11. Beat egg whites until frothy. Gradually add sugar and continue beating until shiny and stiff.

12. Pipe a closely placed lattice over the cooled torta.

13. Dot "kisses" around the periphery to connect the lattice strips of meringue to the baked crust.

14. Bake about 12 minutes more.

15. Cool 1/2 to 1 hour before unmolding.

Serve warm or cold.

Swedish Church-Social Delights

Our children were raised in a Swedish church. Magnusons, Olsens, Carlsens, Petersens and Lundgrens filled the congregation.

Coffee hour following the Sunday services was all-important and eagerly anticipated. Each woman held a family-treasured recipe and was just waiting to serve it forth on her appointed weekend each year. I'll never forget Lillie Lundgren's cardamom rolls: perfectly formed small, blond clouds of cardamom-perfumed heaven.

In our church, events were orchestrated specifically to showcase Swedish specialties. Whole days were devoted to the stuffing of Myrtle Petersen's potato sausage. Before the annual House of Christmas, phone orders were taken for our meatballs, which were famous throughout the county.

The Swedish love of gathering family and friends around the groaning table to share a meal is a tradition that our family has easily embraced. The recipes that follow are characteristically lightly flavored. Swedish baking is distinguished by its simple presentation and dependable quality. Not driven to excessive showiness, the subtle and toothsome wonder that is real Swedish baking is seldom obscured by fruits or glazes.

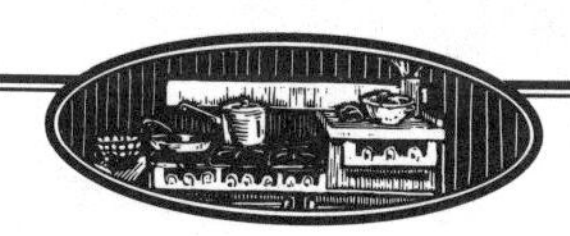

When I have a wonderful recipe for feather-light biscuits or a beautiful vegetable dish with brilliant colors and fascinating taste, I can't wait to tell everybody about it. Don't be afraid to share your joy over good food."

SHILEY O. CORRIHER OF CONFIDENT COOKING IN ATLANTA, GA; TEACHER, WRITER, CONSULTANT

Swedish Cardamom Rolls

Makes 18 to 24

Ingredients

1 quart whole milk
1 cup granulated sugar
1 package (1 tablespoon) yeast
3 cups all-purpose flour (scant)
1 tablespoon salt
6 cardamom seeds, ground
1/2 cup additional granulated sugar
4 egg yolks, beaten
1/4 pound unsalted butter, melted and cooled
Additional flour, if necessary, to achieve a soft dough
2 tablespoons additional unsalted butter, melted and cooled
1/2 cup granulated sugar
2 crushed cardamom seeds

Procedures

1. Bring milk to a boil. Add 1 cup sugar, lower heat, and continue to heat, stirring to dissolve the sugar. Cool to lukewarm.

2. Dissolve the yeast in 3 tablespoons warm water.

3. Gradually blend the yeast with the 3 cups flour, salt, ground cardamom seeds, and cooled milk mixture.

4. Beat the yeasty mixture until it resembles a smooth batter.

5. Allow mixture to rise in a warm place, loosely covered, for 1 hour.

6. Beat in remaining granulated sugar, egg yolks and butter, mixing well.

7. Stir in only enough of the additional flour to make a soft dough.

8. Knead lightly. Allow to rise 2 hours.

9. Form risen dough into braids or small knots and place on buttered baking pans.

10. Let rise, covered, 1 more hour.

11. Bake at 375°F 15 minutes, until pale gold.

12. Remove from the oven and brush lightly with this additional melted butter.

13. Sprinkle with granulated sugar mixed with crushed cardamom seeds.

Danish Butter Cookies

Makes 5 dozen

Ingredients

2 cups unsalted butter
1 cup granulated sugar
4 cups all-purpose flour
Pinch salt
1 egg, beaten well
Additional sugar

Procedures

1. Knead ingredients together until a 2-inch-diameter roll can be formed. Refrigerate roll, wrapped, 1 to 2 hours.
2. Cut off 1/4-inch slices. Place on greased sheet.
3. Brush cookie surfaces with egg.
4. Sprinkle with additional sugar.
5. Bake at 375°F about 12 minutes, until pale golden.

Almond Coffeecake

Serves 12

Ingredients

For Cake

3 to 3 1/2 cups flour
1 package dry yeast
1 cup milk
6 tablespoons unsalted butter
1/3 cup granulated sugar
1 teaspoon salt
1 egg, slightly beaten

For Almond Filling

1 can Almond paste
2/3 cup granulated sugar
4 tablespoons unsalted butter, softened
1/2 teaspoon almond flavoring

For Glaze

1 cup powdered sugar
1/2 teaspoon almond extract
Water

Procedures

For Cake

1. Put 1 cup of flour in a mixing bowl.

2. Heat yeast, milk, butter, sugar and salt to about 110°F, stirring to dissolve sugar. The mixture must be only *lukewarm* to not kill the yeast.

3. Stir the warm liquid mixture into the 1 cup flour until smooth.

4. Add egg and beat 1 minute.

5. Scrape the bowl to collect all ingredients in the bottom again, and then beat for 3 minutes more.

6. Knead the mixture while adding remaining flour.

7. Allow the dough to rise 1 hour, covered.

8. Punch dough down, let rest 10 minutes.

9. Carefully roll dough into an 18-inch-by-12-inch rectangle.

10. Spread with almond filling and roll the filled dough into a log from one long side of the rectangle to the other.

11. Dampen dough edges and pinch along the seam to seal.

12. Make an oval with the dough, sealing ends together to connect.

13. Slit the dough at 1/2-inch intervals, nearly cutting all the way across the dough log.

14. Lift alternate slices and arrange them above the stationary slices, keeping them still attached to the ring of dough.

15. Let rise 45 minutes more, covered.

16. Bake in a 375°F oven for about 25 to 30 minutes, until golden brown.

For Almond Filling

17. Mix all ingredients together, beating until spreadable.

For Glaze

18. Make a creamy mixture of the powdered sugar, almond extract and just enough water to make the glaze drizzleable

SUMMER

Summer—a time for easier living. Less scheduling, more exercise, casual entertaining, picnics, hiking. Abundance and satisfaction are the keys to healthful summertime cooking. A relaxed approach to meals and flavorful summer produce compliment the desire for less total volume of food on the long, hot days. Crisp salads, garden-fresh vegetables, ice creams, herbs and fresh berries are available and affordable. The cook's desire for culinary simplicity is achievable. The time for control cookery is now.

APPETIZERS, FIRST COURSES, SALADS AND SOUPS

Braised Leek Salad	100
Celeriac Salad	100
French Onion Tart	106
Fromage du Jardin	65
Herbed Cream Soups	66
Mushroom Salad	99
Pasta with Sun-dried Tomatoes	113
Pasta with Tuna Fish and Italian Tomatoes	112
Pork and Veal Pâté with Herbs	78
Radish Salad	101
Rice Salad in Tulips	64
Salade Niçoise	108
Spinach Salad	99
Tian of Roasted Sweet Peppers	95
Tian of Swiss Chard or Celery	97
Zucchini *Tian*	96

FISH AND MEATS

Chicken Vegetable Terrine	80
Ham Terrine with Aspic	81

BREADS

Sourdough Corn Bread	93
Sourdough French Bread	91
Sourdough Starter	90

SWEETS

Almond Apple Tart	104
Brazilian Coffee Custard	85
French Apple Tart	103
German Raspberry Pudding	69
Italian Chocolate Mousse	86
Ladyfingers	88
Lemon Blueberry Muffins	83
Peaches with Rose Petals	63
Poppy Seed Coffeecake	84
Raspberry Pie	71
Rhubarb Ice Cream	74
Tiramisù	87
Vanilla Nutmeg Ice Cream	73

ACCOMPANIMENTS

Crème Fraîche	64
Quick Provençal Tomato Sauce	107
Raspberry Liqueur	70
Sun-dried Tomatoes	111

BASICS

Edible Flowers	62
Pastry for Pies and Tarts	109
Sourdough	90
Vinaigrette Dressing	98

Just Help Yourself to the Flowers!

What's poisonous? What's palatable? How do you prepare it?

Flowers on the dinner plate are the rage. These tasty and cheery accents, used as garnish and ingredient, have been cultivated for the table by British gardeners for centuries.

Old gardens grew herbs and flowers for perfume, medicinal and culinary uses. The tisane, referred to in English literature, is a medicinally beneficial flower tea. Flower-flavored beverages, jellies and pastry creams were served throughout the British Empire. Fragrant spikes and blossoms contributed their character to vinegars and oils.

My first encounter with flowers as food was at Brusseau's garden, cooking school and restaurant in Edmonds, Washington. Blue borage flowers and orange calendula petals painted my salad. Ruby nasturtiums floated in the sorrel (*Rumex scutatus*) soup. Rose petals perfumed butter and peaches. Rice salad tumbled from zucchini flowers onto a bed of buttery spinach sprinkled with chive flowers. I was enchanted.

I investigated my own garden's offerings with some garden experts. I found I had edible leafy greens and nasturtiums, pansies, violas, calendulas, roses and herb flowers.

Flower infusions and jams may not meet our contemporary taste or time requirements, but I have found many uncomplicated ways to adorn and flavor my foods with edible flowers. To test my creativity, I served a dinner in which all courses featured flowers. I "pinned" dill florets on pats of butter. Nasturtiums were embedded on my crusty bread before baking—they browned and desiccated during baking, but retained their lovely shapes! Blossoms and petals studded the fresh garden salad of mixed greens. Sprigs of sweet woodruff—mint would have done the same—were dipped in powdered sugar to garnish the dessert.

Mustards become extra table-worthy when chopped flowers are added. Served from a glass pot, herbs and chopped blossoms become obvious. Dill flowers add a delicate fragrance to sauces for fish and veal. Minty mustard is nice with ham, pork and lamb. Herb sage flowers enliven mustards to accompany sausages and pâtés.

Flower butters descend to us from the gracious days of tea, tea sandwiches and leisure time. I think they are particularly well-suited to brunches and showers. Chopped fragrant petals, added to unsalted butter, are an aromatic delight between fingers of brioche or melting into a homemade muffin. Try serving homemade lemonade infused with mauve mint flowers, or float rose petals in glasses of chilled white wine.

I was delighted to discover that tulip flowers are a lovely edible holder for rice, fish, and vegetable salads, and are tasty chopped into stuffed eggs. Dandelion petals and leaves are a spicy addition to salad greens. Rose petals, layered with apples, subtly perfume the all-American apple pie.

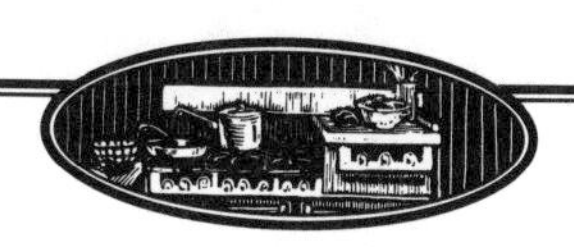

Peaches Poached with Rose Petals

Serves 10

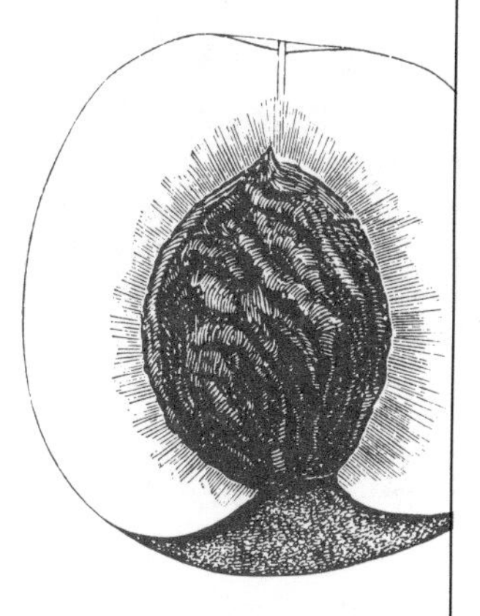

Ingredients

10 roses (don't use roses from the florist—they may have been sprayed)
1 1/2 cups sugar
3 cups water
Juice of 1 lemon
1/2 vanilla bean (split in half), or 1 teaspoon pure vanilla extract
10 firm peaches
1/2 cup raspberry or currant purée, sieved (to remove most seeds)
1/4 to 1/2 teaspoon almond extract

Procedures

1. Pick petals from roses and wrap in cheesecloth.
2. Dissolve sugar in water and simmer 10 minutes with rose petals.
3. Add lemon juice and vanilla, and allow mixture to steep 1/2 hour.
4. Remove cheesecloth and vanilla bean (if used).
5. Blanch peaches, to remove skins, peel, cut in half and take out stones.
6. Poach peach halves and seeds together in rose petal-flavored sugar syrup until peaches are nearly tender.
7. Remove peaches from syrup. Cool peaches and syrup, separately, at room temperature.
8. Mix the purée and almond extract with the syrup.
9. Refrigerate the peaches in the syrup until serving time.

Garnish with fresh rose petals before serving.

Rice Salad in Tulips

Serves 6 to 8

Ingredients

6 to 8 large edible tulip flowers, pistils and stamens removed
3 cups long grain and/or wild rice, cooked
Vinaigrette as needed (see Basic Salad Dressing recipe on p. 98)
1/2 green and/or red pepper
1/4 cucumber
3 radishes
2 tablespoons black and/or green olives
2 green onions

Procedures

1. Toss cooked and cooled rice with vinaigrette so all is lightly moistened.

2. Dice or mince vegetables to desired size (I prefer tiny pieces of vegetables).

3. Toss rice with vegetables and more vinaigrette, if desired.

4. Chill. Remove from refrigerator 1/2 hour before serving.

Serve inside any large edible flowers.

May be served at room temperature.

USING EDIBLE FLOWERS

A few rules must be observed in using edible flowers:

❦ Be positive about flower identification. Consult dependable resources, such as Rosalind Creasy's *Complete Book of Edible Landscaping*, Sierra Club Books, 1982.

❦ Use flowers you *know* have not been sprayed with insecticides.

❦ Taste *all* flower varieties before using. There is a difference between edibility and palatability.

❦ Remove the calyx, pistils and stamens.

❦ *Never* garnish a plate with anything inedible.

❦ Here are some edible flowers:

Bachelor Buttons (*Centaurea cyanus*)

Chrysanthemum (*Chrysanthemum* species)

Cultivated herb flowers

Hyssop (*Hyssopus officinalis*)

Lavender (*Lavandula* species)

Nasturtium (*Tropaeolum, majus*)

Pansy (*Viola x wittrockiana*)

Pot Marigold (*Calendula officinalis*)

Primrose (*Primula vulgaris*)

Rose (*Rosa* species), old fragrant varieties

Sweet Violet (*Viola odorata*)

Fromage du Jardin

My own fresh cheese! Great for the times when herbs and edible flowers are young, pulpy and most flavorful.

Prepare 24 hours before you wish to serve.

Serves 12

Ingredients

1 24-ounce carton creamed cottage cheese
1 clove garlic, mashed with 1 teaspoon salt
1/3 cup fresh herbs, minced with some flowers
1 large egg white, beaten to soft peaks
1/3 cup whipping cream, lightly whipped
Fresh herbs and herb flowers
Lemon rind, freshly grated (optional)
Black pepper, coarsely ground (optional)

Procedures

1. Rub the cheese through a strainer.

2. Stir the garlic and herbs into the cheese.

3. Gently fold the egg whites and cream into cheese.

4. Line cheese molds, a sieve, or cottage cheese cartons perforated with 1/16-inch holes with cheesecloth and fill.

5. Place molds over a pan to drain in a cool place for 24 hours.

6. Refrigerate molds until ready to serve.

7. Unmold cheese carefully onto serving plate or into decorative bowl.

8. Remove cheesecloth and garnish with fresh herbs and herb flowers.

9. Optional: Freshly grated lemon rind and coarsely ground black pepper may be added to pep up this pleasant herbed cheese.

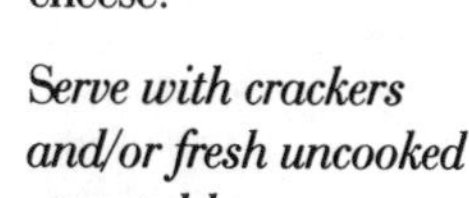

Serve with crackers and/or fresh uncooked vegetables.

Herbed Cream Soups

This soup requires short preparation on 2 days followed by a 4-hour final chilling.

Serves 4 to 6

Ingredients

For Herbed Infusion

3 1/2 ounces mixed (compatible) fresh herbs
1 1/2 pints lightly salted water

For Soup

3 large egg yolks, beaten together
4 tablespoons crème fraîche (see recipe on p. 68)
Salt
Freshly ground black pepper
Additional herbs and herb or other edible flowers

Procedures

The first day: Make an herb infusion

1. Reserving some sprigs for garnish, separate leaves from branches of herbs.

2. Place leaves in a large bell jar.

3. Simmer branches in the lightly salted water for 10 minutes.

4. Strain this liquid into "leaf jar" and cover immediately. Allow to infuse a minimum of 10 hours.

The second day: Make the soup

5. Strain the infusion into a saucepan and squeeze leaves to remove the flavorful liquids.

6. Mix yolks and crème fraîche in a bowl.

7. Bring infusion to a boil. Stir 1/3 cup hot liquid into egg mixture.

8. Return this mixture to the saucepan and, over low heat, stir until it almost boils.

9. Remove soup immediately from the hot cooking pan and correct seasonings. Pour into soup dishes.

10. Chill 4 hours.

Garnish with remaining herbs and edible flowers.

Raspberry Season

Each summer I am astounded by the bounty of fresh raspberries available in Jackson Hole. I thought that all summer berries came from California and Michigan. The first time I was contacted by a local berry distributor I was overjoyed.

As groceries have never been something I was willing to budget, I had no hesitation in responding, "I'll take two flats!" The immoderate side of me became even more glaring when I realized that I had eaten two pints on the five mile ride between Hungry Jack's general store and my south Wilson home.

Jams and jellies splattered all over my stove. Generous bowls of gleaming edible rubies appeared at all meals. Oh Bounty! How I love it!

To wash the berries, either spray them lightly with cold water or (inside a colander) dip them briefly into an icy water bath. Drain them with a gentle shake. Shimmy them gingerly in a terry cloth towel. Pick out any visibly soft fruit and leaves. Serve immediately, or freeze them in a single layer, on cookie sheets, to be bagged when frozen.

HOW TO USE CRÈME FRAÎCHE

This is a trendy concept with its roots deep in France. A dairy culture is added to whipping cream to thicken the cream. Crème fraîche may be used as it is, whipped to serve on berries, pies and tarts or added to hot liquids (such as creamed soups and sauces) without curdling. Though it isn't fat-free, crème fraîche is very user-friendly.

Crème Fraîche

Make at least 24 hours before serving.

This recipe may be made in larger quantities.

Makes 1 cup

Ingredients

1 cup whipping cream
1 tablespoon buttermilk, sour cream or yogurt (I like buttermilk.)

Procedures

1. Thoroughly mix the ingredients.
2. Pour into a clean container and cover tightly.
3. Allow the mixture to sit, undisturbed, 24 to 36 hours, until visibly thickened.
4. Refrigerate (it will continue to thicken as it chills) and use as desired.

To accelerate this process, heat whipping cream until just tepid. Then begin with Step 1 and proceed as directed. Crème fraîche should then thicken visibly within 12 to 18 hours.

Crème fraîche can be stored up to two weeks, tightly sealed and refrigerated.

Kaethe Quarck's German Raspberry Pudding

A part of Ed's dowry, this is an Opler family favorite.

Serves 8

Ingredients

1 pound fresh raspberries or combination of berries, such as currants and raspberries
4 cups water (approximately)
1/3 cup cornstarch
1 cup granulated sugar

Procedures

1. Combine berries and water in a saucepan. Bring to a boil.

2. Simmer 5 minutes.

3. Pass through a sieve over a bowl and press to separate all juices and pulp from seeds.

4. Measure juice and pulp together.

5. Add water to make 5 cups liquid.

6. In a small bowl, combine cornstarch with 3/4 cup of this cooled juice to make a thin paste.

7. Pour remaining juice into a saucepan and bring the liquids to a boil.

8. Reduce heat to medium and stir in sugar and the cornstarch paste.

9. Cook, stirring constantly, until thickened and sugar is dissolved.

10. Cover the pan and cool for 1/2 hour.

11. Pour into a serving bowl and cover with a skin of waxed paper or cling film.

Serve chilled with a drizzle of cream, whipped cream, ice cream, crème fraîche (see recipe above) or a silken custard sauce.

One of life's great pleasures is sharing food with friends, whether at an informal outdoor meal or candlelit dinner. For me, it is wholly satisfying to create something that will bring pleasure. Australia has a wealth of marvelous ingredients that require little assistance to allow their intrinsic qualities to shine through."

JOAN CAMPBELL FOOD EDITOR VOGUE PUBLICATIONS, AUSTRALIA

JOYCE WARNER'S RASPBERRY LIQUEUR

Requires 6 weeks of steeping

Makes approximately 3 quarts

INGREDIENTS

8 pints fresh raspberries, washed
190 proof alcohol (Everclear)
1 1/2 quarts distilled water
5 pounds granulated sugar

PROCEDURES

1. Fill a wide-mouthed gallon jug with the raspberries.
2. Pour in enough alcohol to cover the berries. Tightly cover the bottle.
3. Give the jug an easy shake to mix the ingredients.
4. Steep the jug in a sunny place for 6 weeks.
5. Strain the berries through cheesecloth and squeeze the pulp to remove the maximum quantity.
6. Heat the distilled water with granulated sugar until dissolved. Cool.
7. Add sugar syrup to the strained juices and then pour into clear bottles. Cork the bottles.
8. Store this ambrosial treasure in cool, dark surroundings.

Raspberry liqueur can be served alone as a drink, drizzled over fruit, crepes, or ice creams, combined with custard sauces, added to ice cream mixtures. I make it to give as Christmas gifts, too.

Raspberry Pie in a Pecan Meringue

Serves 8

Ingredients

For Shell

4 large egg whites, room temperature
14 Nilla Wafers, crushed
1 cup granulated sugar
1 teaspoon baking powder
1/2 cup finely chopped pecans

For Filling

20 ounces frozen raspberries, defrosted and drained over a bowl, reserving juices.
Cold water or other juice
2 tablespoons cornstarch

For Topping

3/4 cup whipping cream
1 teaspoon powdered sugar
1 teaspoon pure vanilla extract

Procedures

For Shell

1. Beat egg whites until stiff, smooth and glossy.

2. Fold crumbs, sugar, baking powder and nuts into beaten whites.

3. Spread this mixture into a greased 8-or 9-inch glass pie plate.

4. Bake 40 minutes in a preheated 350°F oven. Cool.

For Filling

5. Add cold water or other compatibly flavored juice to reserved raspberry juice to equal 1 cup liquid.

6. Stir cornstarch into juice and cook in a saucepan over medium-high heat until thickened. Cool.

7. Stir berries into thickened juices.

8. Fill the cooled meringue crust and refrigerate.

For Topping

9. Whip cream with powdered sugar and vanilla just before serving pie.

10. Mound topping onto chilled pie. Serve.

Summer's Highlight: Homemade Ice Cream

Homemade ice cream is one of my family's favorite refreshers on a summer evening. Somehow we just aren't interested in ice cream with the same frequency or enthusiasm in the winter.

Wonderful new ice cream machines make the process much more inviting than it used to be. Other than the ritual "communal churning," I never could muster the same excitement about making this American staple when children had to be coerced to churn beyond the endurance of their interest, and often my supply of salt. I'll never forget the Christmas when my mom gave me my first manual ice cream freezing tub. Thoughtfully, she also gave me the ice cream mixture—ready to churn—for dessert, that evening! Imagine the project of churning dessert on Christmas! Fancy countertop freezers and miraculous glycol gel-insulated churning bowls make this job easier and more fun.

In ice-cream making, texture is the magic word. We all notice when ice creams are grainy or icy. Minimizing the development of ice crystals while freezing ice cream will ensure a smooth texture. A few simple steps will help home ice-cream makers achieve the smoothness we all desire:

❦ Always chill the ice-cream-freezing bowl and dasher in the freezer before proceeding.

❦ Chill the ice-cream mixture until *almost* frozen before putting it into the machine bowl.

❦ Remove any ice crystals with a spoon before churning begins.

❦ Use half-and-half instead of milk or whipping cream to further ensure a silky smooth texture.

With these hints, homemade ice cream will surely be better than store-bought!

Vanilla Nutmeg Ice Cream

Serves 6 to 10

Ingredients

2 cups whole milk
1 vanilla bean, split lengthwise (1 tablespoon pure vanilla extract may be substituted and added with cream in step 7)
1 cup granulated sugar
1 teaspoon nutmeg, freshly grated
6 large egg yolks, room temperature
1 cup whipping cream

Procedures

1. Bring milk and vanilla bean to boil with 1/2 cup of the sugar.

2. Remove from heat and cover to steep for 30 minutes.

3. Scrape vanilla bean seeds into the milk. Add nutmeg and whisk the mixture.

4. Beat egg yolks with remaining sugar until light yellow and visibly thickened.

5. Pour hot milk onto beaten eggs and whisk.

6. Return the custard mixture to a saucepan and stir over low heat until the mixture smoothly coats the back of a metal spoon.

7. Strain the mixture into a bowl. Add cream. Chill.

8. Refrigerate as directed in "tips" before freezing in ice cream machine as directed by manufacturer.

"I was bitten by the food bug over 30 years ago and I still love food as much today as I did then. I believe cooking well is the best way of showing people you care. Let's face it: eating is a daily adventure, so it's important to do it properly."

Elise Pascoe, author of three cookbooks, food writer for the *Sydney Morning Herald, Food Arts Australian* contributor, and principal of the Elise Pascoe Cooking School

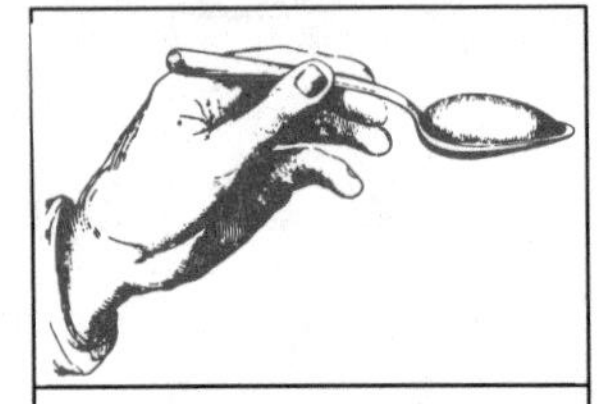

CURDLING CAUTION

Take care to prevent boiling any custard mixtures, like those in the vanilla nutmeg and rhubarb ice cream recipes. Eggs will curdle and consistency will be sacrificed. If curdling does begin, pour mixture immediately through a sieve. If curdling ceases and mixture is smooth, congratulations. If not, sorry, begin again.

Rhubarb Ice Cream

Serves 4 to 8

Ingredients

1 bunch (5 to 6 stalks) rhubarb
2/3 cup granulated sugar
3 to 4 tablespoons fresh lemon juice
6 large egg yolks
2/3 cup additional granulated sugar
1 1/2 cups whole milk
3/4 cup whipping cream

Procedures

1. Scrub rhubarb and cut into 1-inch pieces.
2. Place rhubarb in a non-corrosive pot with 2/3 cup sugar and lemon juice.
3. Cook slowly for about 1/2 hour and then push fruit through a sieve. Reserve juice to drizzle over finished ice cream.
4. Beat egg yolks with remaining sugar until light yellow and visibly thickened.
5. Bring milk to a boil and pour over yolks, whisking.
6. Return custard mixture to the stove and cook over low heat until it smoothly coats the back of a metal spoon. (It shouldn't look frothy on the spoon.)
7. Remove custard from the cooking pan to cease its cooking.
8. Allow custard to cool.
9. Combine custard, fruit pieces and cream; cool as directed in "tips" before freezing in ice cream machine according to manufacturer's directions.

TIPS FOR PERFECT ICE CREAM

1. Start with a great recipe.

2. To increase heft of ice cream without increasing butterfat, use sweetened condensed milk (more milk, less water).

3. If fresh fruit is used, coat it in sugar to prevent it from freezing solid.

4. Refrigerate ice-cream mixture 2 to 6 hours before cranking. Then place mixture in freezer for 1 hour, until ice crystals almost form. (Ice creams with alcohol or excess sugar will take longer to reach this stage, and the addition of alcohol will result in softer ice cream.)

5. If using a traditional ice-cream maker requiring salt and crushed ice, increase recommended salt-to-ice ratio to 1:4 or 1:5. Alternate layers of crushed ice with salt. Pour 2 cups water over ice/salt to distribute chilling power. Crank slowly before freezing begins, to prevent whipping air into mixture. When freezing begins (resistance is felt), crank as fast as you can to break up any ice crystals.

6. Eat homemade ice cream immediately! Within 3 days it may become inedibly crunchy.

Pâtés and Terrines: The Glorified Meat Loaf

Before houseguests begin to arrive, I plan menus and choose recipes to make life simpler as I enjoy my visitors. Making breads, salad dressing, pie crusts, soups and pâtés is an old trick. Having these preparations ready makes it possible to spend my days away from home without fear as dinnertime approaches.

Making muffin batter and refrigerating it in tins for morning baking is a magical way to look extra efficient (see The Survival of the "Hostess Cupcake" on page 82). The same tactic is also successful for batter-type coffeecakes.

One of my favorite do-ahead standbys is pâté. A pâté, in its most traditional form, is simply a glorified meat loaf. Another one of those thrifty French culinary ideas, pâtés use up meat trimmings in a palate-pleasing and table-worthy way. Liver sausage and veal loaf are relatives of the pâté. Duck, pork, and cognac-enhanced pâtés are now sold in supermarkets and gourmet food shops throughout the U.S.

Typically, I freeze bits of pork and veal to amass enough quantity for a pâté. (Careful freezer labeling is an important habit to develop.) Like meat loaf, pâté is a mixture of meats and other savory ingredients bound by egg protein. A pâté can be baked, to be eaten warm today, and then chilled for serving at a second meal. Most pâtés can be tightly double-wrapped and frozen. Unfrozen, meat pâtés will keep up to 1 week if tightly wrapped and refrigerated. After each use, remaining pâté should be wrapped with clean plastic wrap and refrigerated. The herb pâté can be frozen successfully if layered decorative strips of meat or vegetables are substituted for the hard-cooked eggs.

One of the obvious differences between a pâté and a meat loaf is additional fat. Fats are not fashionable, but they do convey flavor and ensure a moist loaf. Bacon surrounding the pâté is meant to be eaten, but it can be omitted or removed after cooking is completed.

After removing the cooked pâté from the oven, if desired, carefully remove the hot liquid fat to prevent reabsorption. Baking a pâté in a water bath will ensure the characteristic moist, not crusty, exterior.

Technically, a pâté is a mixture baked in a vessel called a terrine. The pâté may be made of fish, chicken, duck, vegetables and meats. The terrine may be any shape or size, with or without a cover.

Pâté's relatives, ballottines and galantines, are words encountered but rarely explained. Boned fowl, of any size or variety from quail to turkey, is filled with a pâté-like mixture, tied securely to resemble a large sausage, poached and served warm—ballottine—or cold—galantine.

This all sounds far more complex than it should. Pâtés are another deliciously efficient way to use time and ingredients. Today's recipe is one on my favorite summer standbys. I sometimes distribute pistachios, cubes of prosciutto or ham and turkey, or diced cooked vegetables and bright green peas throughout the pâté meat mixture as a simple variation.

The one underlying tenet that all chefs hold and share is that, foremost, always, is the quality of your ingredients. Make sure your ingredients are the freshest, organically grown, the best plant stock, or whatever it takes to obtain the finest quality. Then treat them with great respect, always remembering what Frank Lloyd Wright said—'God is in the details.' "

PETER KUMP, PRESIDENT THE JAMES BEARD FOUNDATION; PRESIDENT, PETER KUMP'S NEW YORK COOKING SCHOOL

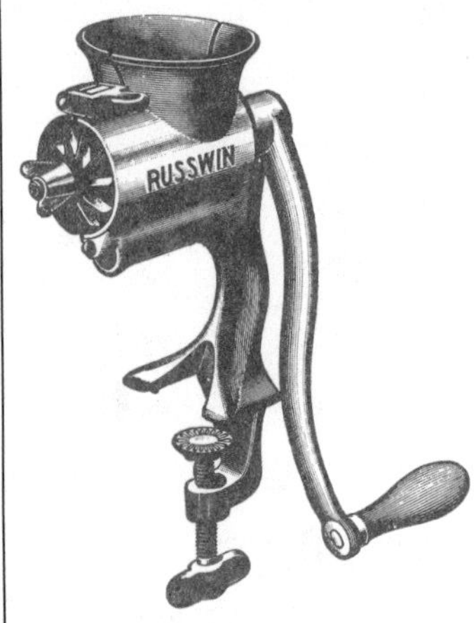

Pork and Veal Pâté with Herbs

Must be prepared at least 24 hours before serving

Serves 8 to 12

Ingredients

1 pound boneless pork
1/2 pound boneless veal
4 ounces pork fat
3/4 cup onion, chopped
2 cloves garlic, minced
1 tablespoon butter or margarine
1 1/2 cups fresh spinach, chopped
3 tablespoons brandy
1 large egg
1 1/2 tablespoons fresh basil, snipped, or 1 teaspoon dried basil leaves
1 1/2 tablespoons fresh rosemary, snipped, or 1 teaspoon dried rosemary leaves
1 tablespoon fresh thyme, snipped, or 1/2 teaspoon dried thyme leaves
1 1/4 teaspoons salt
1/2 teaspoon fennel seeds, crushed
1/4 teaspoon freshly ground black pepper
8 to 12 thin-sliced bacon strips
6 large eggs, hard-cooked (whole)
1 fresh thyme sprig
Drilled gherkins (available in stores carrying imported foods)
Marinated pearl onions

Procedures

1. Cut pork, veal and pork fat into small pieces. Pass mixture twice through fine blade of meat grinder.

2. In a small skillet, sauté onion and garlic in butter about 5 minutes. Add spinach and cook, stirring, about 1 minute. Transfer to a bowl.

3. Stir meat mixture into onion mixture. Stir in remaining ingredients except bacon, hard-cooked eggs, thyme sprig, gherkins and onions.

4. Arrange bacon slices perpendicularly across bottom and up the sides of an 8 1/2-inch by 4 1/2-inch loaf pan. Let slices overhang edges of pan. (To use other terrines, measure water volume held in 8 1/2-inch by 4 1/2-inch loaf pan. Choose a cooking container of similar volume or alter recipe quantities proportionally as needed.)

5. Place half of the meat mixture in loaf pan.

6. Arrange whole, hard-cooked eggs lengthwise in a row down the center of meat mixture, pressing down lightly. Cover with remaining meat mixture. Wrap bacon over top. Place thyme sprig on top.

7. Cover loaf pan with foil or lid and set it into a baking pan with enough hot water to reach 1/3 up the sides of the terrine.

8. In a preheated 350°F oven, bake the pâté 1 1/4 hours or until meat juices run clear and internal temperature is 160° F.

9. Pour off the fat now, or let stand uncovered 20 minutes and then drain off the fat.

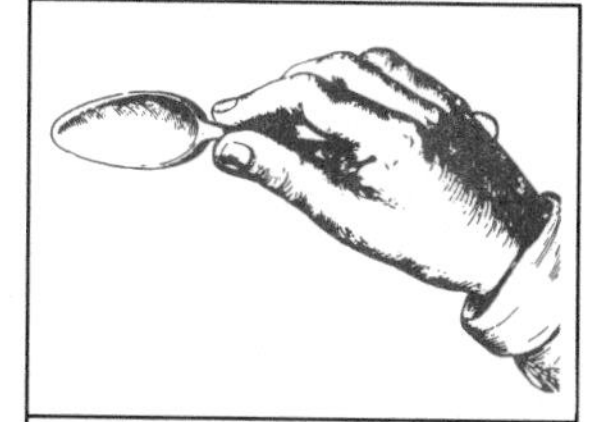

10. To serve in the traditional flattened brick shape, cover and place weight on top of loaf. Refrigerate at least 24 hours. (I weigh my foil-covered pâté down with assorted canned goods whose diameters fit across the top of the meat. To add additional weight, I make a 2- or 3-tiered pyramid with cans. I have even used a brick or a bag of shotgun shot!)

11. Before serving, run spatula around edge of pan and unmold chilled pâté; trim excess fat away. Cut into 1/2-inch slices.

Serve with gherkins and onions.

SERVING SUGGESTIONS

This pâté is perfect fare for an elegant picnic lunch or dinner on the deck. Serve it with French bread, lusty mustard, tiny dilled pickles and onions. A beautiful fresh salad and perfectly ripened cheese (I like Morbier, Raclette or Gruyère) are my favorite accompaniments. Fresh berries or a rich chocolate dessert would be a grande finale.

CHICKEN VEGETABLE TERRINE

Serves 8 to 10

INGREDIENTS

1 1/4 pounds chicken breast meat
1 cup carrots, diced
3/4 cup whole green beans
1 cup green peas
1 tomato
1 1/2 tablespoons butter, melted
1/4 pound mushrooms, sliced
1 1/2 teaspoons olive oil
1 teaspoon salt
1/2 teaspoon ground white pepper
1/4 cup fresh parsley, chopped
1/2 teaspoon fresh thyme,* chopped
1/2 teaspoon fresh tarragon,* chopped
1 cup whipping cream

***Substitute other fresh available herbs rather than substitute dry. Use more parsley and some green onion tops if all else fails.**

PROCEDURES

1. Remove skin and fat from chicken and cut into cubes.

2. Cook carrots 2 minutes and then add green beans for 2 minutes. Next add peas for 1 minute.

3. Drain vegetables, refresh them with cold water, drain and blot dry.

4. Peel tomato, remove seeds and cut into cubes.

5. Sauté mushrooms in melted butter.

6. In bowl, combine all vegetables.

7. Sprinkle with olive oil, salt and pepper.

8. In processor, combine chicken, parsley, thyme and tarragon and purée until smooth.

9. With processor running, pour whipping cream through feeder tube and process until the mixture holds its shape on a spoon held upside-down.

10. Transfer the chicken mixture into a large bowl and gently stir in the vegetable mixture.

11. Pour this mixture into an oiled 8-cup terrine.

12. Cover the terrine with the greased lid or greased foil.

13. Place terrine in a water bath (1/3 up the side of the terrine) in a preheated 325°F oven for about 60 minutes, or until juices are yellow and a meat thermometer registers 190° F.

I like to serve this chicken terrine with a honey-mustard flavored mayonnaise and thinly sliced pumpernickel bread.

Ham Terrine with Aspic

Prepare the day before serving

Serves 8 to 12

Ingredients

3 cans consommé or madrilène
1 bottle dry white wine
2 cups water
1/2 best-quality fully cooked ham with rind and fat removed, boned
3 cloves garlic
1 sprig thyme
Freshly ground black pepper
1 tablespoon gelatin powder
1 1/2 cups parsley, chopped
2 tablespoons fresh tarragon, chopped (optional)

Procedures

1. Assemble liquids with ham, garlic, thyme and pepper in a large stock pot and simmer, covered, 30 minutes.

2. Remove ham from poaching liquids. Reserve and cool 2 cups liquid for the following procedures. Allow this stock to cool while cutting ham into 1/2-inch chunks. (Discard remaining cooking liquid.)

3. Add gelatin to the 2 cups cooled poaching stock and heat to dissolve gelatin. With your fingers, feel the slippery liquid and make sure the gelatin is not all stuck to the bottom of the saucepan.

4. Test the gelling strength by allowing 1/4 cup of this stock to sit in a metal bowl inside another bowl of iced water. It should become firm.

If the testing liquid doesn't gel firmly:

Cool a small amount of the poaching stock and add 1 teaspoon more gelatin. Add this stock and the testing liquid back into the remaining poaching stock and reheat to dissolve gelatin. Retest, as before, for a firmly gelled consistency. Repeat this process until liquid gels to a sliceable firmness.

5. Remelt this testing liquid and add back into warm poaching stock.

6. Add parsley and optional fresh tarragon to the stock.

7. Ladle a layer of stock into terrine. Refrigerate to set the gelatin before layering ham on top.

8. Ladle more stock over ham and refrigerate again to set gelatin before repeating. Continue until the terrine is filled with layers of ham and stock.

9. The terrine must chill several hours, or preferably overnight, in the refrigerator before serving.

It may be served sliced from the terrine or unmolded whole onto a chilled platter.

If unmolded, an electric knife is especially helpful. Slicing and immediate serving must be done while aspic is cold.

THE SURVIVAL OF THE "HOSTESS CUPCAKE"

I have learned through experience that having house guests can either be an exhilarating experience or it can become a drudgery, depending on how I manage the meals.

No one could have approached the task of sharing Jackson Hole with her visiting guests more earnestly. I did everything. The table was set before guests awoke. The croissants were hot and fresh from the oven. Rooms were waiting, bedecked with garden-fresh flowers.

I've learned a lot in my 13 summers in that beautiful valley. I had to learn the lessons the hard way. I had a reputation to uphold! The house had to be in perfect readiness and all foods had to be fresh and homemade. Little by little, my spontaneous invitations, "Why don't you stay with us? The price is right once you get there!" became less automatic.

I was creating my own dilemma, and a friend's offer to bring and take away her own sheets finally woke me up. I missed skiing for two consecutive years, despite having new skis, because I was—as one good friend put it—"the perfect 'Hostess Cupcake.' "

My entire raison d'etre had become the preparation and execution of the perfect visit to Jackson Hole. Well, let me tell you: The "execution" was my own and I was scaring the guests with my perfectly orchestrated visitor habitat.

I have relaxed a great deal and I am now able to enjoy the valley with my friends. After a full day on the river, we clean the lettuce together. I have even learned to let others make the vinaigrette. Grilling, slow-cooking and virtually unlimited pasta variations are wonderfully simple ways to put together a perfectly cooked meal after a full day away from home. Chocolate sundaes and/or fresh berries are always a popular dessert. Wondrously, I have found that guests really love Fig Newtons and Lorna Doones.

Oh well, I know that they are still anticipating some of the old Pat Opler breakfast goodies. I have solved the conflict between fresh breads for breakfast and enough sleep.

Following are two recipes illustrating that batter breads can be completely made and refrigerated before baking. My delicious lemon blueberry muffins and poppyseed coffee cake have made me look like I was up before dawn. They can do the same for you.

P.S. Never turn down a guest's invitation to go out for dinner!

Lemon Blueberry Muffins

Makes 14 standard-size muffins

Ingredients

1 cup all-purpose flour
2 teaspoons baking powder
1/2 teaspoon salt
2 tablespoons sugar
1 large egg
1/4 teaspoon corn oil
1 cup milk
Rind of 1 lemon, grated
1 1/2 cups fresh or frozen blueberries
Optional:
3 tablespoons unsalted butter, melted
3 tablespoons granulated sugar

Procedures

1. Mix dry ingredients.

2. Beat egg, oil, milk, and lemon rind together.

3. Stir liquids into dry ingredients with a fork. Blend only until all dry ingredients have been moistened.

4. Gently stir in blueberries.

5. Fill greased muffin tins 2/3 full.

May refrigerate overnight before baking at this point.

6. In a preheated 425°F oven, bake 20 minutes or until golden.

7. Remove carefully from muffin tins after cooling 10 minutes.

8. Optional: Dip tops of muffins into hot melted butter and then into granulated sugar while muffins are still warm.

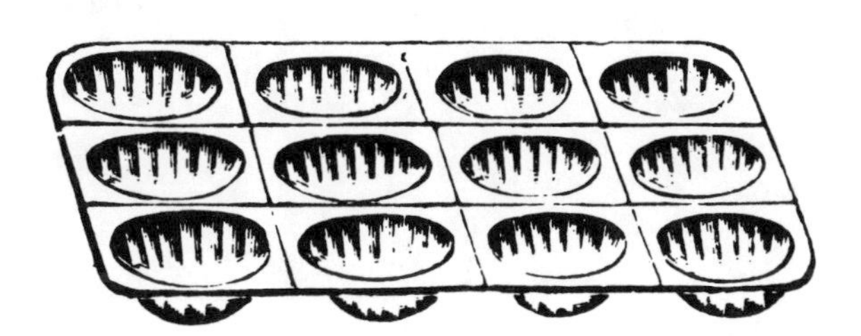

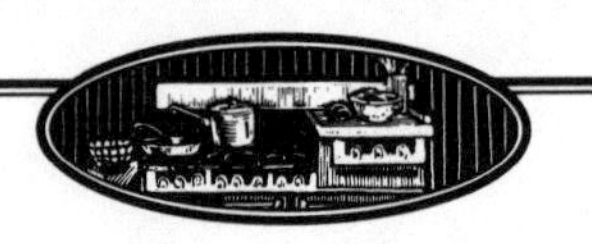

HIGH-ALTITUDE BAKING

At high altitude (above 3,500 feet), I increase flour and decrease sugar slightly for batter breads and cakes. I make no changes for yeast breads.

Poppy Seed Coffeecake

Makes 1 cake in a bundt or angelfood cake pan

Ingredients

1/4 cup poppy seeds
1 teaspoon almond extract
1 cup buttermilk
1/8 cup granulated sugar, mixed with 2 teaspoons cinnamon
1 1/2 cups granulated sugar
4 large egg yolks
1 cup unsalted butter
2 1/2 cups all-purpose flour
1 teaspoon baking powder
1 teaspoon baking soda
1 teaspoon salt
4 large egg whites, room temperature
Powdered sugar

Procedures

1. Soak poppy seeds with almond extract in buttermilk.

2. Reserve cinnamon-sugar mixture.

3. Cream sugar, yolks and butter until light and creamy.

4. Mix the next 4 dry ingredients together.

5. Beat egg whites until soft peaks form.

6. Combine buttermilk mixture with egg yolk mixture.

7. Stir in flour mixture to moisten the dry ingredients.

8. Fold in egg whites until smoothly blended.

9. Butter and flour a tube pan.

10. Distribute 1/2 of batter in pan and sprinkle 1/2 of cinnamon-sugar mixture over the top of the batter, taking care not to get the cinnamon-sugar on the cake pan.

11. Distribute remaining batter and sprinkle with the rest of the cinnamon-sugar.

May be refrigerated overnight at this point.

12. In a preheated and accurate 350°F oven, bake 1 to 1 1/4 hours.

13. Cool 30 minutes, then invert coffeecake onto a serving plate after loosening cake edges where possible.

14. Dust with powdered sugar.

A Half-Empty, or Half-Full Coffeepot

Oh bounty! How I love it!

I just love the aura of abundance that comes from my kitchen and its offerings. Those of us with a tendency toward excess must work creatively to deflect criticism. My husband and I regularly differ regarding the appropriate number of bottles of wine to "breathe" prior to a dinner party. I usually win. I have developed several recipes to make the unconsumed wines look intentional.

The following recipes justify the half-full or half-empty (depending on your sense of justification) coffeepot. Just about the time the second pot of coffee is ready, everyone decides to leave for work or play. Good quality strong coffee, either high test or de-caf, will benefit any of these recipes. We always use Medaglia d'Oro coffee. I've never understood or enjoyed stewed beans.

Nina Bégué's Brazilian Coffee Custard

Serves 8 to 10

Ingredients

1/2 cup unsalted butter, softened
1 cup granulated sugar
1/2 cup brown sugar
3 large eggs
1/4 cup hot coffee
1 tablespoon heavy cream
1/2 teaspoon pure vanilla extract

Procedures

1. Beat butter with sugars until smooth.

2. Add eggs 1 at a time, beating.

3. Blend coffee, cream and vanilla.

4. Fill 8 to 10 ramekins or custard cups 2/3 full and place on a jellyroll pan or cookie sheet.

5. In a preheated 350°F oven, bake 20 to 25 minutes until puffy, crusty and golden on top.

Serve warm or at room temperature. We like it served with ice cream.

Italian Chocolate Mousse

Serves 8

Ingredients

4 large eggs, separated, room temperature
2 teaspoons granulated sugar
2 tablespoons orange juice (yes, fresh does make a difference!)
6 ounces sweet dark chocolate
1 tablespoon unsalted butter
1/4 cup strong coffee
1/2 ounce candied orange peel (traditional, but not required)
2/3 cup whipping cream

Procedures

1. Beat egg yolks and sugar until thick and light yellow. Reserve egg whites.
2. Add the orange juice and cook in a double boiler until visibly thickened.
3. Melt the chocolate, butter and coffee together in a double boiler or in the microwave for 2 minutes on high. If microwaving, stir to incorporate chocolate with coffee and butter after melting.
4. Stir the 2 mixtures together.
5. Add candied orange peel, if desired.
6. Beat the egg whites until stiff but still shiny.
7. Stir 1/3 of white into the chocolate mixture. Then carefully fold chocolate into the remaining whites.
8. Beat the cream until almost whipped, then fold into the mousse.
9. Chill and enjoy.

Garnish with chocolate shavings, candied orange peel, sliced toasted almonds or a bit of whipped cream.

Tiramisù

The Italian "pick-me-up"

From my first day in Milanese restaurant kitchens, I wanted to know how to make this wonderful dessert. To my dismay, I discovered that tiramisù is nearly always made commercially and delivered to restaurants each morning. I hope you like my version.

Serves 9 to 12

Ingredients

24 ladyfingers, slightly dried (see recipe on next page), leftover cake chunks or commercial biscotti
8 ounces sweet dark chocolate
Optional: 1/4 cup Amaretto
1 cup cooled strong coffee
6 large egg yolks
6 tablespoons granulated sugar
6 large egg whites
1 pound Mascarpone cheese, or a combination of 1/2 cup Ricotta blended well with 1 cup whipping cream will substitute nicely.

Procedures

1. Grate chocolate coarsely by hand or in food processor with the steel blade running.

2. If using Amaretto, mix it with the coffee. (If not, use slightly sweetened coffee for step 7.)

3. Cream yolks and sugar together until light yellow and thickened.

4. Beat egg whites until stiff but still shiny.

5. Stir 1/3 of egg whites into the cheese.

6. Fold cheese back into remaining whites.

7. Dip flat side of ladyfingers into coffee and line the bottom of a 9-inch square Pyrex baking dish or other comparable or individual serving dishes.

8. Spread 1/2 of cheese mixture over ladyfingers.

9. Distribute 1/2 of chocolate over cheese layer.

10. Repeat layers, ending with a generous layer of chocolate.

11. Chill, covered, at least 2 hours.

This dessert does not serve in neat little squares. Spoon the tiramisù into dessert bowls or wine glasses and watch the way it picks up your guests!

From Milano . . . Ristorante Francesco expresses the spirit, style, refined cuisine and friendly atmosphere of Italy's business capital with 'la buona cucina italiana.'

Grazie Di totto amore, Irene Sanna, owner Ristorante Francesco, Milano Italy

LADYFINGERS

Makes approximately 4 dozen

INGREDIENTS

5 large egg yolks, room temperature
9 tablespoons granulated sugar
1 scant cup flour
5 large egg whites, room temperature
1 1/2 tablespoons additional granulated sugar
Powdered sugar

PROCEDURES

1. Beat 9 tablespoons sugar with egg yolks until mixture is light yellow and thickened.

2. Blend the flour thoroughly with the egg yolk mixture.

3. Beat egg whites at high speed for about 1 minute. Add 1 1/2 tablespoons sugar and beat 1 minute more.

4. Stir 1/4 of the beaten egg whites into egg yolk mixture to lighten it.

5. Fold the yolk mixture back into the remaining beaten whites.

6. Smear a small amount of batter onto the cookie sheets. Stick pieces of parchment (or brown paper from grocery bags) to the sheets—parchment will not move as ladyfingers are piped.

7. Fill pastry bag fitted with a 1/2-inch round-tipped nozzle. Pipe out ladyfingers, about 3 1/2 inches long and about 1 inch wide.

8. Dust ladyfingers heavily with powdered sugar.

9. In a preheated 350°F oven, bake for 12 minutes.

10. Turn cookie sheets around and bake about 5 more minutes, until puffed and barely golden in color.

11. Remove ladyfingers after cooling slightly.

Ladyfingers should be light golden. Accurate oven temperature is important.

Blue-Ribbon Sourdough

There is no doubt that generations of pioneering Americans sustained themselves with the help of a carefully protected, bubbling and aromatic crock of sourdough starter. Before the advent of commercially marketed envelopes of yeast, bakers and brew masters closely guarded their magical organisms. Today the intrigue of sourdough still invites creative bakers throughout the world to develop new ways of instilling the tangy flavor into baked products.

In this age, foods evidencing a life of their own—such as molds—are quietly discarded. We overlook the fact that cheeses, yogurts and beers are "living" foods whose flavor characteristics rely upon the incorporation and nurturing of molds and yeasts.

I like to imagine it was a cooking creature like myself who, in years past, discovered a convenient liquid for making bread was yesterday's potato cooking water. A neat host for airborne bacterial yeasts, the bread dough rises. A loftier product results. Small amounts of the lively dough are saved from each batch. Voila! The discovery of a "sponge," or leavener. Frequent use invigorates this sponge. More flour and water are added to feed and increase its volume. Bubbles assure the baker of its powers. Crocks of starter are taken to bed to prevent a slowing chill. Enter human inventiveness: Pancakes, biscuits, corn bread, doughnuts, gingerbread, fruit breads and rye, white and wheat breads spring from the sourdough discovery.

Sourdough cookery is not an exact science. A healthy sourdough starter is a dependable yeast agent with a long slow-acting schedule. For those of us accustomed to using the "quick-rise" yeasts now available, the less demanding pace of sourdough cooking can be a welcome change.

Starter-power varies from one location to another. Climate affects airborne yeasts. Low humidity speeds rising times. Therefore, starters perk up faster in a dry climate. Temperature also affects rising times and intensity of sourness.

Starters, sponges and doughs thrive on leisurely rising times and eliminate the need to get up in the night or rush home to punch down the dough. Any stage can be manipulated to meet scheduling needs. Rising loaves can be slowed by refrigeration. A healthy starter will best lend its tangy flavor if it isn't rushed. Sourdough cookery works nicely for all kinds of days—the well-regulated, the high speed or the unpredictable.

Sourdough Basics

Most sourdough products are completed in three stages:

1. **Starter**—A fermented batter made from flour plus water or milk, to be made in advance. A portion will be incorporated later into a "sponge." The unused remainder of the starter is replenished with equal parts of all-purpose flour and water, stirred, and allowed to ferment at room temperature for up to 24 hours before refrigerating in a loosely covered jar or crock. Bubbles will develop at room temperature, indicating a reactivated starter.

2. **Sponge**—A soft batter made of some starter with additional flour and water, to be used as the leavener for a dough recipe. Sponges normally activate for 24 hours or longer before being added to remaining ingredients. Chill sponge to slow fermentation.

3. **Dough**—The sponge plus the ingredients to complete the desired product.

Sourdough Starter

Starter must be made a week ahead of planned bread baking day.

Ingredients

1 cup skim or low-fat milk
1 package (1 tablespoon) dry yeast
3 tablespoons unflavored nonfat yogurt
1 cup unbleached flour

Procedures

1. Heat milk to tepid (about 90°F)

2. Pour into glass or stainless-steel container and stir in yeast and yogurt.

3. Cover tightly and allow to rest 18 to 24 hours in a warm place to develop the culture.

4. Pour off liquid from top.

5. Stir in flour until smooth.

6. Cover tightly and rest again in a warm place 2 to 5 days.

Wynne Gensey's Sourdough French Bread

Makes 4 loaves

Step 1. First morning—Make sponge

Ingredients

1 cup all-purpose flour
1 cup warm water
2 cups sourdough starter, made at least one week previous

Procedures

1. Mix all ingredients together gently in a bowl.

2. Cover with a warm, damp towel.

3. Let sponge develop for up to 24 hours. Chilling will slow it down. To reactivate it, bring to room temperature.

Step 2. Replenish starter

Ingredients

Remaining Starter
1 cup flour
1 cup warm water

Procedures

4. To remaining starter, add equal parts flour and water and let stand, covered, at room temperature.

Step 3. 18 to 24 hours later—Make bread

Ingredients

2 teaspoons salt
2 tablespoons sugar
3 cups warm water
Sponge made in Step 1
8 cups flour—unbleached or bread flour

Procedures

5. Dissolve salt and sugar in water.

6. Add sponge, stir.

7. Add flour, 4 cups at a time. Add more flour until a kneadable consistency is reached.

8. Knead at least 10 minutes.

9. Spray a large bowl with non-stick vegetable oil spray.

10. Place dough in bowl and turn over once in bowl.

11. Cover. Let rise until doubled. (Rises will take about 2 hours each. They can be slowed by refrigeration.)

12. Punch dough down, cover again, allow to rise again until doubled.

13. Remove from bowl onto floured cloth.

14. Divide dough into quarters and form into desired loaf shapes.

15. Make diagonal cuts for decoration through loaves with scissors or a sharp knife; cut at least halfway through the loaf.

16. Cover with a damp towel. Let rise again.

17. Refrigerate replenished starter.

Step 4. Bake bread

Ingredients

Butter, melted

Procedures

18. Put loaf pans into cold oven.

19. Set oven to 375°F.

20. Bake 1 hour. Spray with water every 15 minutes.

21. Turn loaves out of pans when baked.

22. Brush with melted butter.

Step 5. To reheat bread

Procedures

23. Reheat in a 350°F oven for 10 minutes.

If freezing, cool before wrapping.

Sourdough Corn Bread

From Wynne Gensey

Makes a 10-inch round skillet of corn bread

Ingredients

1 cup starter (see recipe on p. 90)
1 cup mixed white and yellow cornmeal
1/2 cup all-purpose flour
1 large can evaporated milk
2 large eggs, beaten
2 tablespoons granulated sugar
1/4 cup unsalted butter, melted
1/2 teaspoon salt
1 teaspoon baking soda

Procedures

1. Mix the starter, cornmeal, flour, milk, eggs and sugar.

2. Stir in butter, salt and baking soda.

3. Grease a 10-inch cast-iron skillet or baking dish of similar volume.

4. In a preheated 425°F oven, bake 25 minutes.

The Genseys serve this with butter and maple syrup! I like to add 2 tablespoons chopped green chilies and 1/2 cup cooked corn.

TIPS FOR SOURDOUGH SUCCESS

❦ 1 cup starter = 1 cake or package yeast in leavening strength.

❦ To increase starter quantity, add equal amounts all-purpose flour and water (up to 10 cups each) and let stand 2 days. Refrigerate.

❦ Store starter, covered loosely, in the refrigerator.

❦ Mix ingredients into starter gently to preserve yeast bubbles.

❦ Use starter at room temperature.

❦ If you use all your starter, add equal parts of flour and water to the unwashed starter jar. Allow to ferment several hours, stir, cover loosely, refrigerate.

❦ If starter seems too smelly to you, it is likely too sour. Add 1 cup warm water plus 1 cup all-purpose flour; stir. Pour out all but 1 cup. Let stand several hours and replenish as directed.

❦ Starters like to be used weekly. If this isn't possible:

A. Freeze starter (at its healthiest) 2 to 3 months.

B. Dehydrate by smoothing some onto plastic wrap. Allow to dry. I keep dehydrated starter in the freezer. To use, mix 1/4 cup water and 1/4 cup flour and stir in a little starter. Allow to stand, uncovered, 48 hours. Refrigerate.

Tians Meld Last Flavors of Summer

Here's a culinary topic you never knew you'd be happy to know. The name is alarmingly foreign-sounding, and the chances are that you've never even seen it, let alone pronounced it. "Tian" (pronounced TEE-yan) is appropriate during the harvest months, when garden-ripened vegetables are at their peak of quality and abundance. Simply put, a tian is a casserole of layered vegetables.

Tian is actually the word naming those appealing, oval, reddish earthenware baking dishes associated with gratinéed foods. (Gratinéed refers to the thin crust formed on the surface of dishes which have been browned in the oven or under a broiler.) Such dishes have a comforting home-cooked look and can be served directly from oven to table.

A tian is just as flavorful at room temperature as it is hot and bubbling from the oven. The making of a tian can fit into any schedule.

What could be better than combining the season's bounty in succulent mixtures ready to serve whenever you are. A quickly grilled steak, chicken breast or fish fillet and crunchy salad are all that is needed to make a complete meal. A leftover tian can be eaten as is, bundled into omelettes and crepes, or stuffed into game hens before they're roasted. I've even puréed the last of the tian and combined it with chicken stock for a thick vegetable soup.

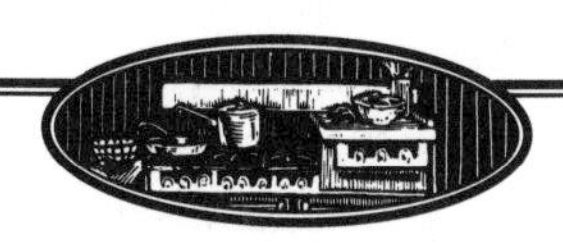

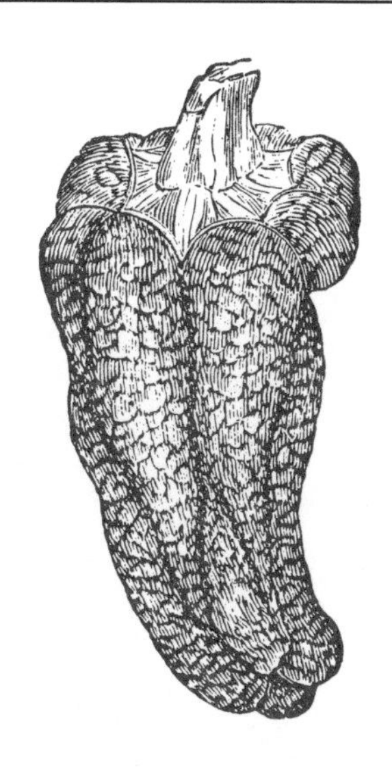

Tian of Roasted Sweet Peppers

Serves 8

Ingredients

1 cup parsley, well chopped
2/3 cup basil leaves, chopped
1 tablespoon fresh thyme leaves
6 large mixed red, green, and yellow sweet peppers, roasted and peeled
12 large, firm red tomatoes, washed, tough core removed
1 to 2 tablespoons olive oil
salt
pepper
2 tablespoons capers
1/4 cup crunchy bread crumbs
1 1/2 to 3 tablespoons additional olive oil

Procedures

1. Preheat oven to 400°F.

2. Chop all herbs together. (Substitute different herbs, green onions, and/or more parsley if necessary to achieve volume indicated.)

3. Roast whole peppers over gas flame or fire until uniformly charred. Steam charred peppers by wrapping snugly in a tea towel 10 minutes. Peel away charred skin while running peppers beneath cold water. Blot dry.

4. Seed and slice peppers into one-inch strips.

5. Slice tomatoes into 1/2-inch thick rounds.

6. Rub earthenware baking dish with olive oil.

7. Distribute 1/3 of tomatoes.

8. Sprinkle tomatoes with 1/3 of mixed herbs.

9. Salt and pepper lightly.

10. Cover with 1/2 of pepper slices.

11. Repeat above, layering until all ingredients are used.

12. Mix capers and crumbs. Sprinkle over vegetables.

13. Drizzle with 1 1/2 to 3 tablespoons olive oil.

14. Bake about 45 minutes, until crumbs form a nice crust.

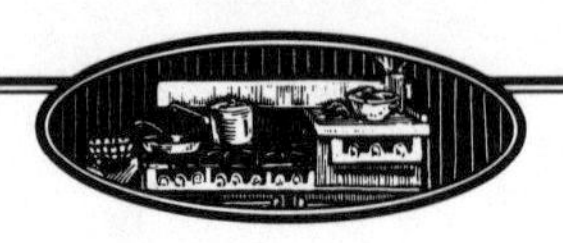

Zucchini Tian

Serves 4 to 6

Ingredients

- **1 tablespoon olive oil**
- **2 tablespoons additional olive oil**
- **1 medium onion, finely chopped**
- **2–2 1/2 pounds zucchini, chopped**
- **2 cloves garlic, minced**
- **2 large eggs, lightly beaten**
- **1/2 cup Swiss cheese, grated**
- **3 tablespoons Parmesan cheese, grated**
- **1/2 cup chopped fresh parsley**
- **3/4 cup cooked rice**
- **1/4 teaspoon fresh thyme leaves**
- **1/4 teaspoon fresh basil, chopped**
- **salt and pepper to taste**

Procedures

1. Preheat oven to 375°F.

2. Oil a 1 1/2-quart casserole or other baking dish.

3. Sauté onion in 2 tablespoons additional olive oil until tender.

4. Add zucchini and garlic and sauté gently, stirring until cooked and most of excess zucchini liquids are evaporated.

5. Beat eggs together with remaining ingredients.

6. Stir in sautéed vegetables.

7. Pour into casserole.

8. Bake at 375°F until liquids are set (as for custard), 40 to 60 minutes.

9. Serve hot, cold, or at room temperature.

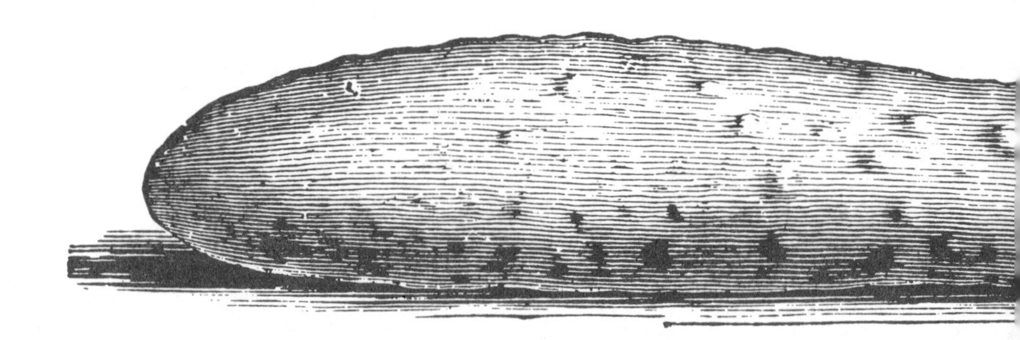

Tian of Swiss Chard or Celery

Serves 4 to 6

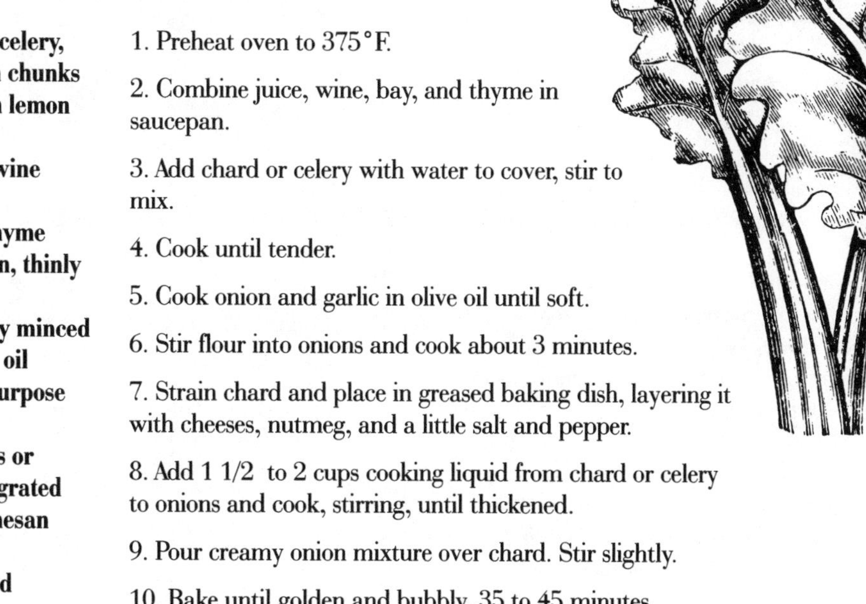

Ingredients

2 pounds chard or celery, cut into one-inch chunks
2 tablespoons fresh lemon juice
1/3 cup dry white wine
1 bay leaf
2 branches fresh thyme
1 medium red onion, thinly sliced
1 garlic clove, finely minced
3 tablespoons olive oil
3 tablespoons all-purpose flour
4 tablespoons Swiss or Gruyere cheese, grated
2 tablespoons Parmesan cheese, grated
1/2 teaspoon ground nutmeg
salt and pepper to taste

Procedures

1. Preheat oven to 375°F.

2. Combine juice, wine, bay, and thyme in saucepan.

3. Add chard or celery with water to cover, stir to mix.

4. Cook until tender.

5. Cook onion and garlic in olive oil until soft.

6. Stir flour into onions and cook about 3 minutes.

7. Strain chard and place in greased baking dish, layering it with cheeses, nutmeg, and a little salt and pepper.

8. Add 1 1/2 to 2 cups cooking liquid from chard or celery to onions and cook, stirring, until thickened.

9. Pour creamy onion mixture over chard. Stir slightly.

10. Bake until golden and bubbly, 35 to 45 minutes.

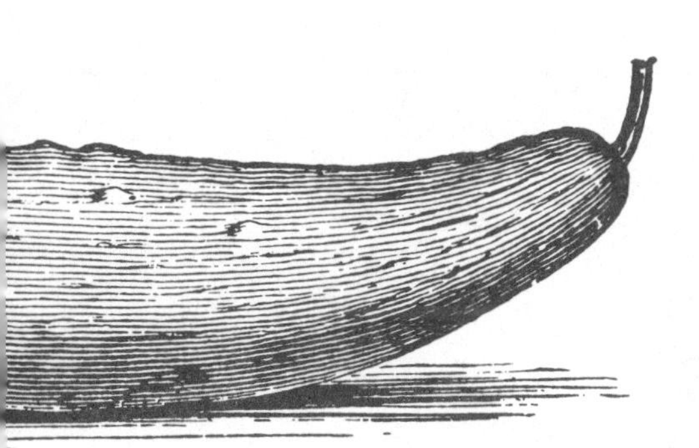

Stamp Out Brown Lettuce

I deplore iceberg lettuce, especially when it gets that telltale "tan." I simply don't consider it real lettuce when bibb, romaine, Boston and leafy lettuces are so readily available. A green salad should be served only when lettuces are fresh, crisp and flavorful.

If there is no unblemished lettuce available, I proudly serve spinach, mushroom, celery root or leek salad. Salads need not always be leafy or simply green, but, they should reflect the spirit and flavors of the seasonal menu. Fresh herbs may be varied to mirror the flavors of the main course.

Personally, I like my salads to follow the main course, as a refresher. They should be of the freshest, crispest ingredients available, and napped with a simple vinaigrette.

The following recipes are alternative ideas for salads, to be used especially when greens look grim. Enjoy the fun of varying your homemade vinaigrette salad dressings to enhance the flavors in your meal.

SALAD DRESSINGS

Vinaigrette Gelée (a delicious no-oil idea to add sparkle to the top of salads)

Cross and Blackwell's consommé with a minimum of vinegar to taste

1. Chill in a thin layer in a Pyrex dish.

2. When jelled firmly (6 hours), run a fork through the jelled dressing.

3. Serve sprinkled on top of salads.

Serve immediately as it will soon melt!

VINAIGRETTE VARIATIONS

3 tablespoons selected oil
1 tablespoon selected vinegar
1/2 teaspoon dry or Dijon mustard
1/2 teaspoon salt
Fresh pepper, ground to taste

Oils:
Walnut oil
Hazelnut oil
Olive oil
Canola oil (rape seed)
Sunflower oil

Vinegars:
Fruit vinegars
Herb vinegars
Red or white wine vinegars, best quality
Balsamic vinegar

Juices: (as an acidic substitute for vinegar)
Orange juice
Lemon juice
Grapefruit juice
Tomato/lemon juice combination

Sandy Buell's Spinach Salad
Serves 4

Ingredients

1 pound fresh spinach, washed and "zipped"
1 clove garlic
1/2 teaspoon salt
1/2 teaspoon lemon rind, grated
1/4 teaspoon freshly ground pepper
1/4 teaspoon sweet paprika
2 tablespoons tarragon vinegar
1/2 cup good-quality olive oil
2 tablespoons sour cream or crème fraîche (see recipes on p. 68)
1/2 pound bacon, cooked, drained and crumbled
1 hard-cooked egg, sieved
croutons (optional)

Procedures

1. Clean spinach, "zip" off the tough stem and central rib (if desired), spin in spinner, roll in dry towel, refrigerate.

2. Pulverize garlic with salt and lemon rind.

3. Put garlic, salt, pepper, paprika, vinegar into blender and blend until nicely combined. Keep machine running and slowly pour in olive oil and then add the sour cream briefly to blend.

4. Toss the solid ingredients and spinach together and then lightly toss with the dressing.

Mushroom Salad
Serves 4

Ingredients

1/2 pound fresh mushrooms
1 sweet red pepper, fresh or canned and roasted
1 green pepper
4 shallots, minced
1 small zucchini, sliced
1 tablespoon parsley (or mixed fresh herbs), chopped
1/4 cup vinaigrette

Procedures

1. Clean and slice mushrooms.

2. Seed and slice washed peppers.

3. Make vinaigrette.

4. Combine all ingredients, toss lightly.

Celeriac Salad

Serves 4 to 6

Ingredients

2 large celery knobs (also known as celeriac or celery root)
Salt
1 teaspoon lemon juice
1 tart, crisp apple, peeled and finely cubed
2 tablespoons coarsely chopped walnuts
freshly ground white pepper
3/4 cup mayonnaise
3 teaspoons additional lemon juice
3 tablespoons cream, lightly whipped
1/2 cup ham, cut into fine strips
1 tablespoon parsley, minced
Some whole walnut halves for garnish

Procedures

1. Bring 4 or 5 quarts of salted water to a boil and cook peeled celery knobs about 20 minutes. They should be easily pierced, but slightly crisp.

2. Drain knobs and cut into small cubes. Place in a serving bowl and sprinkle with a little lemon juice.

3. Add and toss apples, chopped walnuts, salt and pepper to taste.

4. Combine mayonnaise, 3 teaspoons lemon juice, mustard and whipped cream. Pour over salad and toss.

5. Sprinkle the salad with ham strips and parsley. Garnish with walnut halves.

6. Chill salad several hours. Correct seasonings—add more lemon juice if desired.

Braised Leek Salad

Serves 4

Ingredients

4 small thin leeks
2 tablespoons butter
1 teaspoon chicken stock base
6 ounces water
Lettuce leaves
Vinaigrette dressing (see recipe p. 98)

Procedures

1. Cut leeks lengthwise and clean completely.

2. Melt butter in a skillet, add leeks and cook 2 minutes.

3. Add stock and water and bring to a boil.

4. Reduce heat and simmer until tender (about 30 minutes). Cool, then drain.

5. Spoon vinaigrette dressing over leeks arranged on lettuce.

Radish Salad

Serves 6 to 8

Ingredients

For Salad

3 cups radishes, washed and sliced thinly
1/2 cup celery, finely sliced
1 cup Swiss cheese, finely cubed
10 pitted black olives, sliced
3 green onions, chopped

For Dressing

2 tablespoons tarragon wine vinegar
6 tablespoons olive oil
1 teaspoon anchovy paste
1 teaspoon Dijon-style mustard
1 small clove garlic, pulverized
2 tablespoons chives, cut in 1-inch lengths
1 tablespoon tarragon leaves
Salt and black pepper
Parsley, hashed

Procedures

For Dressing

1. Toss radish slices with celery, cheese, olives and green onions.

2. Whisk together vinegar, oil, anchovy, mustard, garlic and scallions. The dressing will be creamy.

For Salad

3. Pour dressing over radish mixture and toss.

4. Season with salt and pepper.

5. Garnish with fluffy hashed parsley.

I serve this salad on a bed of greens. The colors are beautiful and fresh.

Tarts Are Really Just Fancy Pies

I have passed many pleasant hours with my nose flattened against patisserie windows.

One cannot be expected to eat everything displayed in these French pastry shops. But the ladies selling the goodies inside don't seem to understand. They seem proud of their robust silhouettes. They glare unsubtly at me as I jot childlike sketches of spiraling apples, perfectly latticed pastries and precariously mounded fruits "glued" deliciously together with sparkling jellied glazes. They want me to buy. I want to commit these low-calorie encounters with French tarts to memory.

A homemaker in France need not make her own pastry. Why would she? Perfectly executed and delicious treats lie in wait on every shopping street. Often, you don't even have to buy the entire creation. You can buy just one slice—or one of each! This is very exciting to me. They look good. They are good. They are sold every day, every week, all year . . . forever!

We are beginning to move in the right direction in the U.S. In many cities, excellent pastry shops offer Americans this variety and convenience that the French take for granted. Even in our rural areas, restaurants are reflecting the growing interest in traditional French pastries.

Travel, cooking schools and publications have generated an interest in tart making. It is much simpler than it appears. Tarts are really just fancy pies. A good-quality, all-purpose pie pastry is the only indispensable ingredient. Tarts are frequently baked in tin baking pans, of many shapes and diameters, having removable bottoms. This feature permits a pastry to be displayed on, and served nicely from, a serving plate. Most tart recipes can be made in conventional pie plates. Quantities must be adjusted according to the size of baking pans.

French Apple Tart

Makes a 9- or 11-inch tart

Ingredients

For Tart

1/2 to 1 Basic Pastry recipe (see recipe on p. 109)
2/3 cup granulated sugar
4 tart, firm apples (I use Granny Smith apples), cored, peeled and very thinly sliced
2 tablespoons unsalted butter, frozen

For Apricot Glaze

1/2 cup apricot preserves, mixed with 2 tablespoons granulated sugar

Procedures

For Tart

1. Prepare pastry according to directions. Select a 9- or 11-inch fluted tart pan with a removable bottom.

2. Either chill or freeze the flattened dough for later use or roll immediately and line the tart pan. Chill.

3. Distribute 3 tablespoons granulated sugar around the tart bottom.

4. Arrange the apple slices atop sugar in a spiraling single layer.

5. Sprinkle remaining sugar over the apples and shave the butter over the apple/sugar mixture.

6. In the middle of a preheated 425°F oven, bake the tart for 30 to 40 minutes. The juices will form a thick, clear syrup and the tart will be pale, with occasional caramelized specks.

7. Remove the tart to a cooling rack.

For Apricot Glaze

8. Cook apricot preserves and sugar over moderately high heat until a candy thermometer reads 223°F (200°F above 3,000 feet). Strain and use immediately.

9. Brush tart with the apricot glaze or drizzle the glaze in a spiral.

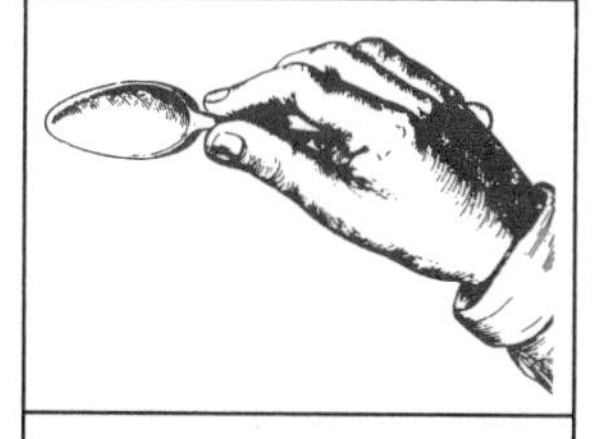

TART-MAKING TIPS

❦ In the oven, preheat a tile or cookie-sheet on the baking shelf. Bake tart directly on this tile or sheet to promote a crisp bottom crust.

❦ To remove the tart from the pan, first cool the baked tart. If using a tart pan with a removable bottom, run a pointed knife around the edge of the pan, knife edge away from crust. Remove the tart pan bottom with the tart. A long, thin knife or frosting spreader, worked in a flat sawing motion between the tart and pan bottom, will release any sticky places. Slide the tart slowly from tart pan bottom to serving plate.

❦ If using a plate without a removable bottom, slice cooled tart and remove slices carefully with a flexible knife, frosting spreader, or spatula.

"There's more to baking than tablespoons and ounces. With an understanding of the basics, you have the tools to be very creative. Experimenting is a great way to learn, even when your attempts don't turn out quite right. And when your creation is a success, that is a sweet reward!"

Katherine de Funiak, executive pastry chef at Ambria and Un Grand Café restaurants, Chicago, IL

Almond Apple Tart

Makes an 8- or 9-inch tart

Ingredients

For Tart

- **1/2 Basic Pastry recipe (see recipe on p. 109)**
- **3 to 4 ripe apples, peeled and halved**
- **6 tablespoons granulated sugar, dissolved in 8 ounces water to make sugar syrup**
- **1/4 cup unsalted butter**
- **8 1/2 tablespoons granulated sugar**
- **2 large eggs, room temperature**
- **2 teaspoons finely grated orange rind**
- **1 1/2 cups ground almonds**
- **3 1/2 tablespoons flour**
- **1/4 teaspoon almond extract or liqueur of choice**

For Apricot Glaze

- **1/2 cup apricot preserves, mixed with 2 tablespoons granulated sugar**

Procedures

For Tart

1. Select an 8- or 9-inch fluted tart pan with a removable bottom, or an 8- or 9-inch pie plate.

2. Prepare pastry according to directions.

3. Line pan with pastry and freeze.

4. Poach apples in sugar syrup until tender and transparent. Drain and cool while making almond mixture.

5. In a medium mixing bowl, cream butter and sugar together until fluffy.

6. Beat in eggs and orange rind. Then stir in almonds, flour and flavoring to complete mixture.

7. Fill frozen pastry with almond mixture.

8. In a preheated 375°F oven, bake tart about 30 minutes. Cool on a cooling rack.

For Apricot Glaze

9. Cook apricot preserves and sugar over moderately high heat until a candy thermometer reads 223°F (200°F above 3,000 feet). Strain and use immediately.

10. Brush cooled tart with hot apricot glaze.

11. Arrange apples, sliced or unsliced, on top; brush again with glaze.

Garnish with toasted sliced almonds.

A Vegetable Tart From Provençe

In Provençe, that region of France facing south to the Mediterranean Sea and away from the chilly Alps, cooking is as colorful as the countryside. Pungent sauces convey the earthy character of this corner of France.

Herbs sprout from crags in rocky hillsides. Vegetables grow abundantly and year-round in sheltered valleys. Close-walled streets of perched mountain villages provide shelter from the relentless sun. Vigorous people and cuisine belie the harsh climate of Provençe.

Vegetable cookery reaches an admirable level of respect in southern France. Vegetable dishes hold their own on elegant menus.

Tomatoes, sweet peppers, onions, olives, garlic, olive oil and anchovies are usually assumed to be in recipes labeled provençal—of Provençe. Amusingly, in *The Taste of France,* Waverly Root reports during the nineteenth century garlic was "used by only those accustomed to meridional cuisine" but now plays a nearly obligatory role in most local preparations. Tomatoes, unmentioned in French cooking until the nineteenth century, are now called traditionally provençal.

Provençal cooking is home cooking, not restaurant cooking. Recipes from Provençe reflect the long months of searingly hot weather. Most dishes are meant to be eaten outdoors. Provençe is the market basket of France and has been strongly influenced by contact with its Mediterranean neighbors.

"The simplicity of what you are cooking keeps the enjoyment of what you are doing. Cooking is a cut of everyday life, a celebration that will be shared. The seasons do offer us celebrations that we should transpose into our everyday cooking and eating around the table. Add ingredients from around the world and you have a cuisine with a new twist and new life."

Monique Hooker, instructor at The Cooking and Hospitality Institute of Chicago, Inc.

French Onion Tart

Serves 8 to 12

Ingredients

For Pastry

1 Basic Pastry recipe, chilled (see recipe on p. 109)

For Filling

2 tablespoons butter
1 tablespoon olive oil
4 large onions, thinly sliced
Salt and freshly ground black pepper to taste
Pinch sugar
2 cups (approximately) Quick Provençal Tomato Sauce (see facing page)
1/2 teaspoon oregano
1/4 teaspoon thyme
1/4 teaspoon basil

To Complete Tart

3 cans anchovy fillets
Greek or niçoise-style black olives

Procedures

For Pastry

1. Prepare pastry according to directions.

2. Roll out chilled dough and line an 11-inch by 14-inch jellyroll pan. Chill well or freeze.

For Filling

3. Heat butter and oil in a large heavy skillet. Add onions and cook slowly with salt, pepper and sugar, stirring occasionally, until caramelized (about 1 hour).

4. Prepare tomato sauce and set aside.

5. Add tomato sauce and herbs to caramelized onions; correct seasonings.

To Complete Tart

6. Spread tomato mixture on pastry and arrange anchovy fillets and olives in a lattice on top.

7. In a preheated 350°F oven, bake 40 minutes until bubbly and crust is deep golden.

Serve hot or at room temperature.

DO-AHEAD METHOD

❦ Caramelize onions—refrigerate.

❦ Make pastry and assemble in tart pan—freeze.

❦ Complete tomato sauce—refrigerate or freeze.

❦ Soak drained anchovies in milk for 15 minutes to remove excess saltiness. Pat them dry. Refrigerate until ready for use. If 3 cans won't completely lattice the tart, slice them in half lengthwise.

❦ Assemble tart just before baking.

Quick Provençal Tomato Sauce

Makes approximately 2 cups

Ingredients

5 tablespoons olive oil
1 to 2 tablespoons shallots, minced
6 ounces tomato paste
1 2/3 cups chicken broth or water
1 bay leaf
2 to 3 teaspoons Herbes de Provençe (Available in gourmet markets or by mail. A mixture of equal parts leaf basil, thyme, savory and oregano will substitute adequately.)
Salt to taste
Freshly ground black pepper
Nutmeg, freshly grated
2 to 3 teaspoons heavy cream or crème fraîche (see recipe on p. 68)

Procedures

1. Sauté shallots gently in oil for 1 minute.

2. Stir in chicken broth, tomato paste, herbs and all seasonings except salt. Simmer 20 to 30 minutes, stirring frequently.

3. Remove bay leaf; correct seasoning.

4. Add heavy cream or crème fraîche to reduce the acidity of the sauce.

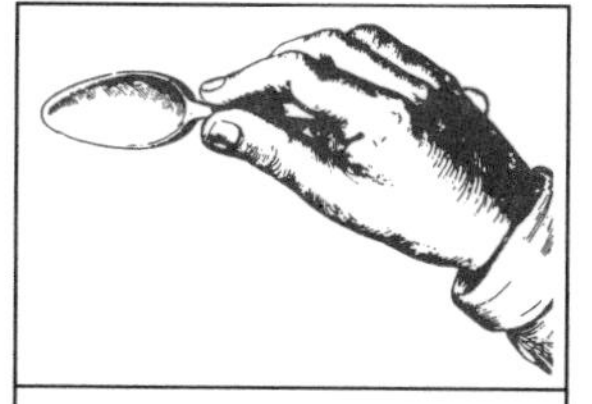

BASIC PASTRY TIPS

❦ Dough discs may be wrapped tightly and frozen up to 2 months.

❦ When a recipe directs you to prick the pastry crust:

Prick the pastry with a fork before chilling the rolled pastry shell. However, while pricking the crust will help keep the pastry shell from undulating and collapsing during baking, pricking holes may permit leaking of ingredients. Leaking sugars and fruit juices, for instance, will caramelize on the tart pan or pie plate and cause sticking.

I rarely prick a pastry shell. Instead, carefully following prebaking instructions for empty pastry shells will alleviate this problem. Freezing unbaked pastry shells before filling and baking is also helpful.

❦ For a double-crust or lattice-top pie, freeze rolled and cut pastry circle for top crust or lattice strips. Assembly will be simpler with firm pieces of pastry.

Salade Niçoise
Salad of Nice, France

"Traditionally innocent of lettuce" (*The Food of France,* Waverly Root), but knowing that the French relish a good culinary disagreement, I offer my version.

Ingredients

Quantities vary according to taste and number of diners.

The "Traditional Musts":

Tomatoes, quartered
Black olives (with pits)
Green and red sweet peppers

My "Traditional Additions":

Hard-cooked eggs, quartered
Chunks of chilled tuna fish
Red potatoes sliced and marinated in vinaigrette
Fresh green beans, cooked whole and marinated in vinaigrette
Red onion rings
Vinaigrette
Use vinaigrette as both marinade and dressing

Procedures

1. Arrange salad artistically on mixed greens, either on a large platter or on individual plates.

Serve as a luncheon, supper or picnic dish.

Basic Salad Dressing—Vinaigrette
Makes enough for 2 to 4 salads

Ingredients

3 tablespoons oil—olive, corn, safflower, canola or a combination
1 tablespoon wine vinegar or lemon juice
1/2 teaspoon dry mustard, or 1 1/2 teaspoons Dijon-style mustard
1/2 teaspoon salt
1/4 to 1/2 teaspoon freshly ground black pepper (it does make a difference)

Choices of vinegars, juices and oils will change the flavor of your vinaigrette.

Procedures

1. Whisk all ingredients together until creamy.

Use with vegetables, salads or as a marinade.

Basic Pastry for Pies and Tarts

Makes enough dough for 1 11-inch tart pan, 1 9-inch double crust pie, 1 11-inch by 14-inch jellyroll pan, 12 4- or 6-inch individual tart pans or 24 to 36 tiny tartlet shells.

May be done in a food processor.

Ingredients

2 cups all-purpose flour
1/2 teaspoon salt
1 tablespoon sugar (for sweet pastries)
1 cup unsalted butter
1 large egg, broken into a 1-cup glass measure, and cold water added to egg to total 1/2 cup liquid

Procedures

1. Mix flour and salt together. (Finely chopped herbs, lemon peel or grated nutmeg may be added now as a dry ingredient.) Add sugar, if using.

2. Cut butter into flour mixture until pieces vary in size from tapioca to peas.

3. Mix egg with water and add to dry ingredients all at once.

4. Blend liquids through the dry ingredients until mixture binds together.

5. Press dough into a disc between waxed paper sheets.

6. Chill 1/2 hour, minimum, before rolling to desired size and shape on a lightly floured surface.

BAKING PASTRY SHELLS

TO PARTIALLY BAKE PASTRY SHELL(S):
Before filling and completing the baking:

1. Freeze rolled pastry in tart pans or pie plate until solid.

2. Remove from freezer and quickly line shell(s) with foil or baking parchment. Fill lined pastry shell(s) with dried beans.

3. In a preheated 425°F oven, bake the bean-filled shell(s) for 10 to 12 minutes.

4. Carefully remove foil or parchment and beans.

5. Bake 2 minutes more, empty.

TO COMPLETELY PREBAKE PASTRY SHELL(S):
Before filling:

1. Freeze rolled pastry in tart pans or pie plate until solid.

2. Remove from freezer and quickly line shell(s) with foil or baking parchment. Fill lined pastry shell(s) with dried beans.

3. In a preheated 425°F oven, bake the bean-filled shell(s) for 12 minutes.

4. Carefully remove foil or parchment and beans.

5. Return shell(s) to oven and bake 5 to 7 minutes more until nicely golden.

TO BAKE FILLED (UNBAKED) PASTRY SHELL(S):

1. Freeze rolled pastry in tart pans or pie plate until solid.

2. Remove from freezer and fill with filling ingredients.

3. Bake as directed in the recipe.

Sun-dried Tomatoes Are Easily Made at Home

Globalization is the cry of the nineties! Children are being encouraged to master foreign languages. Air travel invites curiosity and adventure. Communications technology brings nearly anything one can imagine to his fingertips one way or another.

Glossy food magazines and cookbooks call us to read about, to visit and to taste the exciting discoveries waiting at the end of more comfortable and quicker-than-ever flight. Wise journalists are peeking into previously hidden little cracks of our world. They fax their personal discoveries to their editors and announce the unearthing of a regional specialty.

Those of us who enjoy the kitchen and its witchery are titillated by such local treasures. Following each culinary excavation, *Sunset* Magazine tells us how it can be duplicated at home. *Bon Appetit, Food and Wine,* and *Cook's Magazine* tell us how to use our creation and how to serve it.

One of my favorite culinary discoveries is the sun-dried tomato. An Italian specialty, sun-dried tomatoes are available in specialty stores in jars, tubes and bags. This uniquely tangy ingredient can be made at home, too.

My recipes share nice and easy ways to use them. Their interesting flavor comes from the concentration of tomato acids and sugars during the drying process. Whether chopped and tossed with equal parts of fresh parsley as a salad, combined with pasta, cooked into a tomato sauce, or inlaid in homemade breads or pizza, sun-dried tomatoes will provoke the taste buds. Something new has been added!

Stored in olive oil, tightly sealed and refrigerated, sun-dried tomatoes will keep for months. The intriguingly flavored oil is a nice addition to salad dressings and is delicious rubbed onto the surface of garlic bread or croutons. Try this exciting taste of the Italian countryside while tomatoes are abundant.

Sun-dried Tomatoes

Makes 12 sun-dried tomato halves

Ingredients

6 Italian plum tomatoes
2 teaspoons salt
2 sprigs fresh rosemary (or 1 tablespoon dried)
1 1/4 cups olive oil

Procedures

1. Wash tomatoes.
2. Cut tomatoes in half.
3. Sprinkle cut surfaces with salt.
4. Place tomato halves, cut side up, on a cookie sheet.
5. Bake for 15 to 24 hours in a 125°F oven.
6. Bake only until they are flexible, not brittle.
7. Store, covered with olive oil and flavored with rosemary, in tightly sealed jars.

Pasta with Tuna Fish and Italian Tomatoes

Serves 2

Ingredients

2 tablespoons butter
4 tablespoons olive oil
1 red onion, minced
2 tablespoons chopped sun-dried tomatoes
28-ounce can Italian tomatoes, chopped
2 ounces green olives, sliced in circles
1 ounce capers, coarsely chopped
1 teaspoon anchovy paste
6 1/2 ounces Genoa tuna (in olive oil), drained
1 pound pasta
Few fresh basil leaves

Procedures

1. Melt butter with 1/2 of olive oil and cook minced onions until translucent.

2. Stir in tomatoes, capers, olives and anchovy paste.

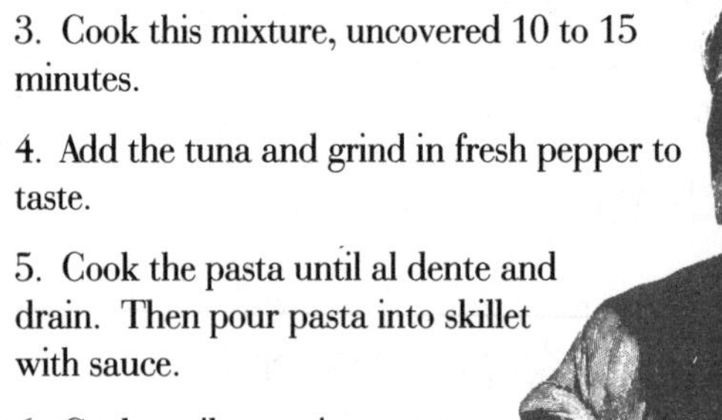

3. Cook this mixture, uncovered 10 to 15 minutes.

4. Add the tuna and grind in fresh pepper to taste.

5. Cook the pasta until al dente and drain. Then pour pasta into skillet with sauce.

6. Cook until sauce is correct consistency and toss in basil.

7. Serve in heated bowls.

Pasta with Sun-dried Tomatoes

Serves 2

Ingredients

2 eggs
1/2 cup dried tomatoes cut in 1/8-inch strips
1/2 cup olive oil from dried tomatoes
1/2 cup good-quality grated Parmesan cheese
1/2 cup chopped parsley (if possible, flat-leaf variety)
2 cloves garlic, minced finely
1 tablespoon lemon juice
1/2 pound pasta

Procedures

1. In serving bowl, whisk eggs, tomatoes, oil, cheese, parsley, garlic and lemon juice.
2. Cook pasta until al dente.
3. Drain pasta and add to ingredients in serving bowl.
4. Toss to mix ingredients and to cook eggs.
5. Season with salt and pepper to taste.
6. Serve on heated plates or flat bowls.

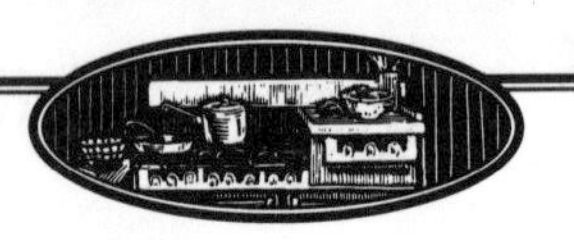

AUTUMN

There is a snap in the air that heralds the fragrant and colorful return of autumn. The squeeze of increased scheduling is felt and kitchen efficiency and planning continue to be important. Autumn's aromas and colors provoke a yearning for heavier seasonings, smoked foods and a heartier fare. Tailgates become tables as wood smoke wafts and frost gleams on the morning's walk. Lunch boxes cry for healthful variety. Soups simmer in pots, breads rise and root vegetables present themselves in all shapes and sizes. A desire for starchy vegetables and legumes replace summer's desire for light carbohydrates. Autumn's harvest frequently cooks at a more patient pace. New opportunities for planning and culinary organization come from the earth.

APPETIZERS, FIRST COURSES, SALADS AND SOUPS

Creamy Curried Pumpkin Soup 137
Finnish Baked Mushrooms 145
Fish Chowder 167
Garlic Potato Madeleines 143
Low-Fat Skillet Soup 140
Marinated Trout Seviche 163
Mushroom Soufflé 147
Pear and Stilton Salad 117
Polenta Tart 128
Potato Soup with Asparagus 140
Potato Soup with Sorrel 141
Potato Soup with Tomato and Basil 142
Smoked Trout Pâté 165

FISH AND MEATS

Chicken with Hazelnuts and Mushrooms 149
Game Birds with Italian Sausage 122
Italian Sausage 123
Pork Tenderloins in Porcini Cream Sauce 148
Ruffed Grouse and Partridge with Artichoke Hearts 125
Sautéed Partridge Breasts 124
Smoked Goose Breast 125
Smoked Trout in Pastry with Horseradish Sauce 164
Steamed Trout Molds with Shrimp 166

BREADS

Crunchy Hazelnut Wedges 151
Pumpkin Spice Muffins 136

SWEETS

Chocolate Mousse Torte 131
Chocolate Pie 130
Chocolate Sheet Cake 132
Hazelnut Cookies 153
Hazelnut Sponge Cake 152
Kugelhopf 156
Macedonia of Fruits 159
Orange Zabaglione, 161
Pear Mousse 120
Pear Tart with Hazelnut Filling 118
Pecan Pumpkin Pie 135
Pumpkin Chiffon Pie 134
Sugar Tart 157
Tart with Pear and Chocolate 119
Tortoni 160

ACCOMPANIMENTS

Chive and Mussel Sauce 166
Horseradish Sauce 164
Jansson's Temptation 143
Microwave Polenta 127
Porcini Cream Sauce 148
Potatoes Fried with Wild and Domestic Mushrooms 146
Toasted Pumpkin Seeds 135
Twice-Baked Idaho Potatoes 139
Wild Rice with Raisins and Almonds 155

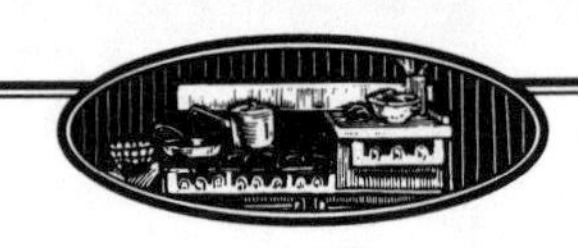

The Pulchritudinous Pear

The appearance of pears in the supermarket signals, to me, the arrival of fall. The cold storage treatment imposed on apples, making me suspicious of early apple arrivals, is inappropriate for pears. Pears must be picked before ripening begins, and I, therefore, am much more trusting and enthusiastic when they appear.

Pears are members of the rose family. Native to Europe and western Asia and introduced into North America in the seventeenth century, pears were probably cultivated in ancient times. There are several thousand pear varieties.

Unlike the other pome fruits (having a compartmented core, i.e., apples), pears ripen from the inside out. Perhaps this explains why pears frequently seem hard.

These aromatic and juicy fruits have a short shelf life. To enjoy autumn's pear harvest fully, purchase relatively hard fruits in usable quantities. Keep them at room temperature until the stem end softens and pears are fragrant. To speed ripening, place pears into brown paper bags with a ripe apple. This will provide the extra ethylene needed to accelerate ripening.

Pears contain carbohydrates and mineral salts, as well as vitamins A, B, and C, which is contained in the peel. They are an excellent energy source, having only 40 calories per 3 1/2-ounce pear, and they are low in sodium.

Bartletts are usually the first pears to appear in the grocery stores. Available from August to December, these bell-shaped fruits have sweet, fine texture with juicy granular flesh. Yellow Bartletts are ripe when they are fully yellowed and have a few "freckles." Red Bartletts are identical to the yellow but are often less flavorful. Comice pears are available from October to March and are larger than most pear varieties. Roundish in shape, they have a rough, mottled, green skin which turns yellow when ripe. Considered the best eating pear, the comice pear is finely textured with a sweet, nutty flavor.

Bosc pears are in stores from October to June. They have a long, tapered shape and a leathery skin which turns yellow-brown when ripe. Excellent for cooking and eating, the bosc pear is appealingly crisp when slightly underripe and smooth when thoroughly ripened.

Pear and Stilton Salad

Serves 8

Ingredients

Stilton cheese, good quality, room temperature
8 firm but ripe Bartlett pears (or other variety of your choice)
Fresh juice of 1/2 lemon or orange
Vinaigrette (see recipe on p. 98)
Watercress sprigs or lettuce, cleaned and chopped
Poppy seeds (optionally, toasted slivered almonds)

Procedures

1. Mash or process the cheese to smooth and soften it.

2. Cut pears in half lengthwise. Peel and core carefully.

3. Rub all cut surfaces with lemon juice to reduce discoloration.

4. Fill pear cavity with softened cheese.

5. Wrap each pear half tightly with plastic wrap. Chill.

6. Whisk any remaining cheese into the dressing.

7. To serve, slice cheese-filled pear halves carefully and arrange on salad plates with crisp greens. Dress with vinaigrette and poppy seeds or nuts.

Pear Tart with Hazelnut Cream Filling

Serves 8 to 12

Ingredients

1/2 Basic Pastry Recipe (see p. 109)
8 ounces water
6 tablespoons granulated sugar (beaten together with the water to make a syrup
4 nearly ripe pears
1/2 stick unsalted butter
1/2 cup plus 1 tablespoon granulated sugar
2 large eggs, room temperature
1 1/2 cup hazelnuts
3 1/2 tablespoons flour
1/4 teaspoon vanilla, almond extract or hazelnut liqueur
Apricot jam glaze (1/2 cup apricot jam plus 2 tablespoons sugar cooked to 200°F and strained)

Procedures

1. Line a 9- or 10-inch tart pan or pie plate with pastry and freeze.

2. Poach fruit in syrup until tender and transparent. Drain and cool while making hazelnut filling.

3. Preheat oven to 375°F.

4. Cream sugar and butter together until fluffy. Add eggs, beating to blend.

5. Stir in nuts, flour and flavoring.

6. Fill chilled pastry with hazelnut filling.

7. Bake tart about 30 minutes. Cool.

8. When cool, brush with hot apricot glaze.

9. Arrange pears on top; brush again with glaze.

Decorate with chopped pistachios and whipped cream, if desired.

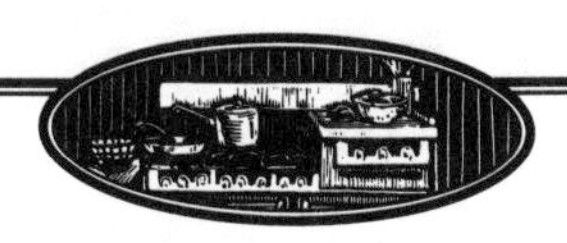

Tart with Pears and Chocolate

Serves 12

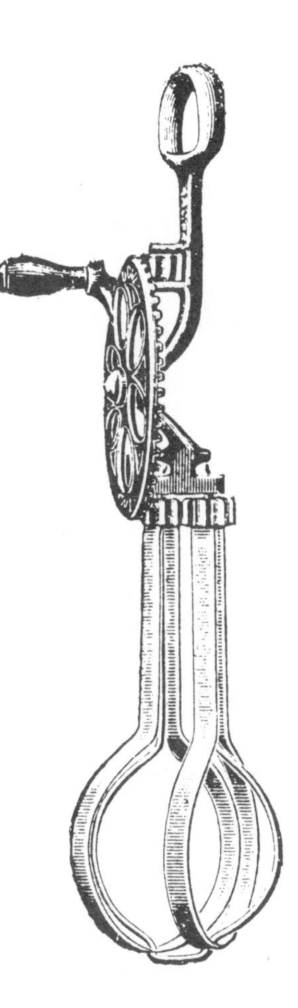

Ingredients

1 recipe Basic Pastry (see p. 109)
4 ounces bittersweet or semi-sweet chocolate
2 tablespoons unsalted butter
5 or 6 barely ripe pears
Juice of 1/2 lemon
1 cup granulated sugar
2 1/2 cups water
1 cup apricot reserves
1 tablespoon brandy
1 to 2 tablespoons sliced almonds, toasted

Procedures

1. Roll out chilled pastry and line an 8-inch tart pan. Chill.

2. Line the chilled pastry shell with foil. Fill it with dried peas, beans or other pie weights. Bake the pie blind at 425°F for 12 minutes. (See tip on p. 109.)

3. Remove pie weights and foil. Bake 5 to 10 minutes more, until deep golden. Cool.

4. Melt chocolate in an uncovered double boiler and, when melted, add room-temperature butter. Stir to blend.

5. Spread chocolate on the tart shell bottom. Chill.

6. Peel, core and halve pears. Rub pear flesh with lemon juice.

7. Heat water and sugar together until sugar dissolves to make a simple syrup.

8. Poach pear halves in simmering sugar syrup until tender. The time required will vary according to ripeness of pears.

9. Drain and cool the pears.

10. Slice pears in 1/4-inch slices. (I slice them across the width.)

11. Place pears over chocolate, pushing the pears slightly to spread the slices apart.

12. Melt the jam and brandy together and strain to remove solid fruit pieces. Drizzle over pears.*

13. Sprinkle with almonds.

**If not serving immediately, coat with jam as close to serving time as possible.*

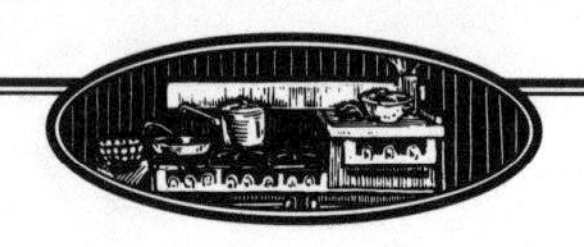

Pear Mousse

Serves 12

Ingredients

For Mousse

5 medium pears, peeled, cored and quartered
3/4 teaspoon cinnamon
1/4 cup peach preserves
1/4 teaspoon freshly grated nutmeg
1/2 teaspoon orange rind, grated finely
4 large egg yolks
1 teaspoon cornstarch
3/4 cup granulated sugar
1 1/2 cups whole milk, warmed
1 tablespoon unflavored gelatin
1/4 cup fresh orange juice
1 teaspoon vanilla extract
1 cup heavy cream, softly whipped

For Sauce

1 cup peach preserves
2 tablespoons grated orange rind
1/4 cup peach-flavored brandy, pear brandy, Grand Marnier, or other
2 tablespoons powdered sugar
1/4 cup pear brandy

Procedures

For Custard

1. Combine pears, cinnamon, preserves, nutmeg and orange rind in a saucepan.

2. Cook slowly until fruit softens, stirring often.

3. Purée mixture well.

4. In an uncovered double boiler, over simmering water, combine egg yolks, cornstarch and sugar.

5. Beat well, over water, until light yellow and fluffy.

6. Stir in warm milk and continue cooking until the creamy mixture coats the back of a metal spoon smoothly. DO NOT ALLOW WATER TO BOIL.

7. Remove cooked custard mixture from the double boiler to a bowl.

8. Heat gelatin with orange juice until gelatin mixture feels slick and no gelatin is coating the saucepan bottom.

9. Whisk this mixture into reserved custard.

10. Chill until visibly thickened, about two hours.

11. Whisk in vanilla and whipped cream.

12. Chill well before serving.

For Fruit Sauce

1. Combine all sauce ingredients, except brandy, in a small saucepan.

2. Heat thoroughly to dissolve sugar.

3. Pass through a sieve to remove solid fruit pieces. Stir in brandy.

4. Chill sauce and serve with mousse.

"Don't Shoot, Miss Pat . . . Them's Tweeties!"

My first bird-shooting experience was traumatic: twelve dove shooters, guns poised and waiting in Jeeps, as we arrived. Me, the prospective bride, still trying to remember the flight pattern differences between robins and doves.

Out into the "dove fields," without even a snack. Rambos everywhere. I stand to take a shot. "Don't shoot, Miss Pat, them's tweeties!"* Shooting holes in the sky to get seven birds, in three days shooting, and a twelve-inch shoulder bruise. Totally intimidating. I'll show them next time. I'll coat my body with sorghum and corn and wring the necks when the birds come in.

The pressure was intense, but the frustration was worth it. Bird shooting—in the right crowds—will yield great bird eating. Game-bird eating is wonderful. Enjoy these recipes with last year's frozen birds or this year's crop. These recipes are superb. Warning: Use no tweeties!

**Tweeties are songbirds.*

Game Birds in Red Wine with Italian Sausage

Serves 3 to 4 (Serving sizes: Men, 3 to 4 birds. Ladies, 2 to 3 birds.)

Ingredients

12 dove or quail breasts
1/2 cup butter
6 green onions, chopped
All-purpose flour for dredging birds
Hearts and livers from cleaned game birds, if available
16 ounces low-sodium chicken broth
1 cup good-quality red wine
1 pound Italian sausage links (see next recipe)

Procedures

1. Pat bird breasts dry and shake in a bag containing flour.

2. Melt butter in a large skillet until bubbly.

3. Sauté green onions in hot butter 1 minute; don't brown.

4. Add floured birds and cook over medium heat in a single layer, turning when necessary to brown evenly.

5. If you have hearts and livers, add them after the birds are browned and cook them only 1 minute, stirring.

6. Add broth and wine and, over medium-high heat, cook birds about 20 minutes to thicken sauce and complete the cooking.

7. While cooking birds, cook and brown the sausages on a grill or in an iron skillet. (This could easily be done in advance.) Add them in chunks to the sauce. Cook about 2 more minutes.

I like to serve this dish on a bed of brown and wild rice or with polenta.

Italian Sausage

Makes 5 pounds of sausage (recipe may be reduced but seasonings must be carefully adjusted. Take particular care in reducing salt.)

Ingredients

5 pounds pork shoulder (4 to 4 1/2 pounds of meat to 1/2 pound fat)
3 tablespoons salt
1 tablespoon paprika
3 tablespoons fennel seeds, rinsed in a sieve to hydrate and to wash off dust
1 to 1 1/2 tablespoons red chili pepper flakes

Procedures

1. Grind meat and fat together to obtain a medium grind.

2. Mix all seasonings together and distribute them over the meat. Blend into the meat lightly without squeezing. Allow seasoning to blend with meat for several hours.

3. Before forming sausages, check the seasoning balance by sautéing a small amount of the meat mixture. Taste and adjust seasoning if necessary.

4. Form sausage links, individual serving size, using plastic wrap as a casing, or make sausage into small patties. If using plastic wrap casing, poach the wrapped links for 12 minutes in simmering water. Drain, cool and unwrap.

5. After removing the plastic, sausages may be sautéed, grilled, broiled or frozen for later use.

George's Sautéed Partridge Breasts

The breast meat from 1 partridge will serve 2 diners nicely.

Ingredients

Whole boneless breast pieces from Hungarian partridge
1 large egg
3 tablespoons milk
1 cup all-purpose flour
1/2 cup Parmesan cheese, freshly grated
Butter (amount necessary for sautéing)
Corn oil (use in a proportion of 1 tablespoon oil to 3 tablespoons butter)
1 to 2 tablespoons corn oil

Ingredient quantities will vary, depending upon amount of meat.

Procedures

1. Using the edge of a plate, pound the breast fillets until uniform in the thickness.

2. Blot breast meat to dry the surface.

3. Beat egg and milk together.

4. Mix flour with Parmesan cheese.

5. Dip fillets alternately into egg/milk, then flour/Parmesan several times, until well coated. End with the dry coating.

6. Heat butter and oil together until bubbly. (The addition of corn oil prevents the butter from burning.)

7. Sauté the whole fillets until they are springy when touched. Make a small slit in the fillet and check the color of the juices. Pink juices mean the meat is not yet cooked. Yellow to clear juices indicate that meat is cooked.

8. Serve hot immediately, or cool to serve as an appetizer, sliced.

Slice against the grain, across the cooked breast piece, to serve as an appetizer.

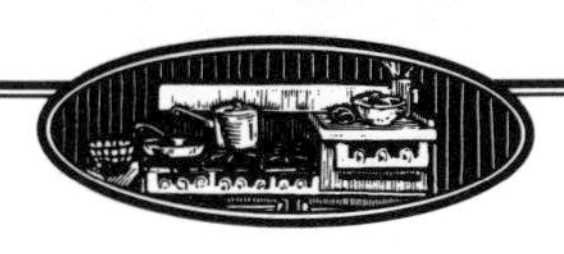

Smoked Goose Breast

From Kathy and Jay Buchner

Plan to make this appetizer at least 2 days before serving.

Serves 4 to 8

Ingredients

1 1/2 tablespoons lemon juice
3 tablespoons Heinz 57 sauce
1/2 cup red wine
2/3 cup cider vinegar
1 1/2 teaspoons ground allspice
1 whole raw wild goose breast (2 halves), skinned

Procedures

1. Mix marinade ingredients in stainless-steel or glass bowl.

2. Marinate goose breast pieces at room temperature for 24 hours, covered in marinating liquids. Add water, if necessary, to increase amount of liquid necessary to cover meat.

3. Blot marinated meat to dry surface and place in smoker with a few hickory chips that have been soaked and drained.

4. Smoke for 8 hours.

5. Remove meat from smoker. Microwave on high for 3 minutes.

Slice very thinly, across the grain, to serve as an appetizer.

Northup-Style Ruffed Grouse and Partridge with Artichoke Hearts

Serves 4 to 6

Ingredients

Breast meat of 2 grouse and/or partridge, cut into chunks
1 cup flour, mixed with 1/4 cup lemon-pepper seasoning
Butter (amount necessary for sautéing)
1 to 2 tablespoons corn oil
Mushrooms, equal in volume to meat
2 small cans sliced water chestnuts
2 small jars marinated artichoke hearts, undrained
1 tablespoon lemon juice

Procedures

1. Blot the breast meat chunks with paper towels to dry.

2. Dip the meat into the flour/pepper mixture, coat heavily.

3. Melt butter with oil in a large skillet until bubbly and hot.

4. Brown the meat pieces in a single layer, to promote crispness. (If pieces are touching, they will steam and be less crisp where they touch.)

5. Remove the meat pieces. Brown the mushrooms in the same skillet.

6. Add the water chestnuts to the mushrooms. Brown well. Then add the marinated artichokes and the lemon juice.

7. Warm the vegetables thoroughly and then add the sautéed meat. Heat entire mixture together before serving.

For a main course, serve on wild rice or pasta. As an appetizer, serve from a casserole dish with toothpicks or forks.

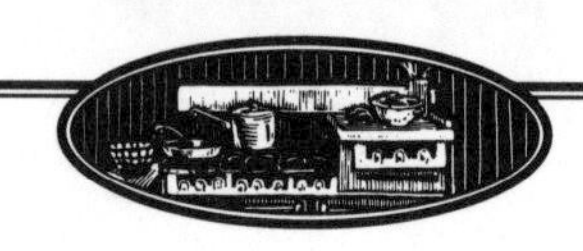

Polenta: A Garnish for Garden Warblers

Polenta is a classic puddinglike mixture of cornmeal and water which has its roots in medieval time. Made originally with various kinds of wheats and other cereals, today's version of creamy yellow cornmeal pudding is made from air-dried corn flour. Polenta is a succulent garnish for meats and fish. As a sunny, steaming mound or cooled, sliced and sautéed, polenta is a versatile accompaniment.

During the Middle Ages, millet, acorn and chestnut flours were milled coarsely to make polenta flour. Buckwheat was often added. Corn was first cultivated in Spain but slid from the national plate when an edict from Charles V declared wheat to be the only truly Christian grain.

The first incentives for wheat farmers followed, and corn cultivators migrated to the Po River Delta near Venice, Italy. Corn became a staple for the poor. From hunger evolved the enduring culinary monarch: polenta. An intriguing connection between fundamental peasant ingenuity and the aristocratic palate was made, with polenta, around 1556, when corn seeds were sent to Florentine aristocrat Ferdinand de' Medici. The homey corn pudding which had softened the peasants' cruel lives soon found itself dressed up and on more noble tables.

Polenta is simply a sturdy version of the American spoonbread found in our southern states. It is made from coarse or finely ground yellow or white cornmeal.

I first became acquainted with polenta in northern Italy, where, in the Piedmont region, it is a staple, served like rice. In southern Italy it is served more like a pasta. The Latin root for polenta is *pulentum* and was the ancient term for gruel. Eastern Europe shares this deeply established love of polenta. This simple and sustaining food may become more familiar as Eastern European tastes spread westward with newly liberated energy.

Versatile, satisfying and nourishing, polenta is a delicious and economical addition to our culinary cache. I use it as an accompaniment for sausages, hearty meat-and-vegetable stews and with grilled chops. It is especially wonderful with game. Try using Quaker cornmeal in these recipes. It works well and is easy to get. Leave it to the French to describe polenta in their own inimitable way: "Polenta is used as a garnish for garden warblers and other similar small birds." Oh, well . . .

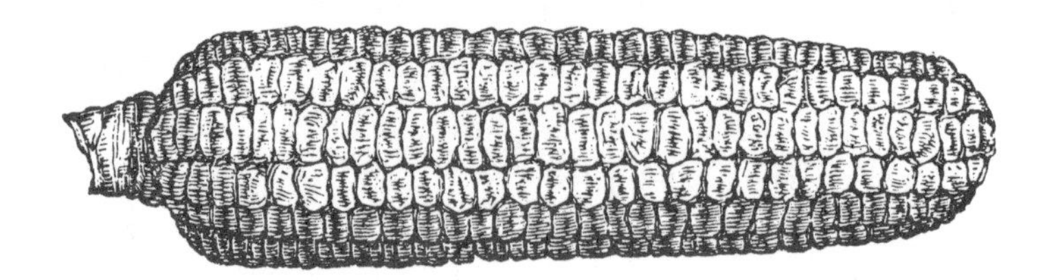

Microwave Polenta

Adapted from Barbara Kafka's *Microwave Gourmet*
Serves 6-8

Ingredients

1/4 cup butter
1 medium onion, coarsely chopped
3 1/2 cups water
1/2 teaspoon salt
1 cup yellow medium cornmeal
4 sprigs hashed parsley
2 ounces good-quality Parmesan cheese

Procedures

1. In microwavable container, melt butter with onion and cook 1 minute at full power.

2. Add 3 1/2 cups water and heat about 5 minutes, until water is very hot.

3. Stir polenta into water and add salt.

4. Return container to microwave and cook about 6 minutes total, stirring every 2 minutes. (Sometimes the polenta will cook more slowly or quickly. Learn to recognize when it is ready and be flexible about the exact time.) When completed, the polenta should be thick and creamy.

5. Add hashed parsley and Parmesan cheese. Add more butter at this time, if desired.

Serving variations:

❦ *For soft polenta, to be served on warmed plates directly from the cooking pot, use the recipe as outlined above.*

❦ *For firm polenta, use 1 1/4 cups liquid. When recipe is completed, pour polenta into an 8-inch loaf pan which has been lined with buttered plastic wrap. Cool to room temperature, then chill up to 2 days.*

❦ *To grill or sauté, slice chilled polenta in 1/2-inch-thick slices and then into desired shapes. Chill. I usually cut polenta into triangle halves or squares. In a skillet, heat 1 tablespoon olive oil with 1 tablespoon melted butter until bubbling. Brown the polenta slices until golden. Turn only once. Serve immediately or keep warm in oven. Top with Italian Fontina cheese for a variation. Warm briefly in a 400°F oven.*

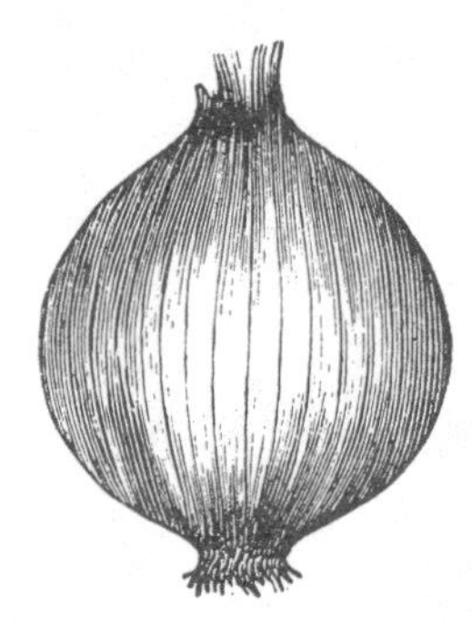

POLENTA TART

Here's a great idea for a light supper or a way to use up leftover polenta. Cook a little extra to make the tart the next day.

Serves 4 to 6

INGREDIENTS

Polenta to line a 10-inch pie plate
2 large eggs
Salt and pepper to taste
2 medium onions, chopped
2 cloves garlic, pulverized
3 tablespoons good-quality olive oil
1 sweet green pepper, roasted, peeled and chopped
6 medium tomatoes, blanched, peeled, seeded and chopped (or 1 28-ounce can of plum tomatoes, drained)
Pinch sugar
2 tablespoons mixed parsley, oregano and thyme, freshly chopped
1/3 cup imported Parmesan cheese, grated

PROCEDURES

1. When polenta is cooked and is a creamy mass, cool it slightly before adding the eggs, beating. Season to taste.

2. Spread the polenta into the well-buttered pie plate.

3. Sauté the onions and garlic in olive oil until soft.

4. Add remaining ingredients and cook at a simmer for about 30 minutes in a skillet, stirring to prevent sticking. Stop cooking when sauce begins to lose its chunkiness. The sauce must, however, be quite dry. To reduce excess liquids, raise heat and, stirring constantly, cook until mixture is no longer runny.

5. Place the topping over the polenta and sprinkle with cheese.

6. Just before baking, dribble 2 tablespoons olive oil over the top.

7. Bake in a 350°F oven for about 45 minutes.

This tart is best served warm, not hot. Great with lamb, grilled chicken, fish, or with a crunchy romaine lettuce salad and crusty bread.

Chocolate: A Way of Life for Oplers

My husband, Ed Opler, is in the chocolate business, so I closely relate to, and am quite fond of, chocolate. But, you know, chocolate really is a source of pleasure for most people.

Admittedly, there are people, even one of my closest friends, who don't care for chocolate. But despite those few, I am continually reminded of the world-wide and historic affection for chocolate. Cortez discovered "chocolate," Montezuma's royal beverage, during his sixteenth-century New World explorations. The Spanish sweetened and kept the joys of his findings to themselves until their monks leaked the tasty secrets to the courts of France. By the mid seventeenth century, English chocolate houses purveyed the pricey delicacy to the wealthy. Mass production later brought the pleasures of chocolate within the reach of the populace.

By the late nineteenth century, a more refined "eating chocolate" was being manufactured in England. The addition of Swiss milk produced the first milk chocolate. The rest is gastronomic history.

Sandra Boynton, author of *Chocolate, The Consuming Passion,* declared that chocolate is only appropriate when served in months spelled with an a, e, or u.

Some people try to substitute carob for chocolate, but in my book, it's no substitute at all. According to Boynton, "Carob is a brown powder made from the pulverized fruit of a Mediterranean evergreen. Some consider carob an adequate substitute for chocolate because it has some similar nutrients (calcium, phosphorus), and because it can, when combined with vegetable fat and sugar, be made to approximate the color and consistency of chocolate. Of course, the same arguments can as persuasively be made in favor of dirt."

Following are some of my favorite ways to use chocolate.

Kathe's Chocolate Pie

From Ed's dowry

Serves 8 to 10

The more I work with chocolate, the more strongly I believe that chocolate has the capacity to awaken even the most dormant artistic spirit in each of us. That's why I approach each class with the zeal of a missionary, intent on sharing my knowledge, my techniques, and my passion for chocolate with my students.

There is nothing that pleases me more than to see a student leave my class with 'chocolate eyes,' 'chocolate wings,' and a newly tapped 'chocolate spirit.' Why it's enough to warm a teacher's 'chocolate heart.' "

Elaine Gonzales of Northbrook, IL: chocolate artist, consultant, and instructor at leading cooking schools; *Modern Baking* contributing editor; author *Chocolate Artistry*

Ingredients

1 9–10 inch pre-baked graham-cracker crust
2 ounces unsweetened baking chocolate
1 cup whole milk
1 envelope Knox gelatin
1/4 cup cold water
2 large eggs, separated
1/2 cup granulated sugar
1/8 teaspoon salt
2/3 cup whipping cream
1 teaspoon vanilla extract
1 tablespoon rum or coffee
1/2 cup additional whipping cream
1 ounce bittersweet chocolate to be used for decoration

Procedures

1. Soften gelatin in water.

2. In an uncovered double boiler, over simmering water, heat chocolate with milk, stirring until smooth.

3. Soften gelatin in cold water. Add softened gelatin to chocolate mixture, stirring to dissolve completely. Test to see that gelatin is completely dissolved by rubbing liquid between your fingers. The liquid should feel slick, not beady. Carefully touch the pan bottom. Gelatin must not be coating the bottom.

4. Beat yolks with half the sugar until lemon-colored. Stir in salt.

5. Slowly stir in chocolate mixture to blend.

6. Chill the chocolate mixture until it begins to have a puddinglike consistency.

7. Beat room-temperature egg whites until frothy. Continue to beat them, adding remaining sugar gradually, until soft, shiny peaks form.

8. Fold whites into chocolate mixture.

9. Whip cream until soft peaks form. Stir in desired flavorings.

10. Fold flavored whipped cream into chocolate mixture.

11. Mound filling into prepared crust.

12. Chill before garnishing with additional whipped cream and chocolate shavings.

Chocolate Mousse Torte
Serves 10–18

Ingredients

2 to 3 dozen ladyfingers (see recipe on p. 188) or comparable quantity of chunks of stale cake or semi-hard cookies, enough to line and layer a 9- or 10-inch springform pan
3/4 pound semi-sweet or bittersweet chocolate
3 tablespoons granulated sugar
3 tablespoons water
3 tablespoons orange-flavored brandy (or coffee)
6 egg yolks, beaten
6 egg whites, room temperature
1 1/2 cups good-quality cream sherry (or sweetened coffee)
1/3 cup slivered or sliced almonds, toasted until golden brown
1 cup whipping cream
2-3 teaspoons powdered sugar
2 teaspoons pure vanilla extract
maraschino cherries or fresh red berries

Procedures

1. Have biscuits, cake or cookies ready.
2. In a double boiler, melt the chocolate with sugar, water and brandy or coffee.
3. Stir chocolate mixture until smooth, and then add yolks.
4. Cool chocolate, off the heat, while beating egg whites to softly firm peaks.
5. Fold beaten whites into chocolate.
6. Dip to moisten ladyfingers in sherry. Line the bottom and sides of a 9-inch or 10-inch springform pan with the ladyfingers.
7. Pour half the chocolate mixture into the pan and sprinkle with 1/3 of almonds.
8. Moisten and layer more ladyfingers atop the almonds.
9. Repeat chocolate and almond layer.
10. Chill the cake for at least 8 hours, lightly covered.
11. Beat whipping cream with vanilla and powdered sugar until softly stiff.
12. Spread flavored whipped cream onto cake.
13. Decorate with remaining almonds and fruits as desired.
14. Keep chilled until ready to serve.

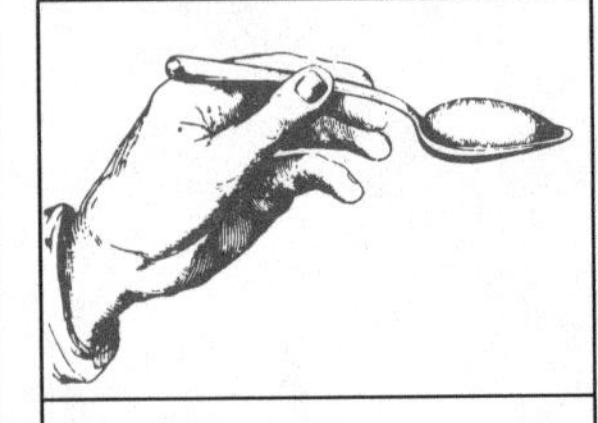

TIP FOR EASY REMOVAL OF CAKE FROM PANS

My experience has led me to *always* butter and lightly flour cake pans—whether or not the recipe calls for it. After distributing flour around the cake pan, turn pan upside down and tap off any excess flour.

Chocolate Sheet Cake

Serves 20 to 25

Ingredients

For Cake

2 large eggs, beaten
1/2 pint sour cream
2 cups granulated sugar
2 cups all-purpose flour
1 teaspoon baking soda
Dash salt
1 cup water
1 cup unsalted butter
4 tablespoons cocoa

For Frosting

6 tablespoons milk
6 tablespoons cocoa
1 cup unsalted butter
1 pound powdered sugar
1 1/2 teaspoons pure vanilla extract

Procedures

For Cake

1. Blend first 6 ingredients well.
2. Boil water, butter and cocoa together 2 minutes.
3. Add cocoa mixture to flour/egg mixture.
4. Spread batter into a buttered and floured jellyroll pan.
5. In a preheated 375°F oven, bake 20 to 25 minutes. Cool slightly.

For Frosting

6. Boil milk, cocoa and butter 3 minutes.
7. Beat in powdered sugar and vanilla until glossy and smooth.
8. Pour frosting over warm cake and spread evenly.

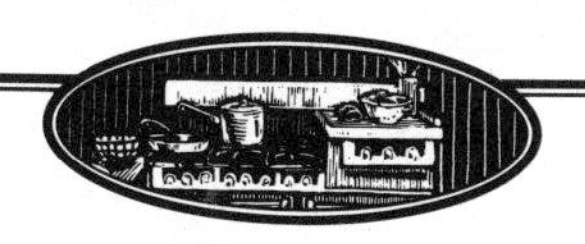

Pumpkin Delights

What would fall be without squash, gourds, pumpkins, and grinning jack-o'-lanterns? First grown in America, pumpkins were cultivated in Mexico and Central America as many as 5,000 years ago.

"Sugar Pie" and "Sweet Spookie" varieties will make the nicest pumpkin pies. "Triple Treat" pumpkins are also great for pie making and contain no seeds. "Sweetnuts" are known for having especially good and prolific seeds. The varieties normally sold as Halloween carving pumpkins are probably the smoothest-skinned and easiest-cutting variety, weighing about ten pounds, or the green-striped "Lady Godiva" (which has hull-less seeds), or the twenty- to sixty-pound "Mammoth Gold." (From *Southern Born and Pumpkin Bred,* published by Graphica, Greensboro, NC.)

To cook fresh pumpkin, just cut whole, washed pumpkin into chunks and boil, steam, or pressure cook. Cook it until it can be easily handled. Scoop out the meat. Pumpkin may be frozen successfully. Pack the cooked, cooled pumpkin (mashed) into freezer containers, leaving one-half inch of head space in the carton.

Pumpkin may be easily cooked in the microwave oven. Peeled, one-inch cubes are cooked 20 to 25 minutes in a little water and covered loosely with plastic wrap. Otherwise, pumpkin may be halved and then baked in a 350°F oven.

One-half cup of cooked pumpkin contains vitamins A, B, and C, potassium, phosphorus, calcium, iron, and twenty-seven calories. One pound of pumpkin has 206 grams of carbohydrates.

PUMPKIN CHIFFON PIE

Makes 1 pie, serves 8

INGREDIENTS

- **1 pre-baked 9- or 10-inch pie shell (see recipe on p. 109)**
- **1 envelope unflavored gelatin**
- **2/3 cup brown sugar**
- **1/2 teaspoon salt**
- **1/2 teaspoon nutmeg**
- **1 teaspoon cinnamon**
- **2 teaspoons creme de cocoa, rum, or vanilla extract**
- **3/4 cup evaporated skim milk**
- **3 large egg yolks**
- **1 1/2 cup canned pumpkin**
- **3 large egg whites**
- **1/4 cup granulated sugar**
- **1/2 pint whipping cream**
- **1 teaspoon maple syrup or vanilla extract**

PROCEDURES

1. Combine gelatin, brown sugar, salt, nutmeg, cinnamon, and creme de cocoa (vanilla or rum) in double boiler.

2. Stir in milk, yolks, and pumpkin. Mix.

3. Cook above mixture over simmering water until mixture is thoroughly heated and gelatin is melted. Feel the bottom of the pan to see that gelatin is not still on the bottom. The mixture should be slick to the touch.

4. Remove mixture from heat and chill until thickened. Mixture should hold its shape when mounded on a large spoon.

5. Beat whites until foamy, then add sugar gradually and beat until the egg whites form a stiff meringue.

6. Fold the whites into pumpkin mixture.

7. Fill the pre-baked pie shell. Chill.

8. Before serving, beat whipping cream with flavoring of your choice until softly stiff.

9. Mound cream on top of chilled pie or serve beside cut pieces. Keep pie cold until serving time.

Swede's Pecan Pumpkin Pie

From a wonderful friend in Daniel, Wyoming

Makes 1 pie, serves 8 to 10

Ingredients

1 well-chilled, unbaked 9-inch pastry shell, made using 1/2 Basic Pastry recipe (see p. 109)
1 large egg, slightly beaten
1 cup canned pumpkin
1/3 cup granulated sugar
1 teaspoon pumpkin pie spice
2 additional large eggs
2/3 cup dark corn syrup (use light if it's all you have)
1/3 cup additional granulated sugar
3 tablespoons unsalted butter, melted
1/2 teaspoon pure vanilla extract
1 cup halved or chopped pecans

Procedures

1. Blend the 1 egg, pumpkin, 1/3 cup sugar and pie spice.
2. Spread over the chilled pastry shell.
3. Combine the additional eggs, corn syrup, additional sugar, butter and vanilla.
4. Stir in the nuts.
5. Spoon over pumpkin mixture.
6. In a preheated 350°F oven, bake pie for about 50 minutes, or until filling is set and a knife inserted into the pie comes out clean.

Serve as is or with whipped cream or ice cream.

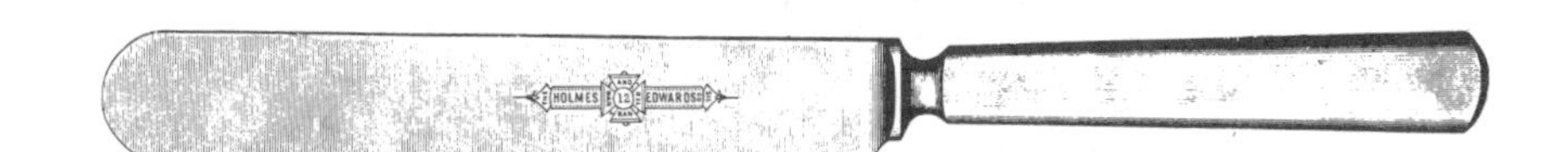

Toasted Pumpkin Seeds

Ingredients

Seeds from 1 pumpkin
2 tablespoons corn oil
Salt to taste

Procedures

1. Rinse and separate seeds.
2. Blot seeds dry and distribute in one layer on a jellyroll pan.
3. Air dry several hours, shaking the pan to promote even drying.
4. Preheat oven to 350°F.
5. In the pan, toss seeds with oil and salt.
6. Toast seeds in oven, stirring every 5 minutes for about 20 to 30 minutes.
7. Remove from pan and cool before serving.

Pumpkin Spice Muffins

Makes 12 muffins

Ingredients

1 large egg
3/4 cup milk
1/2 cup corn oil
1/2 cup canned pumpkin
1/2 cup golden or dark raisins, plumped
2 cups all-purpose flour
1 1/2 teaspoons pumpkin pie spice
1/4 to 1/2 cup chopped pecans (optional)
1 teaspoon freshly grated orange rind (optional)
1/3 cup granulated sugar
3 teaspoons baking powder
1/2 teaspoon salt

Procedures

1. Preheat oven to 400°F.
2. Grease standard-size medium muffin tins well.
3. Beat egg, milk, oil and pumpkin together.
4. Stir in raisins.
5. Blend remaining ingredients. Stir into pumpkin mixture just until blended.
6. Fill muffin cups about 3/4 full.
7. Bake about 20 minutes.

The prepared muffin batter may be refrigerated in muffin tins for up to 12 hours before baking.

Mary Mead's Creamy Curried Pumpkin Soup

Serves 6 to 10

Ingredients

1 large onion, chopped
1 clove garlic, finely chopped
3 tablespoons butter
2 14-ounce cans chicken broth
1 tart apple, peeled and chopped
2 9-ounce cans pumpkin
1 bay leaf
1/2 teaspoon curry powder
1/2 teaspoon thyme
2 cups half-and-half

Procedures

1. Cook onion and garlic in butter.

2. Stir in all remaining ingredients, except half-and-half, and cook slowly until heated through thoroughly.

3. Just before serving, stir in half-and-half and heat, stirring, until heated through. Do not boil.

Garnish with parsley, croutons, or toasted sunflower or pumpkin seeds.

Idaho Potatoes: A Culinary Treasure

Few foods can claim such economy and nutritional value. Eaten perfectly baked with a squeeze of fresh lemon or transformed into endless presentations, Idaho's russet Burbanks are a food for all seasons and reasons in an era when scrutiny often dampens culinary fun.

The words *Grown In Idaho* insure us of the mealy texture and distinctive flavor we assume when we buy Idaho potatoes. Available fresh from October through July, these culinary treasures weigh four to sixteen ounces and reflect the benefits of their home ground: volcanic soil, clean air, plentiful water, warm days and cool nights.

Nutritionally, the Idaho potato is a wonder. Satisfying and low-calorie (100 calories per 5-ounce potato), this tuber supplies protein, iron, thiamine, potassium and vitamin C. High in energy-giving carbohydrates (24 grams per 5-ounce potato) it is almost fat-free and very low in sodium (5 milligrams per 5-ounce potato).

The Idaho Potato Commis-sion recommends soaking spuds before scrubbing. In large quantities, soaked spuds may even be washed in the dishwasher rinse cycle (without soap)!

Twice-Baked Idaho Potatoes

My long-time friend Janis Stevens made these first.
Serves 8

Ingredients

4 large Idaho potatoes, washed
6 strips bacon, cut into 1/4-inch pieces
1/3 cup green onions, chopped
1/3 cup sour cream
2 tablespoons Parmesan cheese, freshly grated
1/2 teaspoon salt
1/2 teaspoon freshly ground black pepper
3 teaspoons butter, melted

Procedures

1. Bake potatoes (see tip). Cool until easy to handle. Cut in half lengthwise.

2. Cook bacon until crispy. Drain and reserve a little fat in a skillet.

3. Cook onions in the fat until translucent.

4. Scoop out potatoes. In the skillet, mash potato with onions.

5. Stir in bacon, sour cream, Parmesan and seasonings.

6. Divide potato filling among potato skins.

7. Drizzle with melted butter.

8. In a preheated 350°F oven, rebake for 20 to 30 minutes before serving.

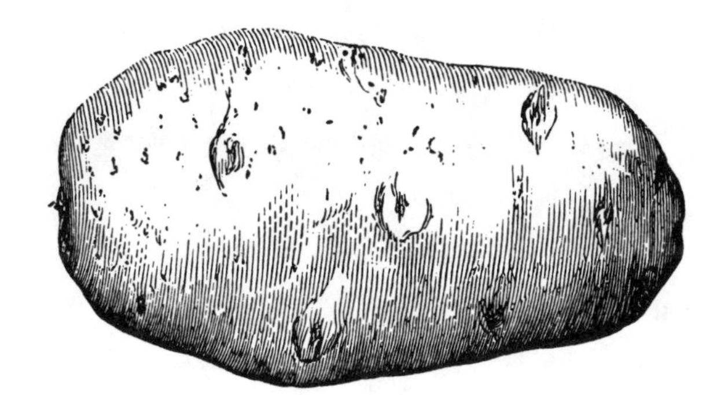

Perfectly Baked Potatoes

1. The ideal way to bake potatoes is at 425°F for 55 to 65 minutes.

2. The potato should be pierced with a fork to allow steam to escape and to assure the desired mealiness. Foil is not recommended for baking. It steams the vegetable and softens the skin. Moisture can't escape and fluffiness will be sacrificed.

3. Overcooking causes natural starches to separate and results in stickiness.

4. To successfully cook spuds in advance, rub skins with olive oil to prevent shrinkage. Skins, however, will not be crisp.

5. Microwaving is a compromise. Its cooking occurs by cellular friction and results in a wetter, stickier product. The best microwave success (600-watt unit) will be achieved by scrubbing and piercing 7- to 9-ounce potatoes and baking them one inch apart on paper toweling. One potato will take about four minutes; three will take eight to ten minutes.

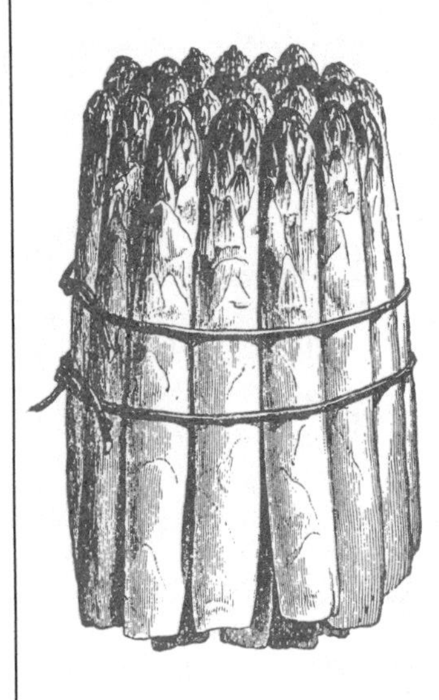

Potato Soup with Asparagus

Makes 3 to 4 quarts

Ingredients

5 Idaho® potatoes, pared and quartered
2 large onions, chopped
2 pounds fresh asparagus, washed and chopped or 2 packages (10-ounce) frozen asparagus
1 tablespoon curry powder
2 quarts chicken stock
1 pint heavy cream
Salt and pepper to taste

Procedures

1. Combine first five ingredients, stir together, bring to a boil and simmer 30–40 minutes.
2. Remove asparagus. Cut off 2-inch tips and reserve.
3. Chop asparagus bottoms.
4. Return bottoms to soup and purée.
5. Return soup to pan.
6. Stir in cream and simmer.
7. Serve hot or cold. Garnish with asparagus tips.

Low-Fat Skillet Soup

Serves 2

Ingredients

1 large Idaho® potato, sliced
1 large onion, sliced
1 cup sliced mushrooms
1 3/4 cups low-fat chicken stock
2 tablespoons chopped parsley
Salt and pepper
Parmesan cheese (optional garnish)

Procedures

1. Layer potatoes, onions and mushrooms in a skillet.
2. Pour stock over all, cover and simmer until tender.
3. Stir in parsley; season to taste.
4. Sprinkle with optional Parmesan cheese.
5. Serve hot.

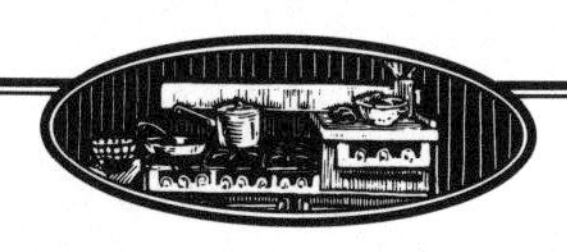

Potato Soup with Sorrel

Serves 4 to 8

Ingredients

- **3 medium all-purpose potatoes, cubed and peeled**
- **6 to 8 cups low-fat chicken stock**
- **1 1/2 pounds fresh sorrel (Spinach can be substituted with 1 tablespoon fresh lemon juice added to step 5.)**
- **Salt**
- **Ground white pepper**
- **1 cup crème fraîche (see recipe on p. 68) or sour cream**
- **2 tablespoons chives, finely minced**

Procedures

1. Cook potatoes in stock for about 20 minutes until tender.

2. Clean and remove stems from sorrel, then cut into strips.

3. Cook the sorrel with the potatoes for 10 minutes, covered.

4. Purée the soup in small batches until smooth.

5. Season to taste.

6. Combine crème fraîche and chives in a small mixing bowl.

7. Pour the soup into serving bowls and top with crème fraîche and chives.

To serve cold, add 2 mashed cloves of garlic to cooking broth and proceed as directed adding 1 cup light cream to finished soup. Correct seasoning and chill 2 hours or more. Garnish with minced herbs and thinly sliced radishes.

"Cooking at home for family and friends can be an experience that goes beyond the kitchen stove. Cooking is the learning experience of different cultures represented by the dishes cooked at home, so from the kitchen one can do lots of traveling. Cooking is also a creating experience. Just as a pianist interprets a Chopin etude, the cook in her kitchen creates her own version of classic dishes. Above all, good cooking is the joy which it brings when the food is appreciated by everyone around the dinner table."

Lydie P. Marshall, owner A La Bonne Cocotte cooking school, New York City; author *Cooking with Lydie Marshall* and *A Passion for Potatoes*

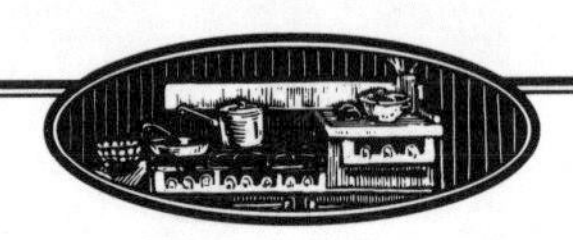

Potato Soup with Tomato and Basil

Serves 4

Ingredients

3 large tomatoes
2 carrots, peeled and thinly sliced
1/4 teaspoon sugar
2 cups low-fat chicken stock
1 medium yellow onion, thinly sliced
1 clove garlic, peeled and pulverized with a little salt
4 red potatoes, peeled and cubed
1 cup crème fraîche (see recipe on p. 68) or heavy cream
Salt
Ground white pepper
1/4 cup coarsely chopped fresh basil

Procedures

1. Remove the seeds from the tomatoes. Chop the tomatoes and place in a sieve over a bowl. Reserve juices.

2. Simmer the tomatoes with the carrots and sugar, adding the reserved tomato juices to prevent sticking. Cook all together until carrots are soft. Pass through a sieve or purée.

3. Simmer chicken stock with onion, garlic and potatoes until potatoes are tender.

4. Purée potato mixture with some stock in a blender. Add crème fraîche. Season to taste.

To serve, swirl the tomato mixture into the potato mixture and sprinkle with chopped fresh basil.

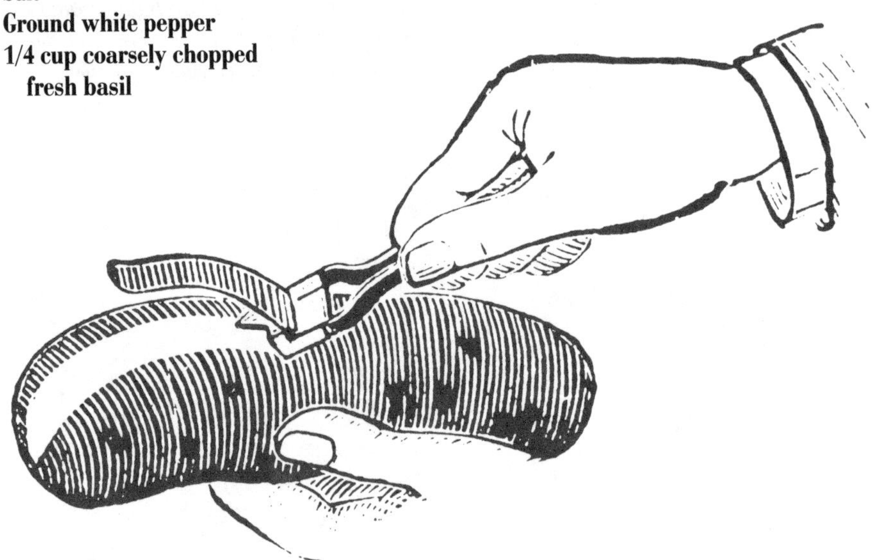

GARLIC POTATO MADELEINES

Serve with sour cream and chives as an appetizer!
Serves 6 to 8

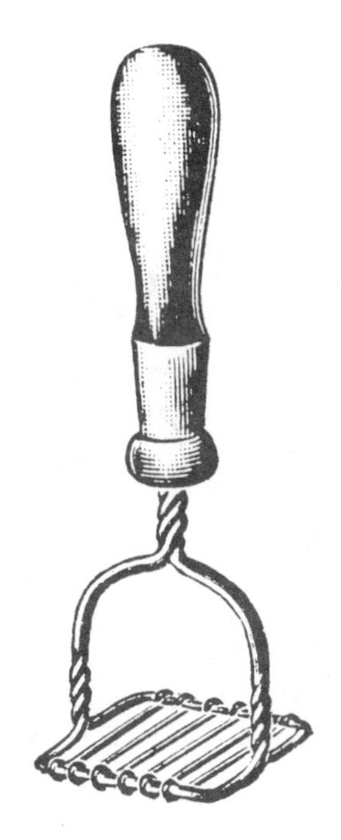

INGREDIENTS

1 pound Idaho potatoes
2 1/3 cups hot milk
2 tablespoons unsalted butter
1 large egg
Salt and pepper to taste
2 teaspoons garlic purée
Seasoned bread crumbs, chopped fine, lightly crisped in the oven

PROCEDURES

1. In a pot, cover potatoes with water and simmer until tender.

2. Drain and cool the potatoes. Peel.

3. Mash or rice potatoes and add other ingredients to taste.

4. Butter madelaine molds well. (Small muffin tins may be substituted.) Sprinkle buttered molds with bread crumbs; tap out excess before filling.

5. Mound potato mixture into the molds, filling 3/4 full.

6. Set the filled molds on cookie sheets in a preheated 400°F oven.

7. Bake about 25 minutes, or until very golden and puffy.

8. Remove each madeleine carefully to a cooling rack.

JANSSON'S TEMPTATION

Serves 10

INGREDIENTS

8 medium potatoes
2 2-ounce cans anchovy fillets
1/2 cup milk
2 tablespoons unsalted butter, room temperature
2 to 3 yellow onions, sliced thinly
1 cup half-and-half
1/2 cup whipping cream

PROCEDURES

1. Peel potatoes and cut into matchstick-size pieces.

2. Soak anchovies 10 minutes in milk to reduce saltiness. Drain. Blot to dry.

3. Cut anchovies into 1/2-inch pieces.

4. Butter a 2-quart baking dish thoroughly.

5. Alternate layers of onions and anchovies.

6. Top with a layer of potatoes.

7. Pour in half-and-half.

8. Bake 25 minutes in a preheated 425°F oven.

9. Pour on remaining cream and bake another 25 to 35 minutes, until golden and creamy.

This dish is a wonderful Scandinavian invention. Serve with grilled fish.

Dried Wild Mushrooms

When I began hunting wild mushrooms, I could identify only a few absolutely. I vowed never to eat one that I (or some better-qualified expert) could not *positively* identify. Friends guided me to the cottonwood bottoms, near the Snake River, where I found two perfectly regal morels. I was excited.

My wild mushroom foragings continued. I even found one on my own. This one I decided to air dry. I suspended it with a thread from my pot rack—my own effort at fungus taxidermy—a public statement of my success. Later my percentages improved. I learned where and how to find chanterelles. I was particularly pleased to discover their affinity for the same season and ground as the huckleberry.

The reason I am recounting the pleasures of wild mushrooms is that I, my hungry friends, have discovered an easy way to perfume meals with the woodsy quality of these elusive fungi: *dried* wild mushrooms. Granted, their prices well represent their mystique, but there are ways to use little bits of them to enhance any dish. When I buy a pricey box of wild mushrooms, I know that they are edible and that they will keep indefinitely.

I hydrate the desired number of wild dried mushrooms in stock or water. Two to four minutes in a microwave oven at high power, covered with plastic wrap, will hydrate the mushrooms and flavor the liquid. I always use the hydrating liquid to flavor soups, sauces, stews, rices or vegetables. I remove the moistened mushrooms with a slotted spoon. Then I strain the pungent liquid through a coffee filter to remove any grit. If I am not using the liquid right away, I freeze it for later use.

A few hydrated wild mushrooms will flavor a whole recipe. I have learned that adding just a few to a pound of cultivated mushrooms spreads the flavor even further. There are several varieties available, each having its own special flavor. I hope these recipes will inspire you to try them and to come up with innovations of your own.

Finnish Baked Mushrooms

Serves 4 to 8

Ingredients

1/4 cup melted butter
1/2 to 1 ounce dried wild mushrooms, hydrated
2 pounds domestic mushrooms, washed and quartered
1 small shallot or 3 green onions, finely chopped
1/4 teaspoon salt
1/2 teaspoon freshly ground pepper to taste
1/4 cup diced ham, prosciutto or cooked bacon
4 tablespoons all-purpose flour
1/2 cup whipping cream or half-and-half
1/2 cup buttered bread crumbs (a mixture of rye with white or whole wheat is nice)

Procedures

1. Butter an ovenproof 2-quart baking dish with 2 teaspoons of butter.

2. Hydrate dried mushrooms 2 to 4 minutes on high power in the microwave oven with 2 cups broth or water. Strain liquid and reserve.

3. Melt remaining butter in a skillet.

4. Then sauté quartered domestic mushrooms with the shallots or onions until cooked and juicy. Remove to the baking dish.

5. Coarsely chop the hydrated mushrooms.

6. Add them to the baking dish with diced ham. Mix.

7. Add flour to skillet with the remaining sautéeing fat. If little fat remains, add 2 tablespoons more butter to skillet and melt it before stirring in flour. Cook flour 2 minutes, stirring.

8. Add cream and 1 cup reserved hydrating liquid. Cook to thicken. Add more liquid, if necessary, to obtain a nice, creamy sauce. Pour over mushrooms.

9. Top with a light crumb layer and bake at 375°F for 20 minutes.

Potatoes Fried with Wild and Domestic Mushrooms

Serves 4 to 6

Ingredients

2 to 3 tablespoons bacon, lard or duck fat
1/8 pound fresh domestic mushrooms, sliced or quartered
1 1/4 pound cubed red potatoes to fill skillet in 1 layer
1/2 ounce dried wild mushrooms, hydrated and then chopped or sliced
1 large garlic clove, finely chopped
Italian parsley, chopped with garlic coarsely

Procedures

1. Melt enough fat to coat the bottom of your skillet.

2. Sauté fresh mushrooms until cooked and golden. Remove from skillet.

3. Blot the potato cubes and place in skillet with mushrooms.

4. Brown the potatoes and season them, adding the hydrated wild mushrooms. Cover with a lid. Cook 1/2 hour, stirring occasionally.

5. Chop the parsley and garlic and stir them into skillet with potatoes and sautéed mushrooms.

6. Complete the cooking time, stirring occasionally.

Serve piping hot.

Mushroom Soufflé

Serves 6 to 8

Ingredients

For Soufflé

4 tablespoons unsalted butter
3 tablespoons fresh lemon juice
2 pounds domestic mushrooms, finely chopped
1/4 pound finely chopped prosciutto or bacon, cooked crisp, drained and crumbled
4 tablespoons mixed chopped parsley, thyme and chives
4 tablespoons additional unsalted butter
3 shallots, finely chopped
1 clove garlic, finely chopped
3/4 cup good-quality brandy
1/4 cup crème fraîche
4 large eggs
2 additional egg yolks, reserving whites
1/4 teaspoon freshly ground nutmeg
1/2 ounce dried mushrooms, hydrated, drained (reserving liquid) and finely chopped
2 egg whites
Salt and white pepper to taste

For Sauce

2 tablespoons butter
3 tablespoons flour
1/3 cup mushroom hydrating juices
2 tablespoons tomato paste
2/3 cup half-and-half
Salt and pepper to taste
1 tablespoon fresh chives, minced
1 tablespoon fresh tomatoes, skinned, drained and chopped

Procedures

For Soufflé

1. Melt 4 tablespoons butter in a large skillet until bubbly.

2. Add domestic mushrooms with lemon juice and cook until juices are released. Strain and reserve cooking liquids. Remove mushrooms to a bowl.

3. Toss cooked, drained mushrooms with prosciutto or bacon and herbs.

4. Cook shallots and garlic in 4 tablespoons butter for 5 minutes with brandy.

5. Add mushroom cooking liquids and cook over high heat to reduce liquids and concentrate mushroom flavor with shallots and garlic.

6. Add cooked shallot/garlic mixture to mushroom mixture with créme fraîche.

7. Beat 2 eggs with 2 additional egg yolks until well mixed. Stir with nutmeg and hydrated chopped wild mushrooms. Bring to room temperature.

8. Beat remaining whites until stiff but not dry. Fold into mushroom mixture carefully.

9. Taste. Use salt and white pepper, seasoning to taste.

10. Butter a 2-quart soufflé dish or equivalent, and spoon in mushroom mixture.

For Sauce

11. Melt butter from sauce ingredients in a 1 1/2-quart saucepan.

12. Stir in flour and cook, stirring, 1 to 2 minutes without allowing it to brown.

13. Stir in reserved wild-mushroom hydrating liquid, tomato paste and half-and-half.

14. Simmer about 10 minutes or until nicely thickened.

15. Add more half-and-half if mixture seems too thick.

16. Season to taste and stir in chives and tomato bits.

Serve sauce under soufflé servings, with a tiny bit drizzled over the top. A sprig of herbs, chives or chopped tomatoes are nice garnishes.

Pork Tenderloins in Porcini Cream Sauce

Serves 8

Ingredients

2 whole pork tenderloins, trimmed of excess fat
4 tablespoons unsalted butter
1 tablespoon corn oil
1/2 ounce dried Porcini mushrooms, or other available variety
1/2 pint heavy cream
16 ounces good-quality consommé
1 stick unsalted butter
2 to 4 tablespoons Madeira wine
1 tablespoon Worcestershire sauce

Procedures

1. Slice pork tenderloins with 3/4-inch-thick slices.

2. Melt butter with oil in a large skillet until bubbly.

3. Blot slices of pork dry and sauté until golden brown on both sides. Remove from skillet.

4. Pour out excess fat and cook a little of the broth in the skillet, lightly scraping the bottom with a wooden spoon to remove flavorful bits.

5. Hydrate dried mushrooms in the microwave on full power for 3 minutes with 1 cup of water, covered with plastic wrap.

6. Remove hydrated mushrooms and strain, reserving liquid.

7. Coarsely chop the hydrated mushrooms. Add cream, remaining consommé, butter, Madeira, Worcestershire sauce, mushroom pieces and liquids to the skillet.

8. Cook until liquids are reduced and a thin creamy sauce results.

9. Add browned pork to skillet and heat quickly to reduce sauce and coat meat evenly. Serve immediately.

Chicken with Hazelnuts and Mushrooms

Serves 8

Ingredients

3 tablespoons unsalted butter
6 tablespoons walnut oil
3 to 4 pounds chicken breasts, skinned and blotted dry
1/4 pound thickly sliced bacon, cut into 1/4-inch strips
1 medium onion, finely chopped
3/4 pound domestic mushrooms, trimmed and quartered
5 shallots, finely chopped
1 clove garlic, finely minced
1/2 ounce dried porcini mushrooms pieces (or other wild varieties), hydrated and coarsely chopped
1/2 pound hazelnuts, skins removed (see p. 151), blanched and coarsely chopped
2 sprigs fresh thyme
3 sprigs fresh parsley
1/4 cup good-quality brandy
1/2 cup good-quality port
3/4 cup crème fraîche (see recipe p. 68)
Salt and pepper to taste

Procedures

1. Melt the butter and the oil together in a large skillet until bubbly.

2. Over medium-high heat, brown the chicken lightly on both sides. Remove from pan to drain.

3. In the same skillet, brown bacon pieces with onion until crisp. Remove bacon and onion pieces to drain.

4. Pour off all but 3 tablespoons fat from skillet and sauté quartered mushrooms with shallots and garlic until golden.

5. Add chopped hydrated wild mushrooms with hazelnut pieces, herbs and brandy.

6. Heat the mixture and flambé it to remove the alcohol.

7. Add port, chicken and bacon to the skillet.

8. Cover and cook about 30 minutes to cook chicken through.

9. When chicken is cooked, remove it with bacon, hazelnuts and mushrooms to a *heated* serving platter. Keep warm.

10. Add crème fraîche to skillet liquids and stir until creamy and thickened.

11. Correct seasoning with salt and pepper to taste.

12. Pour sauce over chicken to serve.

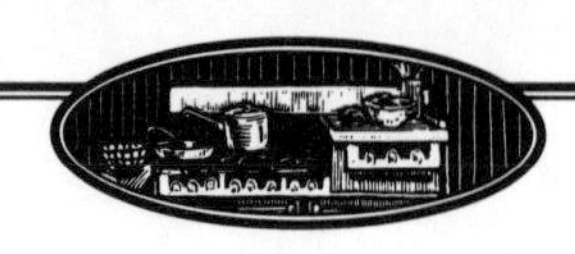

HAZELNUTS: AMERICA'S CULINARY OUTCAST

Perhaps we have never been properly introduced. Or maybe a wary confusion still lingers, from our mixed-nut days, between this round and daintily dimpled little nut and the too-large and oily Brazil nut. Whatever the reasons, Americans have never fully invited the hazelnut to be a regular player in the kitchen.

European restaurant menus feature ice creams, pastries, cakes, custards and breads commonly infused with the distinctive flavor and texture of hazelnut (alias *filbert*). Though almonds and walnuts are popular among European bakers, hazelnuts are a veritable staple. Hazelnuts are a tree nut, indigenous to the Northern Hemisphere. Growing in temperate climes, it was known in China over 5,000 years ago and was collected by the Romans. The European-grown filbert—named possibly for St. Philbert, whose birthday is during harvest time—is closely related to the American hazel tree. Today hazelnuts are planted extensively in the Pacific Northwest. But you certainly wouldn't know this by looking in the supermarkets.

Hazelnuts have no cholesterol (*American Heart Association Cookbook*, 3rd edition) and are high in protein. This sophisticated little nut will become an exciting addition to your kitchen—once you find it. You will enjoy its flavor and texture.

Whether called *noisettes, nocciole,* filberts or hazelnuts, these wonderful nuts deserve an invitation to lunch and dinner.

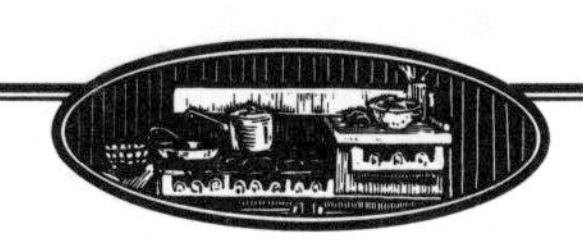

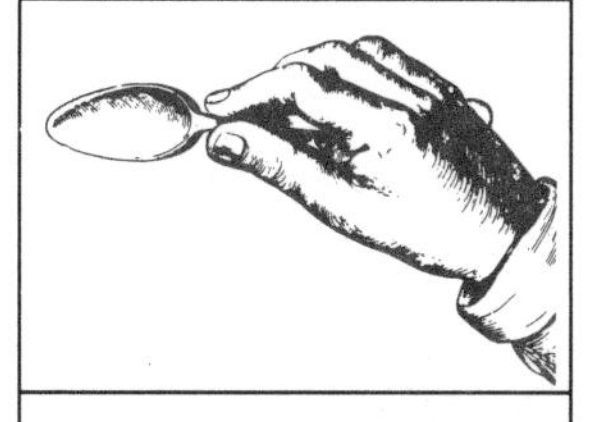

Crunchy Hazelnut Wedges

Makes 10 to 16 wedges

Ingredients

1 1/2 cups coarsely chopped hazelnuts
1 stick plus 5 tablespoons unsalted butter, melted and warm
3/4 cup plus 1 tablespoon granulated sugar
1 1/4 cup plus 1 tablespoon all-purpose flour
Pinch salt

Procedures

1. Mix all ingredients together with your fingers or a wooden spoon until mixture is well blended and crumbly.

2. Line a 9- or 10-inch cake pan with aluminum foil, pressing it flatly into the pan and up the sides to overhang the edges.

3. Butter and flour the foil lining well.

4. Press the crumbly mixture compactly into the foil-lined pan.

5. Preheat an accurate 350°F oven.

6. Bake the "biscuit" 40 to 50 minutes, until nicely golden around the edges.

7. Cool biscuit in the pan before lifting it out to remove the foil.

8. Cut or break the biscuit into pieces.

A Few Nutty Hints

For successful nut use and storage:

❦ Keep nutmeats in the freezer, sealed tightly.

❦ Toast nuts *lightly* to bring out their flavor characteristics character before including them in recipes. Do this in a 300°F oven, turning frequently.

❦ To blanch hazelnuts (or other nuts), oven roast them at 350°F for 10 to 15 minutes. Rub the nuts inside a towel or brown bag to loosen skins. If some skins don't come off, further roasting *won't* help. Just use them as they are.

❦ To prevent chopped nuts from sinking to the bottom of cakes or muffins, lightly toss nuts with flour before adding them to the batter.

The challenge of teaching, answering baking queries, making recipes bake as directed has put me in contact with some of the most enthusiastic, intelligent people I have ever met—my students. It has been their feedback that has spurred me to gather more baking information. It's ironic that I have been the teacher, supposedly the one giving, yet I am the beneficiary because I have learned so much from my students."

Flo Baker, Palo Alto CA; author *The Simple Art of Perfect Baking* and *Sweet Miniatures*

Donna's Hazelnut Sponge Cake

Serves 8 to 12

Ingredients

8 eggs, separated
1/2 pound sugar
1 teaspoon vanilla extract
2 tablespoons fresh bread crumbs
3 cups hazelnuts, blanched and finely ground

Procedures

1. Beat egg yolks with sugar until thickened and pale yellow.
2. Add vanilla extract and bread crumbs.
3. Add nuts, stirring with a wooden spoon to blend.
4. Beat egg whites to form soft peaks.
5. Fold whites into batter.
6. Grease the *bottom only* of a 9-inch springform pan.
7. Bake cake in the center of an accurately preheated 325°F oven for 1 hour.
8. Turn off oven heat and open the door.
9. Leave cake in oven 10 more minutes.
10. Remove cake from oven to serving plate.
11. Sprinkle with powdered sugar.

Serve with whipped cream and/or fresh berries.

My Mother-in-law's Hazelnut Cookies

Makes about 4 dozen

Ingredients

1 cup unsalted butter, softened
1 1/2 teaspoon almond extract
1 cup plus 3 tablespoons powdered sugar
2 cups all-purpose flour
1 cup hazelnuts, blanched or unblanched, finely ground
2/3 cup additional hazelnuts, finely ground
Additional powdered sugar

Procedures

1. Cream butter, extract and sugar together.

2. Add flour and 1 cup ground hazelnuts.

3. Blend well to combine evenly.

4. Form cookie dough into "logs" 2 inches in diameter.

5. Roll logs in additional ground nuts.

6. Wrap tightly in plastic wrap and refrigerate 2 hours or more.

7. Slice 1/4-inch-thick cookies from logs and place on buttered baking sheets.

8. Bake 12 to 15 minutes in a preheated 350°F oven, until edges are golden.

9. Remove cookies immediately to a cooling rack. Cool, then dust well with powdered sugar.

Raisins are Something to Dance About

Besides being portable, packable, nutritious, energy-giving and easy to enjoy, raisins are one of nature's most versatile foods. Quick and simple to use, raisins add taste, texture, flavor and interest in food combinations and, important particularly in drier climates, they help to retain the moisture in baked goods.

Raisins are one of those rare foods requiring no peeling or cooking. They are also a no-waste food. With raisins, there is nothing to throw away and, with 70 percent natural fruit sugars, they are a concentrated energy source easily used by the body. Potassium, phosphorus, calcium, magnesium, some B vitamins, and iron in highly usable form are essential minerals readily available from raisins.

Raisins retain nearly all the food value of grapes but weigh 75 percent less. Popular with Middle Eastern nomads and Mediterranean peoples from the fifth century B.C., raisins keep well because of their high sugar content. Spanish missionaries brought the first grapes to the United States (to California) for use in sacramental wines. Settlers to California's San Joaquin Valley dug canals to irrigate their grapes in an area where only 9 inches of rain fell in an average year. Today one of the earth's most extensive irrigation systems brings water to this rich, fertile, sun-drenched soil and quenches a grape crop that supplies nearly half of the world's raisins.

Not all grapes are suitable for raisins. Today Thompson seedless grapes are the source of both the sun-dried natural seedless raisins and the golden seedless raisins we buy in our markets. Tiny Zante currants, available for baking, come from the Black Corinth grape variety.

Raisins first became available when, in 1872, a vicious heat wave struck the summer-plumped and sweetened grape crop just before harvest time. One resourceful grower took his shriveled crop to market and introduced San Francisco to the ancient delicacy—raisins. This accident spawned one of the most successful and carefully controlled food industries in the world.

California raisin clusters are hand-picked and then sun-dried for two to three weeks to reduce moisture content to about 15 percent. After vibrating conveyor belts separate raisins from their grape stems, raisins are put into "sweat boxes," where drier raisins mingle with wetter ones to assure even moisture distribution. Then off they go to the packing plants and on to us as a favorite snack and cooking staple.

Wild Rice with Raisins and Almonds

Serves 12

Ingredients

2 cups Uncle Ben's wild/brown rice mix
1/2 cup olive oil
2 tablespoons chopped onion
4 1/2 cups chicken broth
3/4 cup slivered almonds, toasted
1/3 cup raisins, plumped in a sieve over simmering water for 10 minutes (or in the microwave as directed in tip #4)

Procedures

1. Wash and drain rice.

2. Sauté onion in olive oil.

3. When onion is translucent, stir in rice and cook, stirring until golden.

4. Stir in broth, seasoning packet, almonds and raisins.

5. Place in a buttered casserole with a cover.

6. Bake, covered, at 250°F for 1 1/4 to 2 hours, until all the broth is absorbed by the rice.

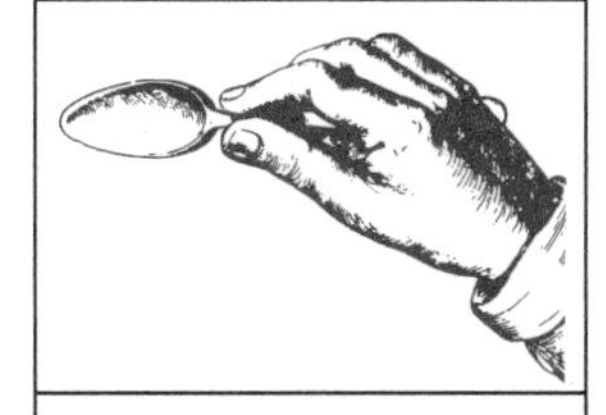

TIPS FOR USING RAISINS

1. To chop or grind raisins, freeze them first. If using a blender or food processor, brush blades and container with a little vegetable oil before grinding or chopping, processing only 1/2 cup at a time.

2. For chopping unfrozen raisins with a knife, toss 1 teaspoon of vegetable oil with one cup of raisins before chopping.

3. To assure even distribution of raisins in cakes or puddings, reserve 1/4 of the raisins from the mixture to be distributed over the top before baking. They will sink in during the baking.

4. To plump raisins, place in a measuring cup with a little water. Cover with plastic wrap and microwave on high for 2 minutes. Drain off the liquid if you are not planning to use it in the recipe.

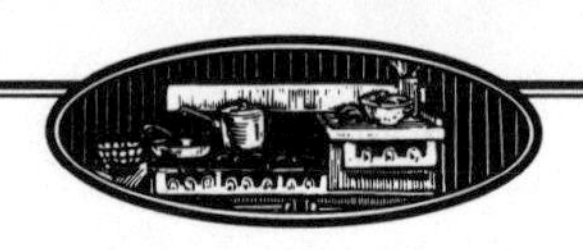

Kugelhopf

Serves 12 to 18

Ingredients

1/2 cup dark raisins, plumped
1/2 cup dried currants, plumped
1 1/2 cups blanched almonds, finely chopped
1 tablespoon grated lemon peel and orange peel mixed
1 tablespoon brandy
1 cup whole milk
1/4 cup granulated sugar
1 package active dry yeast
1/2 cup warm water
3 1/2 cups all-purpose flour
16 whole blanched almonds
1 cups unsalted butter, softened
3/4 cup additional granulated sugar
1 teaspoon salt
6 large eggs
1 1/2 to 2 1/2 cups additional all-purpose flour
1/4 cup unsalted butter, melted
Powdered sugar for decoration

Procedures

1. Combine raisins, currants, chopped almonds (reserving 1/4 cup for later use), peel, and brandy. Toss. Reserve.

2. In a small saucepan, heat milk until bubbles form around edge. Remove from heat and stir in 1/4 cup granulated sugar. Cool.

3. Dissolve yeast in warm water. Add cooled milk mixture. Stir in 3 1/2 cups flour and beat until smooth.

4. Allow dough to rise until doubled.

5. Butter a 4-quart tube mold (10 1/2-inch diameter). Sprinkle remaining chopped almonds around inside. If mold has indentations, press one whole blanched almond into each indentation.

6. In a large bowl, beat softened butter with remaining 3/4 cup granulated sugar and the salt until fluffy. Beat in eggs, one at a time, until blended well.

7. Beat in 1 cup flour and the risen batter until smooth.

8. Stir in remaining flour and the reserved fruit-nut mixture. Combine well.

9. Distribute batter into prepared mold. Tap mold firmly on flat surface to remove air bubbles.

10. Cover and allow to rise in a warm place until doubled or the dough nearly reaches the pan top.

11. Preheat oven to an accurate 350°F.

12. Bake Kugelhopf 50 to 60 minutes, until cake tester comes out clean.

13. Cool Kugelhopf 20 minutes before unmolding.

14. Brush with 1/4 cup melted butter when unmolded.

15. Sprinkle with powdered sugar before serving.

Grandma Larmoyeux's Sugar Tart

A treasured recipe shared by good friends

Makes 2 9-inch tarts

Ingredients

2 eggs
1/2 cup unsalted butter, softened
1/2 teaspoon salt
1 tablespoon lard
1/2 cup whipping cream
2 teaspoons dry yeast
1/4 cup warm water
2 1/2 to 3 cups (generous) all-purpose flour
1/4 cup additional unsalted butter, softened
1/2 cup brown sugar
1/4 cup dark raisins, plumped
1/4 cup walnuts, pecans or almonds, chopped
1/4 cup sweetened coconut

Procedures

1. Mix eggs, butter, salt and shortening.

2. Add cream and mix again.

3. Dissolve and proof yeast in 1/4 cup warm water. Add to egg mixture.

4. Add enough flour to form a biscuit-type consistency. Begin with 2 1/2 cups, adding more if necessary.

5. Allow dough to rise 1 hour.

6. Knead dough lightly and gently pat into two greased 9-inch pie plates.

7. Preheat oven to 350°F.

8. Allow tarts to rise 30 minutes.

9. Prick tarts with a fork.

10. Top with a mixture of 1/4 cup butter and 1/2 cup brown sugar, mixed with any desired combination of raisins, nuts and coconut divided between the two tarts.

11. Bake 25 to 30 minutes, until beautifully golden.

Italian Sweets to Tempt Even the Hardhearted

My very first visit to Milan was a gastronomic event which registered near ten on my tummy's Richter scale. It was love at first bite. From the antipasti, I merrily slid through the pasta and right on through the main course, coming to a halt only after the magnificent *grappa* (strong Italian spirit).

Each day I ventured deeper and deeper into the culinary paradise of the Italian *cucina* (kitchen) From restaurants both *piccolo e grande*, (small and large) I felt the Italian love of fresh and wonderful foods reflected on every menu, on the lips of every waiter and on every plate. The flavors and spirit of Italy were infectious.

There was only one little imperfection in my Italian eating adventure. I never quite seemed to hit the right dessert. Never having been enamored of candied fruits, I unluckily encountered them in nearly every *dolce* (sweet) I tried. It wasn't really a disappointment that clouded my meals. I usually avoided the let-down by ordering a chunk of some obscure Italian cheese with a bowl of perfect *fragolini* (tiny wild strawberries).

Subsequent visits served up the opportunity for me to work in Italian restaurant kitchens and to scour the shelves of local bookstores for cookbooks. I became aware of the *tiramisù* (pick-me-up: sweet biscuits, dried leftover cake or ladyfingers (see p. 88) layered with Amaretto, creamy sweet Mascarpone cheese and chunkily grated sweet dark chocolate, see recipe on p. 87) which was delivered each morning and consumed during the lunch hour, redelivered again before dinner. *Tortoni*, the frozen almond custard, appeared unviolated by candied fruit but nicely accented with toasted slivered almonds.

Even a "lite" dolci alternative was quickly assembled each day: *macedonia* (a maceration of varied fruits tossed with lemon juice, floated in dry Italian white wine and sweetened ever-so-slightly with granulated sugar).

Easily duplicated at home, the recipes which follow offer the kind of Italian dessert which makes reaching your culinary goals easy. All of the recipes are best when made ahead of time. *Buono appetito.*

Macedonia of Fruits

1/2 to 3/4 cup makes a nice size serving

Ingredients

1/2 to 1 fresh lemon
Good-quality dry Italian white wine
Sugar to taste
Suggested fruits:
Pears
Bananas
Strawberries
Apples
Oranges
Grapefruit
Kiwis
Pineapple
Cantaloupe
Honeydew
Peaches
Berries

Procedures

1. Cube, slice and wedge any fruits that are desired. Peeling should be done as desired.

2. Squeeze the juice of 1/2 to 1 lemon over the fruits to prevent darkening while preparing.

3. Toss the mixture and pour wine over to cover.

4. Flavor to taste with granulated sugar. The mixture should not be *very* sweet.

5. Allow fruits to macerate a minimum of 3 hours.

Delicate fruits such as berries, kiwis and bananas may be added just before serving. They get mushy if macerated for a lengthy amount of time.

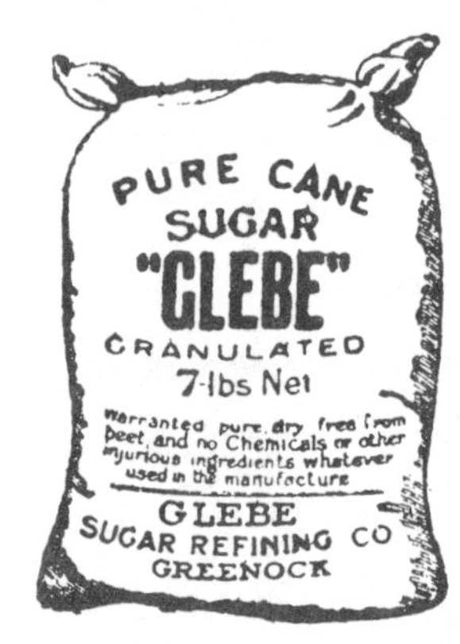

Tortoni

Makes 18 1/2-cup servings

Ingredients

- **6 yolks from large eggs**
- **3/4 cup granulated sugar**
- **1/4 teaspoon salt**
- **1 cup light cream (half-and-half)**
- **1/8 cup sweet sherry**
- **1/4 teaspoon almond extract**
- **1 cup slivered almonds, toasted and chopped**
- **1 cup almond macaroon crumbs (see recipe on p. 186) or used purchased red-tinted Amaretti di Saronno**
- **3 cups heavy cream**

Procedures

1. Beat egg yolks until thickened with the sugar. Mixture will be light yellow.

2. Add salt and light cream.

3. Cook above in a double boiler until mixture readily coats the back of a metal spoon. *Do not allow water in double boiler to boil.*

4. Cool the egg mixture slightly before stirring in the sherry, extract, nuts and crumbs.

5. Whip the cream until softly stiff.

6. Fold cream into egg mixture.

7. Freeze in glasses, custard cups or ramekins for several hours.

Orange Zabaglione

Zabaglione is an Italian pastry cream, flavored with a sweet wine and used as a filling or a sauce. An ultra-rich dessert, it may be "lightened" when combined with whipped cream.

Serves 4

Ingredients

4 large oranges
3/8 cup granulated sugar
2 tablespoons Marsala or other sweet wine
2 large egg yolks, beaten lightly
1/8 cup additional granulated sugar

Procedures

1. Peel and seed oranges.

2. Chop the oranges coarsely.

3. Combine chopped oranges with the 3/8 cup sugar.

4. Cook the mixture about 10 minutes over medium heat to create a syrupy mixture.

5. Purée this mixture and strain it through a sieve to yield a syrup.

6. Add the Marsala, egg yolks and the remaining sugar to the syrup.

7. Place this mixture in a double boiler.

8. Beat it continuously over a simmering pot of water until tripled in volume.

Serve mounded in clear stemmed glasses.

Making the Most of Our Freshwater Trout

About the only time we kill the wild trout we catch today is when fishing with our grandchildren. A freshly caught trout cooked and served streamside is the perfect reward for novice or young fishermen whose skills and success provide game for the table.

For other trout dishes I turn to the farm-raised trout available in supermarkets having a fish department. Single-serving sized, these fresh trout are firm-fleshed and well-cleaned. They are perfect for the preparation of the following recipes, as well as for an outdoor picnic beside your favorite stream.

I can smell the aromatic pine branches burning into a perfect bed of cooking coals. Bacon fat begins to sizzle in our old, long-handled skillet. New potatoes, precooked, await a bit of butter and parsley. Cold trout are bathed in a seasoned mix of flour and cornmeal. Sizzle—swish: the trout begin to turn color immediately. Crispy and browned, our streamside picnic is complete with a crunchy salad and the warmed parslied potatoes. A garnish of lemon and a slip of wild onion are the eye-pleasing finish. Don't forget to take the cooled wine from the rippling stream.

Trout is versatile, nutritious, low calorie, economical and delicious. As with all fish, trout can be simply baked in a 400°F oven for 10 minutes per inch of thickness. If two fillets are sandwiched around a filling and measure three inches in thickness, they will cook properly in 30 minutes.

A preheated oven will ensure success. A meat thermometer will boost confidence. (Be certain that the tip of the thermometer reads the temperature of the fish rather than the filling or the baking pan!)

The smoked trout pâté is a fish spread or dip that is nicely served with crunchy fresh vegetables and crackers. The smoked trout in filo pastry is good as an appetizer. Trout seviche is my adaptation of a Central American favorite. The elegant molds of fish and shrimp are the recipe of an Australian colleague whom I consider to be the world's best food stylist. They are served perfectly as a light lunch or as a first course before dinner.

Marinated Trout Seviche

Begin this tasty appetizer two days before serving.
Serves 6 to 8

INGREDIENTS

2 pounds fresh water trout, filleted and skinned
Coarse salt
6 tablespoons fresh lemon juice
Zest of 1 lemon, finely chopped
3 tablespoons fresh parsley, chopped
2 tablespoons chives, chopped
Chive flowers, when available
2 tablespoons good quality olive oil
3 tablespoons capers, coarsely chopped
2 teaspoons black pepper, coarsely ground

PROCEDURES

1. Ribbon trout meat into 1/2-inch-by-2-inch pieces.

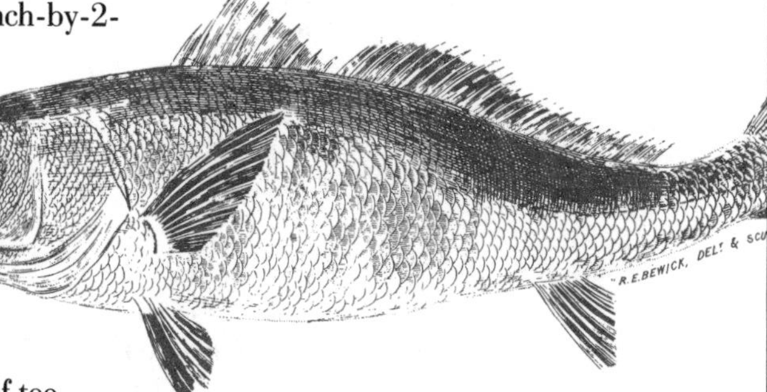

2. Toss trout with salt and refrigerate, covered, 24 hours.

3. Taste trout to check for excessive saltiness.

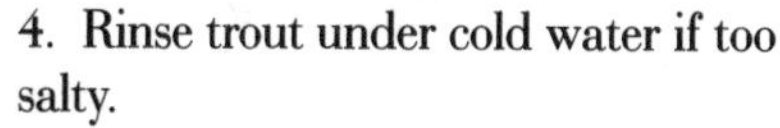

4. Rinse trout under cold water if too salty.

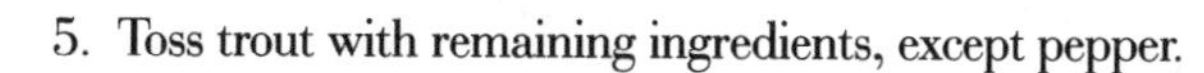

5. Toss trout with remaining ingredients, except pepper.

6. Arrange on serving plate.

7. Grind pepper over trout.

8. Cover tightly and refrigerate 4 to 6 hours before serving.

Serve on greens or with crackers.

Smoked Trout in Pastry with Horseradish Sauce

Adapted from *Australia's Vogue Entertaining Guide*

Serves 4 to 8

Ingredients

For Trout in Pastry

2 1 to 2-pound trout, cleaned
Salt
2 handfuls fresh dill
Filo pastry
Butter, melted

For Sauce

2 tablespoons softened unsalted butter
2 large egg yolks
1 cup whipping cream
Salt
Freshly ground black pepper
1 tablespoon prepared horseradish
3 teaspoons capers
2 to 3 tablespoons fresh dill, chopped
8 small sprigs fresh dill for garnish

Procedures

For Trout in Pastry

1. Rub the trout inside and out with salt. Spread dill inside cavities.

2. Smoke fish in a smoker about 8 minutes.

3. Allow trout to cool. Fillet and skin the fish.

4. Split each fillet in half widthwise and remove any bones.

5. Brush 4 layers of filo with melted butter; stack them. Cut stacked filo into rectangular sized pieces to accommodate the smoked fish pieces.

6. Wrap filleted pieces individually.

7. Place packets seam-side down and brush with butter. (Packets can be formed, buttered, covered and refrigerated for later baking.)

8. In a preheated 425°F oven, bake 7 to 9 minutes until nicely golden and crisp.

For Sauce

9. Whisk together butter, eggs and cream in a small saucepan over medium heat. Do not boil or eggs will scramble.

10. When sauce thickens, remove from heat and stir in salt, pepper, horseradish, capers and chopped fresh dill.

11. Warm sauce gently when ready to serve.

Serve the smoked trout packets with sauce, garnished with fresh dill sprigs.

Smoked Trout Pâté

Serves 4

Ingredients

Whole smoked fresh water trout to yield 8 ounces smoked trout meat
1/2 cup dry white wine or dry vermouth
1 cup water
1/2 cup unsalted butter
2 teaspoons gelatin
1/2 pint sour cream
Salt
Freshly ground black pepper
1 ripe avocado, sliced
Lemon juice
Homemade Melba toast (see Using Sliceable Bread on p. 29) or crackers

Procedures

1. While reserving smoked meat, remove skin, bones and head of fish and place into a skillet with water and wine.

2. Bring fish and liquids to a boil, reduce heat and simmer 5 minutes; strain, reserving liquids.

3. Return liquids to a saucepan and add butter and gelatin. Stir over low heat until butter melts and gelatin dissolves.

4. Place trout meat and liquids in food processor or blender and purée finely. Chill.

5. Fold in sour cream. Season to taste with salt, pepper and lemon juice.

6. Divide among 4 serving dishes and refrigerate.

7. Garnish with avocado slices tossed with lemon juice.

Serve with homemade Melba toast or crackers.

Joan Campbell's Steamed Trout Molds with Shrimp in a Chive and Mussel Sauce

A woman whose work and artistry I greatly admire

Serves 4

Ingredients

For Molds

12 to 16 ounces fresh spinach, washed and deveined
16 to 24 medium shrimp, shelled and deveined
Butter for sautéing (about 2 tablespoons)
Salt
Freshly ground black pepper
2 trout, filleted and skinned

For Sauce

20 mussels (clams may be substituted)
White wine to cover mussels in a skillet
1/4 cup additional dry white wine
1/3 to 1/2 cup crème fraîche (see recipe on p.

1 bunch chives or green onion tops
2/3 cup unsalted butter
Lemon juice
Freshly ground black pepper

Procedures

For Molds

1. Steam the washed spinach until wilted. In a sieve, run immediately under cold water to stop cooking and set color. Squeeze spinach in a damp tea towel to remove excess liquids.

2. Chop the spinach finely.

3. Cut shrimp into 1/2-inch pieces and sauté quickly in butter.

4. Toss shrimp with spinach and season lightly with salt and pepper.

5. Butter molds, ramekins or custard cups. Cut a circle of cooking parchment or buttered waxed paper to fit mold bottoms. Lay this in place.

6. Line the mold with the trout fillet, skinned side facing into mold center.

7. Fill with shrimp mixture.

This dish can be prepared to this point and refrigerated several hours before cooking.

For Sauce

8. Scrub and de-beard mussels. Place into a skillet.

9. Pour wine over mussels just to cover the bottom.

10. Cover the skillet and steam the mussels just until they open. Discard any unopened mussels.

11. Remove the mussels from their shells.

12. Strain mussel cooking liquid into a saucepan. Add wine and crème fraîche. Boil to reduce by 1/3.

13. Blend chives and butter in food processor until very green and smooth.

14. Add chive butter to the reduced sauce and season with lemon juice and pepper.

The above steps can be completed ahead and the mussels reserved until serving time.

When ready to serve

15. Steam the molds, covered, over boiling water for about 8 minutes.

16. Steam the cooked mussels, just until reheated, about 1 to 2 minutes.

17. Warm the sauce; coat serving plates with warm sauce.

18. Invert molds carefully to drain off excess liquid. Unmold drained trout molds onto serving plates.

Garnish with mussels and serve at once.

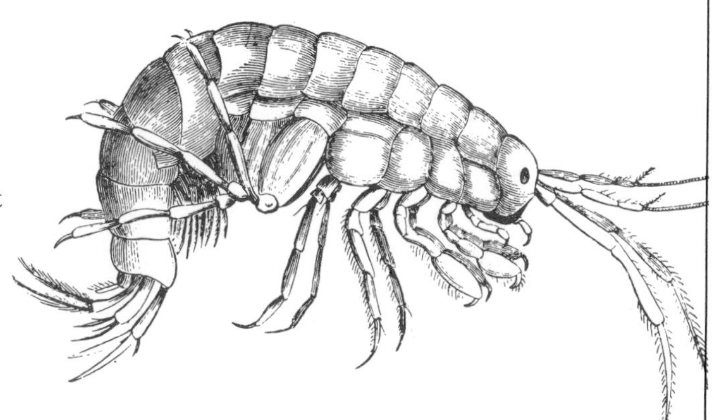

Fish Chowder

Serves 6 to 10

Ingredients

6 strips bacon
1 large onion, peeled and coarsely chopped
2 quarts water
3 to 4 medium red potatoes (peeled or unpeeled), cubed
1 pound fish fillets, skinned
1 can whole kernel corn (drained), or 1 cup fresh corn kernels, cooked
1 large can evaporated milk
1 cup red and green sweet pepper strips
1/4 to 1/2 cup butter
Salt and freshly ground black pepper (lots of pepper!) to taste

Procedures

1. In a Dutch oven, sauté bacon until nearly crisp.

2. Add chopped onion to pot and cook over medium heat until soft and translucent.

3. Add cubed potatoes and water. Cook until potatoes are nearly tender.

4. Add fish fillets. Heat until fish is just cooked.

5. Add corn, evaporated milk and sweet peppers. Heat through.

6. Stir in butter and season to taste.

7. Reheat to desired temperature. Serve at once.

Feel free to improvise. I think the only "must" ingredients are the fish, bacon, onions, and evaporated milk.

WINTER

A need for warming and nurturing flavors the spirit of the winter kitchen. Bodies battle cooler temperatures. Even in these comfortable 1990s, there are physical and psychological considerations in maintaining health and energy levels in winter that differ from those of other seasons. Entertaining takes on a cozy "gathering" character. Long-simmering soups, stews and ethnic dishes fill homes with comforting smells. The chill and damp of winter is kept at bay by more leisurely time spent near the stove. Opportunities to practice techniques and to investigate recipes present themselves in winter as lives move more slowly. Holiday baking and gift making provide an excuse to take the little extra time needed for trying something new.

APPETIZERS, FIRST COURSES, SALADS, AND SOUPS

Busy First Lady's Soup 194
Chicken Vegetable Soup 196
Cream of Mixed Mushroom Soup 197
Lamb Shank Soup 193
Risotto Barolo 172
Risotto Parmesan 172
Risotto Primavera 172
Risotto with Artichokes 174
Risotto with Cheese Fondue 173
Roquefort Soup 195
Veggie Turnovers 201

FISH AND MEATS

Braised Veal Shanks 175
Salmon or Tuna Turnovers 200

BREADS

Brioche à Tête 189
Cracked-Wheat Bread 181
Croissant 182
Focaccia 178
French-Style Whole-Wheat Baguettes 180
One-Rise Italian-Style Bread 179
Polish Turnovers 198
Poppy Seed Coffee Bread 204
Poppy Seed Pancakes 203
Scones 191

SWEETS

Almond Macaroons 186
Chocolate-Tipped Oatmeal Crescents 187
Moravian Gingersnaps 186
Poppy Seed Cookies 203
Swedish Cream Wafers 185

ACCOMPANIMENTS

Kiwifruit Jam 191
Risotto Milanese 171

BASICS

Bread Baking 177
Croissant 182
Scones 191

A Lust for Rice: Creamy Risotto

At last, rice is commanding the attention it deserves in American restaurants and homes. Many flavorful varieties of rice are now available to intrigue the American cook. Blah quick-cooking rices never held my interest. And my consumption of the familiar, dry, individual grains of rice plummeted after my very first mouthful of risotto—the creamy Italian cooked rice.

Approximately 2,500 varieties of rice have been cultivated since antiquity. Rice is the principal food for nearly half of the world's people. "Converted" rice—a 2,000-year-old process—is precooked before milling to ensure nutrient absorption by the rice grain. The whole grain is steeped in water, steamed and dried before milling. Milling removes the hull from the grain. Brown rice remains and is the intact kernel covered by bran. An abrasive process follows to remove the bran, yielding milled, unpolished rice. Polishing removes a fat-containing layer to prolong shelf life and to reduce the possibility of rancidity during storage.

Today, polished rice is fortified by the addition of vitamins and then coated with protein powder. Converted rice should not be rinsed before cooking and should be cooked in enough liquid for full absorption. Converted rice supplies B vitamins, thiamine, riboflavin, and niacin.

The risotto cooking method retains nutrients in a luscious dish commonly served in Italian homes since the sixteenth century. Classic risottos are made with pearl-shaped Arborio rice grains, which are grown in the Italian region of Piedmont. Converted long-grain rices may be used with moderate success.

Risottos make up an entire category of first courses on the traditional Northern Italian menu. Rice grains are cooked and then flavored with cheeses, butter, wine, vegetables, herbs and sometimes even strawberries!

Gastronomically, risotto occupies a niche somewhere between soup and pasta. Accompanied by an antipasto salad, crusty Italian bread (see recipe on page 179) and dessert, this creamy rice creation is served proudly alone on a dish or in a flat-rimmed soup plate.

Exact measurements and cooking times will vary because of differences in quantities, sizes of saucepans and amounts of rice. The following guidelines can be used as a master recipe to ensure the unctuous and al dente consistency desired. Once the basic technique is understood, combinations and variations are endless.

From Riso to Risotto

SERVING SIZES

2 to 4 Servings: 1 cup rice, 1 1/2-quart saucepan

4 to 8 Servings: 2 cups rice, 2-quart saucepan

8 to 10 Servings: 1 pound rice, 4 1/2-quart saucepan

Ingredients

Olive oil
Onion slice
Arborio rice (riso)
Italian dry white wine
Low-salt chicken broth
Unsalted butter

Exact ingredient quantities will vary according to servings required. Follow procedural directions.

Procedures

1. Coat the bottom of a saucepan with 1/4 inch olive oil.

2. Caramelize an onion slice in this oil over moderately high heat. (This flavors the oil.)

3. Remove the onion and add the rice. Stir the rice over the heat for 1 minute to heat and coat the rice. Do not brown.

4. Stir in enough wine to cover the grains by 1/2 inch.

5. Stir rice continually over moderately high heat to evaporate the wine until liquid no longer obscures the saucepan bottom when stirred.

6. Pour in the stock (usually chicken) to cover the grains by 1/2 inch.

7. Cook, stirring as in step 5, to evaporate the liquid and to concentrate flavors.

8. Repeat step 7, stirring until liquid is absorbed.

9. Risotto is finished when rice is a creamy mass and grains are al dente.

10. Stir in 2 teaspoons butter per serving.

Offer freshly grated Parmesan cheese.

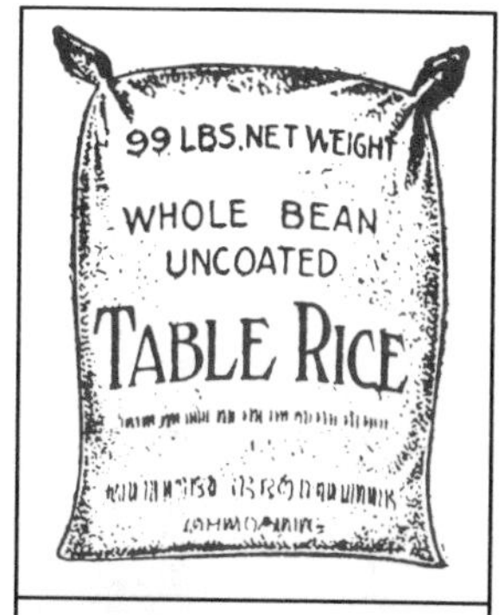

FOR CONVENIENCE: THE INTERRUPTED METHOD

Rice, which has been cooked through step 7, may be tossed with a small quantity of olive oil (about 2 tablespoons for 1 pound of rice) and then stored, covered lightly and refrigerated, for up to 2 days before completion.

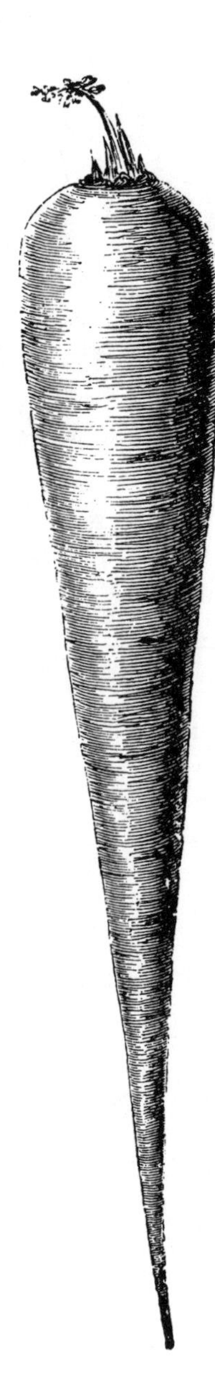

SUGGESTED RISOTTO VARIATIONS:

RISOTTO PARMESAN

Stir freshly grated Parmesan cheese into risotto just before serving.

RISOTTO PRIMAVERA

Add diced vegetables, such as zucchini, carrots, peas, asparagus, to risotto with last addition of broth. Cook to creamy texture. Stir in butter.

RISOTTO BAROLO

Use red wine for half of the last cooking liquid (with equal part chicken broth). Stir in butter when creamy. Omit Parmesan.

RISOTTO MILANESE

This is the only risotto traditionally served with a meal—Braised Veal Shanks (see recipe on p. 175). Steep saffron threads in the last chicken broth to be used. Rice will be yellow. Add butter when creamy.

Risotto reheats nicely in the microwave covered with a light wrapping of plastic wrap. It can also be reheated quickly in a heavy saucepan by adding a little chicken broth and constantly stirring over medium-high heat until the proper consistency is achieved. When rice is heated through, quickly pour it directly from the pan onto serving plates.

Risotto with Cheese Fondue

A specialty of the Aosta Valley of Italy

Serves 6 to 8

Ingredients

2 cups uncooked Arborio rice
1 to 1 1/4 ounces whole milk
4 ounces Italian Fontina cheese or a mild white Cheddar, diced or grated
3 large egg yolks
Salt and freshly ground black pepper to taste

Procedures

1. Cook rice as directed in risotto technique through step 5 (see recipe on p. 171).

2. Heat the milk and cheese together. Gentle microwaving will work nicely.

3. Allow the milk/cheese mixture to stay warm 30 minutes.

4. Begin to finish the process of converting the rice into risotto (steps 6 through 10).

5. At the same time, beat the yolks into the milk/cheese.

6. When the risotto is nearly cooked, turn it into a well-buttered baking dish.

7. Season the egg mixture with salt and pepper, keeping in mind the saltiness of the Fontina.

8. Pour the egg mixture over the risotto and place into a preheated 350°F oven for about 25 minutes, or until the egg mixture is cooked to a custardlike firmness.

Serve immediately. Can be used nicely as a luncheon dish.

Risotto with Artichokes

Serves 8 to 10

Ingredients

1 pound Arborio rice, cooked through step 7 of risotto technique (see recipe on p. 171)
Juice of 1 lemon
3 fresh globe artichokes
8 tablespoons good-quality Italian olive oil
3 cloves garlic, finely slivered
1 cup light chicken stock
2/3 cup Italian parsley, hashed
1 teaspoon freshly ground black pepper
4 tablespoons unsalted butter
3/4 cup aged, imported Parmesan cheese, finely grated

Procedures

1. Rub all broken or cut surfaces of the artichoke with lemon juice throughout the process to prevent discoloration.

2. Cut off artichoke stems and remove tough outer leaves until only pale green and more tender inner leaves remain. Cut 1 1/2 inches off artichoke tops.

3. Cut each artichoke in half lengthwise and, with a paring knife, cut around the choke. Use a teaspoon or melon baller to dig out the fuzzy fibers. Use a damp towel to wipe the heart clean.

4. Rub artichokes with lemon juice to prevent discoloration.

5. Slice each artichoke half as thinly as possible.

6. Heat the olive oil in an enamel 2-quart saucepan.

7. Sauté the artichoke slices and garlic until soft, over medium heat.

8. Add stock, 1/2 cup parsley and pepper. Simmer for 30 minutes.

9. Add the above mixture to the risotto, along with 1 cup stock to continue step 8 of risotto technique.

10. When risotto is al dente, stir in butter and 1/2 cup cheese.

Serve immediately on heated plates, sprinkled with the remaining cheese and parsley.

Braised Veal Shanks

Serves 6 to 8

Ingredients

For Braising Shanks

1/4 cup unsalted butter
2 tablespoons olive oil
1 medium onion, chopped finely
2 medium carrots, chopped finely
2 stalks celery, scraped and chopped finely
1 clove garlic, pulverized
2 1-inch-by-2-inch pieces lemon rind or orange rind
6 to 8 pieces veal shank, sawed into 2-inch lengths, tied to hold meat on the bone while cooking
Salt and freshly ground black pepper
All-purpose flour for dredging the veal shank pieces
1/2 cup olive oil plus more, as needed, to brown meat
1 cup Italian dry white wine
1 28-ounce can Italian tomatoes, drained
3 sprigs fresh thyme, or 1/2 teaspoon dried thyme
2 bay leaves
3 sprigs fresh Italian parsley
3/4 cup meat stock

For Gremolata Garnish

1 tablespoon lemon peel, chopped
1 teaspoon garlic, minced
4 tablespoons parsley, chopped

Procedures

1. In a large, covered Dutch oven, melt butter with 2 tablespoons oil. Cook the chopped vegetables, garlic and rind over medium heat until transparent. Remove the vegetable mixture from Dutch oven and reserve.

2. Season and flour the shanks.

3. Heat 1/2 cup oil in Dutch oven until it is hot. Brown the meat in a single layer. Add and heat more oil, if necessary, between batches.

4. Remove the shanks and add the wine to the Dutch oven. Cook wine over medium-high heat, stirring to lift flavorful bits from the bottom. Cook only until liquid volume is reduced by 1/2.

5. Return vegetable mixture to the Dutch oven and top with browned shanks.

6. Add tomatoes, seasonings and broth to come halfway up the veal shanks.

7. Cook, covered, in a 350°F oven for 1 to 1 1/2 hours.

8. Garnish with the gremolata—a mixture of lemon peel, garlic and parsley chopped together.

Served traditionally with Risotto Milanese (see recipe on p. 172).

Bread Baking Can Be Fun!

Among culinary tasks, the baking of raised breads seems to be one of the most intimidating. Two factors may contribute to this situation: the unwieldy and demanding amount of time required by recipes and the disappointing results of previous bread-baking attempts. Amazingly, bread making can be easily divided into workable time slots. What a difference a little information makes!

Basically, making raised bread consists of adding water and yeast to flour to make a dough, manipulating the dough to develop texture, letting the dough rise and baking the dough. An understanding of flours and yeast is primary to consistent success.

By understanding what is happening in the bread-making process, you should have more confidence and success. Give it another try, take control of the ingredients and I'm sure you'll enjoy the results. Happy baking!

HOW TO TELL WHEN BREAD IS DONE

❦ An oven thermometer, to verify temperature, will ensure that the bread is baking at the proper speed.

❦ If bread is browning too fast, lightly cover with foil and complete the baking time.

❦ A loaf is baked when tapping on the bottom produces a hollow, rather than dense, sound.

Some Basic Bread-Baking Information

No one ever told us, but flours differ in moisture content from one bag to the next. Flours milled in the spring are "wetter" than those milled in the fall. "Wet" flour will understandably require less liquid to achieve the proper consistency. For bread making, I usually use unbleached all-purpose or bread flour. When a dough is too sticky or dry after adding all of the required ingredients in a recipe, it isn't our fault! Get up your courage and add flour or water (1 tablespoon at a time) until the proper consistency is achieved.

Wheat is a grain whose proteins—called gluten—when combined with water, interact to form an elastic network strong enough to produce raised breads. These elastic strands, after kneading, stretch during the rising process. Starch granules, naturally present in flour, are held within this protein network and provide food for the yeast.

Yeasts are a group of single-celled fungi whose CO2-producing metabolism is the secret to the leavening and flavoring of breads. They are living cells which must be invigorated in warm (95°F to 110°F) water. ("Quick-rise" yeasts are engineered to use 120°F water.) A bread thermometer is good insurance against killing yeast in too hot water. Water that is too cool may not adequately energize yeast. Active yeast cells consume starches and sugars, produce CO2, multiply and contribute to flavor and texture during rising. Salts may inhibit yeast activity and should be added with the flour. Sugars, in moderation, increase yeast fermentation. They, too, are normally added with the flour.

Kneading bread dough is very important and can be done by hand or machine. The goal of kneading is the development of a highly elastic dough to ensure desired loaf volume and texture. Properly kneaded dough is smooth, shiny, elastic and cleans the counter or bowl in which it is kneaded.

During rising, fermentation continues as yeasts multiply, consume starches and sugars and give off CO2; 80°F is the optimum rising temperature.

Rising should not be hurried; flavor development may be impaired.

To meet schedule demands, rising dough may be slowed by refrigeration. Before I knew this, I had been known to go to town with my bread rising in a cooler in the back of my car! I now know that breads can be kneaded and then successfully refrigerated overnight, covered.

Second risings are usually suggested to further develop gluten and flavor. They may take less time than the first rising. Most bread recipes require two full risings before baking. The Focaccia (see recipe on page 178) and the One-rise Italian-style Bread (see recipe on page 179) are convenient exceptions to the rule.

Higher altitudes, having less atmospheric pressure, may speed the rising time required for dough to double.

When dough is properly raised, fingers poked into its surface will leave a dent.

After the dough rises, press it down to release stress in the gluten strands, let out excess CO^2 and redistribute the yeasts and their food supply. Next, form loaves and place dough in pans or on a lightly floured surface. Let it rise at least 10 minutes. This sets the structure of the bread before the shock of oven heat completes the final expansion.

Yeast activity accelerates during the first quarter of baking time before an internal temperature of 140°F kills it.

Focaccia

Try this wonderful one-rise Italian flat bread I learned to make while teaching with Richard Nelson in Astoria, Oregon.

Serves 2 to 6

Ingredients

2 1/2 cups all-purpose flour
1/2 teaspoon salt
3/4 teaspoon dry yeast
1 cup warm water
Cornmeal or Wondra flour
2 tablespoons good-quality olive oil (vegetable oil will suffice if you don't like olive oil)
2 cloves garlic, thinly slivered
1/4 cup Mozzarella, thinly sliced
1/8 cup fresh herbs, finely chopped (I like basil and rosemary. Green onions and parsley will do nicely if others are unavailable.)
Coarsely ground salt and freshly ground black pepper

Procedures

1. Combine flour, salt, yeast and water in a bowl.

2. Blend well and knead until dough is elastic and cleans the kneading surface.

3. Turn dough into a bowl greased with olive oil and cover the bowl lightly. Allow dough to rise about 1 1/2 hours, until doubled.

4. Preheat a cookie sheet or baking tile in a 425°F oven.

5. Press risen dough into a 14-inch circle on a cookie sheet sprinkled with cornmeal or Wondra flour.

6. Rub surface of the dough with olive oil; distribute the flavoring ingredients over the dough.

7. Allow dough to rise 10 minutes.

8. Slide dough directly on to the preheated cookie sheet or baking tile. Bake 12 to 15 minutes, until unevenly golden and slightly puffy.

Cut into wedges and serve hot.

One-rise Italian-style Bread

Makes 2 loaves

Ingredients

1 package (1 tablespoon) dry yeast
2 cups warm water (95°F to 105°F)
1 tablespoon sugar
1 1/2 tablespoons salt
6 to 7 cups unbleached flour

Procedures

1. Dissolve yeast in water. Allow 10 to 12 minutes for yeast to proof.

2. Combine sugar and salt with flour; add to yeast mixture 1 cup at a time. Use a mixer with a dough hook, an electric mixer at low speed or a wooden spoon. Add enough flour to make fairly stiff dough.

3. Knead dough until satiny in texture and somewhat elastic.

4. Place dough ball in a bowl and cover. Let rise until doubled in bulk.

5. Preheat an unglazed terra cotta baking tile, pizza stone or empty cookie sheet in a 400°F oven.

6. When doubled, turn dough onto a board and shape into 2 loaves. (If flour is used to prevent stickiness, keep it minimal.) I make this bread into 2 round or oval loaves. I have also shaped it into individual Italian rolls. In this case, baking time must be reduced.

7. Allow to rest 5 minutes, covered.

8. Slash loaf tops at least 1 inch deep.

9. Arrange on the preheated tile, stone or baking sheet.

10. Bake 40 to 45 minutes. Remove to cooling rack.

I have enjoyed adding prosciutto cubes, olives, garlic, cheeses and pepper to vary this bread. Whole-wheat flour may be substituted for about 1/3 of the white flour.

*"**B**aking is a relaxed art. There is no step in the bread baking process that cannot, in some way, be delayed or moved ahead just a bit to make it more convenient to fit into a busy schedule. It is also an inexact art, a forgiving one. A few grains more or less of sugar or salt or yeast will make little difference in the results."*

BERNARD CLAYTON, JR., BLOOMINGTON, IN; AUTHOR *BERNARD CLAYTON'S NEW COMPLETE BOOK OF BREADS* AND OTHER COOKBOOKS

FRENCH-STYLE WHOLE-WHEAT BAGUETTES

Makes 4 long loaves or 24 individual rolls

INGREDIENTS

1 package (1 tablespoon) dry yeast
2 1/2 cups warm water (105°F to 115°F)
5 to 5 1/2 cups unbleached white flour
2 tablespoons sugar
1 tablespoon salt
2 cups whole-wheat flour

PROCEDURES

1. Stir yeast into water to dissolve. Add a pinch of sugar.

2. Pour the yeast mixture into the large bowl of mixer with a dough hook and add 2 cups white flour with remaining sugar and salt.

3. Add the whole-wheat flour. Add more white flour, but only enough to result in a dough which, as kneaded, cleans the kneading surface.

4. Knead the dough about 4 minutes on a moderate speed until it appears glossy and elastic; or knead dough by hand until elastic and shiny.

5. Place dough ball in a large bread bowl which has been greased. Swirl the dough in the bowl and then turn the greased side up. Cover the bowl with a damp towel and allow dough to rise until doubled.

6. When doubled, turn dough out onto counter and gently press to remove air bubbles. When flattened into a casual rectangle, cut dough into quarters and form into long, thin loaves.

7. Fill greased baguette pans or shape long, free-form loaves. Cover. Allow the loaves to rise again until nearly doubled. Slash loaves on the diagonal in several places.

8. Preheat the oven to an accurate 450°F. If loaves are to be baked free-form, preheat 2 cookie sheets, too.

9. Bring a kettle of water to boil. Just before baking begins, put a pan onto the lowest oven shelf and carefully fill it with the water.

10. Place loaves, either in baguette pans or on the preheated sheets, on a shelf above the hot water.

11. Bake 15 minutes, spraying the loaves with water 3 times.

12. Turn oven heat down to 350°F and continue baking for about 30 minutes more. If loaves are browning too quickly, cover them lightly with a sheet of aluminum foil.

13. When loaves are completely baked, remove them from their pans to a cooling rack.

14. Wrap cooled loaves in foil and, if desired, freeze, double wrapped, for later use.

15. Warm unfrozen, unwrapped loaves at 300°F for 20 minutes. Reheat frozen loaves, wrapped in foil, at 350°F for 25 minutes.

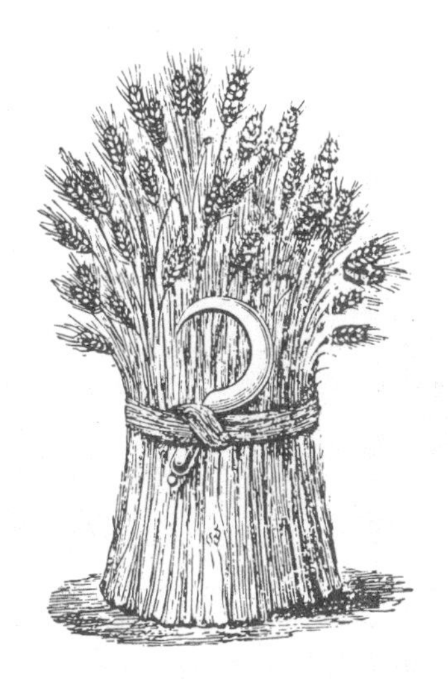

Cracked-Wheat Bread

Makes 2 loaves

Ingredients

1 cup 100% whole cracked-wheat berries
3 1/4 cups water
1/3 cup honey
3 tablespoons butter
2 teaspoons salt
2 cups whole-wheat flour
2 packages (2 tablespoons) dry yeast
1/3 cup powdered milk
4 cups unbleached flour

Procedures

1. Bring cracked wheat and water to a boil in a saucepan.

2. Cover the saucepan, reduce heat to medium and cook about 8 minutes.

3. Stir honey, butter and salt into cooked cereal.

4. When cereal mixture is lukewarm (100°F to 110°F), add whole-wheat flour, yeast and milk powder.

5. Beat mixture for 3 minutes.

6. Add 2 cups unbleached flour and continue to beat the mixture, while adding more flour, until mixture is no longer sticky.

7. With remaining unbleached flour nearby, knead the dough, adding flour by the 1/4 cupful until it is glossy and elastic when pushed.

8. Allow dough to rise, covered, 1 hour or until doubled.

9. Push out air from dough and allow to rest, covered, 10 minutes to relax elasticity.

10. Form 2 loaves and place in greased 9-inch loaf pans. Cover lightly.

11. Allow to rise again until doubled (about 45 minutes).

12. In a preheated 400°F oven, bake loaves about 30 minutes.

CROISSANT . . . KWA-SAWN . . . CRESCENT

I love baking more than any other task, and I am especially fond of the real, wonderful, tangy, crispy, flaky, buttery croissant (pronounced kwa-SAWN). With the advent of such fast-food threats as the croissandwich, I am turning into a croissant preservationist!

The croissant was a simpler, buttery crescent roll when it entered France late in the seventeenth century after the Austrian-Turkish war. Having expertise with puff-pastry work, a French chef tried making the merry crescent roll with puff-pastry techniques early in the 1900s. The flaky, golden miracle became the rage in France by the 1920s and has had a mystical romance with bread lovers to the present. The French eat light breakfasts: café au lait, preserves and pastry. The croissant is revered. Even the French Museum of Bread in Paris has croissant-shaped door handles. This delicate flaky pastry, made of hundreds of very thin layers, is an example of the French willingness to sacrifice all speed and practicality for the sensuous pleasure of something perfect on the palate.

Read all steps and tips carefully before beginning. Note the opportunities to slow the process by chilling the dough—use this technique to work the overall task into your own schedule. Enjoy the feel and smell of this unique dough. The satisfaction of making and eating these flaky masterpieces will be worth following the careful directives.

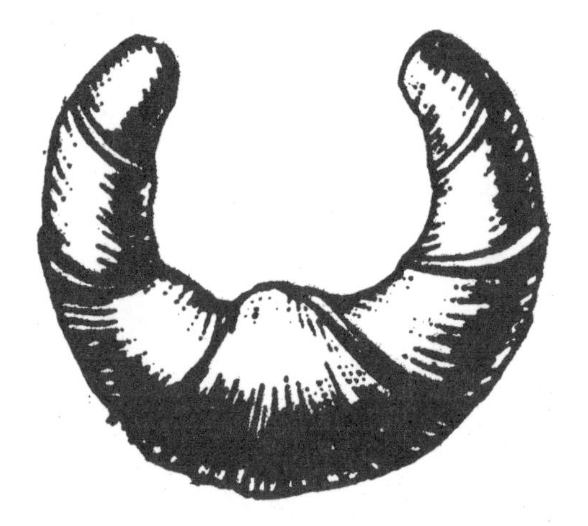

CROISSANTS

Adapted from Barnard Clayton's *Breads of France*

Making croissants is a long process which can easily and successfully be interrupted after steps 4, 9, 10 & 16.

Makes 3 to 4 dozen rolls

INGREDIENTS

For Rolls

8 cups all-purpose flour
4 teaspoons salt
1/4 cup granulated sugar
1/2 cup nonfat dry milk
1 package (1 tablespoon) dry yeast
3 1/2 cups warm water
1 pound unsalted butter, softened slightly

For Glaze

1 large egg
1 tablespoon milk

TIPS FOR SUCCESSFUL CROISSANTS

1. Knead dough very little.

2. The first rising should be only long enough to double the volume of the dough.

3. When rolling the dough, press it with the rolling pin to lengthen it. Roll only when absolutely necessary. Rolling activates the elastic proteins in the dough and will result in a rubber band reaction. When dough is too elastic to be forced to the proper measurements, give it a cool rest cover with a damp cloth.

4. In steps 9 and 10, refrigerate "book of dough," wrapped, if rests need to be longer than 15 minutes. (This keeps butter cold and intact, and retards rising.)

5. Cooled croissants may be frozen and reheated directly from the freezer at 350°F for about 10 minutes.

Procedures

1. In your mixer, or by hand, blend half the flour, all the salt, sugar, dry milk and yeast.

2. Stir in the water and beat until smooth and shiny. If using a mixer, change to dough hook. Slowly incorporate more flour to make a soft dough that will appear too soft. (It will firm in the chilling.)

3. Do not knead.

4. Place the dough in a rising bowl and cover tightly with plastic wrap. Chill 1 to 2 hours, minimum.

5. Roll the butter between sheets of waxed paper or foil to result in a 6-inch by 12-inch sheet of thin butter, 1/4 inch thick. Chill.

6. Remove dough from refrigerator and place on a floured surface.

7. Roll dough into an 8-inch by 20-inch rectangle. Place chilled butter onto the upper 2/3 of dough, leaving a 1-inch border around edge. Fold the unbuttered bottom 1/3 up. Then fold the upper 1/3 over. This will result in all buttered layers being separated by dough layers.

8. From this point forward, always treat your dough package like a book: Binding (the solid folded edge) is always on the left; page edges (open sides) are on the top, right and bottom.

9. Roll your dough "book" into a 12-inch-by-36-inch rectangle (see tip 3). Use a tape measure—you will be rewarded later for the bother. Fold and turn the dough "book" as before. Repeat the rolling and turning process. You will have now completed turns 1 and 2.

10. If the dough is too elastic to roll to the proper dimensions or if the dough is warming and soft butter is coming to the surface, wrap it in a cold, damp towel and refrigerate for 2 hours. After this rest period, complete 2 more turns. If you don't have time to let the dough rest, try to complete 2 more turns now.

11. Refrigerate overnight, tightly wrapped. Overnight chilling allows the dough to develop the flavor characteristics of the true croissant.

12. On a floured surface, roll dough to a 10-inch-by-44-inch strip. Often this is cumbersome. In this case, divide dough in half and roll each half to measure 10 inches by 22 inches.

13. Cut these strips in half lengthwise—having then 4 5-inch wide strips. Cut triangles from these dough strips.

14. Stretch and flatten the triangle with your rolling pin. It will be larger in all dimensions—and thinner. (I like my dough 1/8 to 1/4 inch thick.)

15. Form the croissant by rolling up the dough from the triangle base to the apex. Bend into the croissant (crescent) shape and place on baking sheet with the tip on the underside of croissant.

16. Allow the croissants to rise in a cool room, covered lightly, until doubled and puffy (about 2 hours). Rising may be slowed by refrigeration, to be completed later at room temperature.

17. Prepare glaze: Beat egg and milk together.

18. Brush croissants with egg glaze after rising is completed.

19. Preheat oven to 450°F and again glaze the croissants.

20. Bake about 10 minutes and check. Baking time can take up to 18 minutes, but I prefer them somewhere between 10 and 15 minutes usually. Ovens vary in temperature accuracy and circulation. I often rotate and turn the sheets.

21. Remove baked croissants immediately to cooling racks. (Or eat!)

In Search of Better Christmas Cookies

Too often, anticipation exceeds reality. Where Christmas cookie exchanges are concerned, this is sometimes true.

Each holiday season I receive invitations to cookie exchanges. I immediately imagine the smell of my cookies baking and the doily-covered plate laden with beautiful, buttery holiday cookies. Add to this image a simmering pot of hot spiced cider or wine and friends gathered around . . . savoring my splendid assortment of cookies. I will bake dozens of one delicious cookie recipe and then return from the exchange with a variety worthy of the Neiman-Marcus catalog.

Slowly, like the memory of vanilla's smell and the bitter disappointment of its taste, the ghastly memory of green cornflake wreath cookies, adorned with red hot candies, begins to creep into my mind. The vision of the inviting plate of cookies begins to fade. I remember that each year my cookie tin and I seem to arrive at the cookie table to find only the dreaded green things and assorted orphaned crumbs remaining.

Following are some recipes offered as an effort to raise the numbers of exchange-worthy cookies.

Swedish Cream Wafers

Makes 4 dozen

Ingredients

For Cookies

1 cup unsalted butter, softened
1/3 cup whipping cream
2 cups all-purpose flour

For Filling

1/4 cup unsalted butter, softened
3/4 cup powdered sugar
1 large egg yolk
1 teaspoon pure vanilla extract
Rind of 1/2 lemon, grated

Procedures

1. Blend the first 3 ingredients well and wrap tightly. Chill at least 1 hour.

2. On a lightly floured surface, roll the chilled dough to a thickness of 1/3 inch.

3. Cut the dough into 1- to 1 1/2-inch circles (approximately).

4. Transfer the rounds to a sugared surface and toss to coat them.

5. Place rounds on a cookie sheet and prick each twice with the tines of a fork.

6. In a preheated 375°F oven, bake cookies for 7 to 9 minutes until puffy and pale gold on edges.

7. Cool the cookies on a rack.

8. Prepare filling: Cream all the filling ingredients together.

9. Sandwich pairs of cookies together with the filling.

Food has everything to do with giving, nurturing and rejoicing in the bounty of life. I love being part of the international food community because it attracts people with a similar spirit.

My food philosophy:

❦ Use the finest quality ingredients

❦ Do as little as possible to change their purity and character

❦ Do as much as necessary to blend and enhance them

❦ Bake and cook with love and pleasure—it will show"

Rose Levy Beranbaum, New York City; author *The Cake Bible* and *Rose's Christmas Cookies*

Almond Macaroons

These cookies are often called for in old recipe books but are not readily available. They freeze beautifully and keep very well when sealed. Ground or chopped, they are a perfect addition to ice creams or tortoni (an Italian frozen dessert, see p. 159) or as coffeecake fillings or stuffed inside baked apples.

Makes 5 dozen

Ingredients

8 ounces almond paste (not prepared almond pastry filling)
1 cup superfine sugar (sold in a 1-pound silver box; easily duplicated with granulated sugar processed in a food processor or an electric coffee grinder—remeasure after grinding)
2 large egg whites, room temperature

Procedures

1. In an electric mixer, beat almond paste and sugar until light and creamy.
2. Beat in 1 egg white at a time—twice—at high speed until batter stiffens.
3. Using a pastry tube or moistened teaspoon, place cookies the size of a quarter on the cookie sheet.
4. In a preheated 300°F oven, bake 30 minutes, until nicely golden. (They should not be sticky.)
5. When slightly cooled, remove cookies to a lightly oiled rack to complete cooling.

Anna's Moravian Gingersnaps

To slice these cookies thinly, the dough must be chilled several hours.

Makes 9 dozen

Ingredients

3 1/2 cups all-purpose flour
1 cup sliced almonds
1 cup sugar
1 tablespoon ground ginger
1 tablespoon ground cinnamon
2 teaspoons ground cloves
1 teaspoon baking soda
1 cup unsalted butter, room temperature
1/2 cup dark molasses
Water, if necessary

Procedures

1. Combine the first 7 ingredients.
2. Blend butter and molasses into this dry ingredient mixture.
3. If dough is too dry to hold together, add water, 1 tablespoon at a time, until dough is moist enough to form into 2-inch-by-2-inch-by-9-inch logs.
4. Wrap tightly and refrigerate for at least 6 hours.

The dough can be made ahead and frozen. Thaw frozen dough in the refrigerator.

5. Slice dough as thinly as possible with a very sharp knife (1/3 inch thick maximum).
6. Arrange cookies in rows on a baking sheet, 1/2 inch apart.
7. In a preheated 325°F oven, bake 10 to 12 minutes.
8. Remove cookies from the sheet while still warm.

Mom's Chocolate-tipped Oatmeal Crescents

Yummy memories.

Makes 2 to 3 dozen

Ingredients

For Cookies

1 cup unsalted butter, room temperature
1/2 cup powdered sugar
2 teaspoons pure vanilla extract
2 cups all-purpose flour
1/2 teaspoon salt
1 cup quick-cooking oats
Water, if necessary

For Chocolate Icing

6 ounces semi-sweet chocolate
2 tablespoons milk

Procedures

1. Cream well the butter and sugar. Add vanilla and blend.

2. Mix remaining dry ingredients and blend with butter mixture.

3. Form dough into crescent shapes with your hands. If dough is too dry, add water by the teaspoonful until dough holds together. Make crescents about 3/4 inch thick and 2 to 2 1/2 inches long.

4. In a preheated 325°F oven, bake about 30 minutes, until medium-golden on the bottom and edges.

5. Prepare chocolate icing: Melt chocolate and milk together and stir until smooth.

6. Fill a shot glass with liquid chocolate mixture and dip 1 end of each cookie.

7. Place on a rack until the chocolate cools and sets.

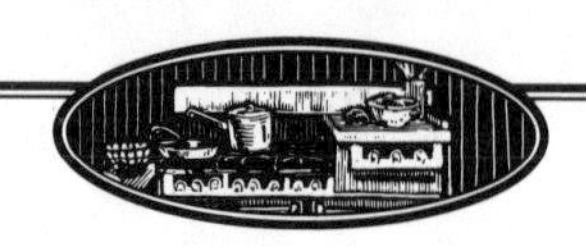

Making Brioche: A Heady Effort

"Hello, Pat, this is the *Chicago Tribune* food editor calling. I understand that you are giving a deli party. What a clever idea, what will you be serving? We'd like to do an article on it."

At that exact moment I was elbow deep in brioche. I didn't have much time to chat. I'd been working for years to make the perfect brioche. Flavor was important, but form was everything. The revered brioche à tête has a saucily cocked head. I'd seen them in French pastry shops. Japanese pastry-making technology had over-popularized the croissant but hadn't yet conquered the brioche, noted for its buttery, yeasty flavor, crumbly texture and perky appearance. I wanted baskets bulging with golden brioches for our party. This was my only day to polish them off. I remained calm as I described our party plan and menu. The scene would be as close to the sights, sounds, smells and tastes of the Place de Madeleine as we could recreate. "Could you give me the time and address for your party?" She asked. I was stunned. "You're coming to our party?" I blurted. My brioche had to be perfect, now.

Brioche is a bread dough enriched with butter and eggs. It can take many forms. I often make a double recipe. I let it rise through step 10, form some for immediate use and freeze the remaining dough in flattened portions for later use. Slowly defrosted until workable, this luscious dough can be rolled flat and filled, rerolled and cut into spirals for sticky buns, pinched and nestled together for pull-apart rolls or simply formed into loaves for slicing and/or toasting. Whatever the use, forming, rising, glazing and baking are all that is required.

At first glance, brioche appears time-consuming. The total time is lengthy, but necessary, for characteristic flavor development. You can control this process to accommodate your schedule.

A traditional breakfast brioche is baked in buttered fluted molds—or muffin tins—and sports a golden topknot. Lashings of butter, jam and/or honey magically transport me to a busy café where I don't speak the language well—and I don't care. Brioches are simple to make, easily frozen and more easily eaten.

Brioche à Tête

The dough may be chilled for hours or even days at steps 8 and 10.

Adapted from my favorite bread authority Bernard Clayton's *Breads of France*

Makes 12 to 20 individual rolls

Ingredients

For Rolls

5 cups unbleached flour
2 teaspoons salt
2 packages (2 tablespoons) dry yeast
1 tablespoon granulated sugar
1/3 cup dried milk
1 cup water, 95°F to 110°F
5 large eggs, room temperature
1 1/2 cups unsalted butter

For Glaze

1 large egg
1 tablespoon whole milk

Procedures

1. In the mixer, blend 2 1/2 cups flour with salt, yeast, sugar and milk.
2. Add water and beat to blend well.
3. Break eggs into batter 1 at a time and beat well after each addition.
4. Soften butter between your fingers and add to the batter.
5. Beat well to incorporate butter.
6. Add remaining flour by the 1/2 cupful until dough can be kneaded by hand on the counter.
7. Turn dough out onto a lightly floured surface and knead vigorously.
8. Allow dough to rise for 2 hours in a tightly covered bowl.
9. Press dough down and turn it over in the bowl.
10. Allow dough to rise 1 hour more, covered, then press down once again and refrigerate at least 6 hours.
11. Press cold dough out onto a lightly floured surface.
12. Divide dough into workable quantities; keep the rest covered and cold.
13. Roll the portions into ropes (determine this by the size of your brioche molds).
14. Form brioche by cutting the ropes into appropriately sized pieces.
15. Roll the pieces into egg-shaped ovals, one for each brioche roll.
16. With the side of your hand, roll the oval back and forth to create a shape having a "neck," separating an imaginary "head" and "body."
17. Lift this dough shape by the "head" and place it "body" first into the buttered brioche mold. When doing this, push the tips of your fingers beneath the "head" and through the "body" until you can feel the bottom of the mold. Let the head rest there.
18. Allow brioches to rise until they fill their molds.
19. Prepare glaze: Beat egg and milk together.
20. Brush the brioche with glaze, taking care not to get any glaze in the "neck" area. (Glaze may inhibit independent rising of "head" and "body" which contributes to individuality of brioches.)
21. In a preheated 375°F oven, bake brioche about 15 minutes, until richly golden.

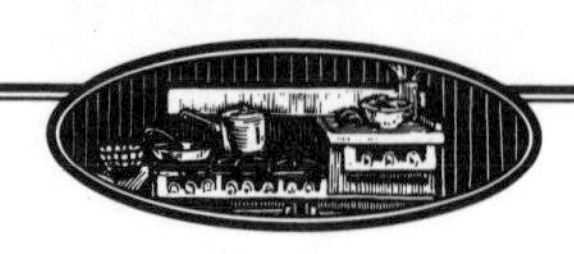

Tea & Scones: A Civilized Indulgence

The fattening, but very civilized, tradition of taking Devonshire Tea—tea served with scones, cream and jam—seems especially appropriate for a winter holiday such as Valentine's Day, when we expect certain indulgences. Tea drinking in Europe began in the mid-sixteenth century when Portuguese traders brought it from Macao. But the pleasure of "taking tea" was polished to a fine art by English royalty late in the seventeenth century. Today the habit of taking morning and afternoon tea remains alive throughout the remnant offspring of British colonialism. Used as a simple break from work, a casual time for conversation or an excuse to display grandmother's china and silver, a relaxed "cuppa" is an indulgence we all deserve.

While visiting New Zealand, I was reminded of the warming ritual of tea and scones. At a business meeting, colleagues adjourned for morning tea and I joined them for a chat. Trays of raisin-filled scones appeared. My conversation flagged. I was distracted. Gleaming bowls of crimson preserves and clouds of whipped cream waited, poised and anticipating.

The ritual of morning tea began: Split the tender scone, then slather with butter, heaps of cream and finally, inlay the jewel of strawberry jam. A decadent habit and the perfect Valentine treat! With a little fast talking, I soon found myself in the Christchurch Park Royal Hotel kitchen watching the scone makers.

Two days later I again encountered the "distinguished biscuit" aboard the Trans-Alpine Express. As I feasted on the scenery of the Southern Alps of New Zealand, my teeth again sank into fluffy scones. Pudgy matrons and rosy-cheeked children knew how to dress their scones properly: butter, cream, jam, mouth, butter, cream, jam, mouth—a good technique! Scones by definition are really very simple and austere little biscuits. But treated with well-deserved

respect, they become positively aristocratic.

The less the dough is manipulated, the better the scones are. They freeze beautifully—if there are any left.

Strawberry jam is not required, but it is traditional from England to New Zealand, from the Ritz and to the Puyallup Fair near Tacoma, Washington. Follow the easy recipe for light and buttery scones. Try the Lake Brunner kiwi jam when kiwifruit are on sale. Then invite someone special to share the pleasures of taking tea.

Basic Scones

Scone is pronounced "sconn" (as in gone) by "Kiwis."

Makes approximately 16

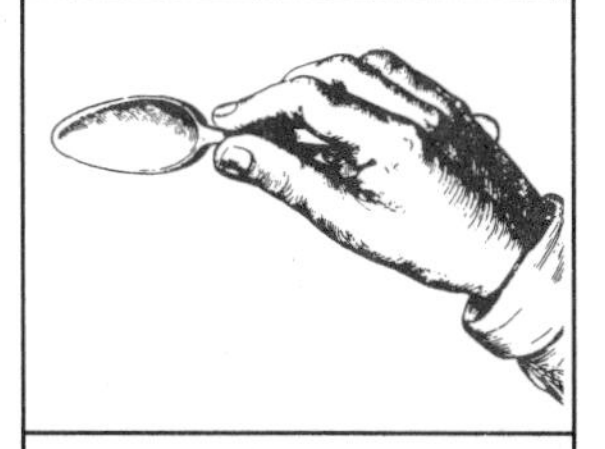

How to Determine Gelling Point

A candy thermometer (if accurate) should read about 194°F at an altitude of 5,000 feet or about 220°F at sea level. The gel point will be 8 degrees above the local boiling temperature.

Ingredients

3 cups all-purpose flour
4 1/2 teaspoons active baking powder (check date)
1/4 teaspoon salt
4 tablespoons butter, room temperature
1 to 1 1/2 cups milk (I use low-fat)
1/2 cup raisins, optional

Procedures

1. Sift dry ingredients together. (Sifting is important this time!)
2. Work butter into the flour with your fingers until uniformly distributed.
3. Add milk and raisins, if desired. Stir quickly with a fork, just to bind ingredients. (Dough will be frighteningly soft!)
4. Turn dough onto floury surface and pat lightly into a circle 3/4 inch thick.
5. Cut the dough with a circular cutter of desired diameter (mine is about 3 inches).
6. Place scones on a cold, ungreased cookie sheet.
7. In a preheated 425°F oven, bake about 10 to 12 minutes, until lightly golden.

For "Devonshire Tea," serve scones with butter, whipped cream and jam. They make exceptional fruit shortcakes, and with the addition of herbs or cheese, they are lovely with salads and soups.

Kiwifruit Jam

From Marion van der Goes of Lake Brunner Lodge near Greymouth, New Zealand.

Makes 9 1/2-pint jars

Ingredients

3 pounds kiwifruit, peeled, finely cubed and measured
1 cup granulated sugar for each cup kiwifruit
1 cup water
Juice of 1/2 lemon

Procedures

1. Mix all ingredients together in a non-aluminum pan.
2. Cook until sugar dissolves and the mixture will gel on a chilled plate. (See tip to determine correct gelling temperature.)
3. Distribute jam among canning jars.
4. Wipe jar edges clean with a cloth moistened with hot water.
5. Allow jams to cool slightly in the jars before sealing with a layer of melted paraffin.

Soup: The Whole is the Sum of its Parts

In soup making, parts are not necessarily just parts. Soups will mirror the qualities of their ingredients. As flavors marry inside the soup kettle, ingredient quality will magnify in importance.

The boiling of broth-based soups is often desirable to evaporate excess liquids and to intensify flavor. Certainly I am not suggesting that Thanksgiving's turkey carcass, accumulated poultry bones or the remains of the devoured beast do not make excellent soups. I am saying that cleaning the freezer and refrigerator crisper drawer will yield a soup with a quality directly proportional to that of the ingredients.

Don't freeze bones, herbs and vegetables for posterity. They will not improve with age. Freezer-burned meats will toughen during cooking. Keep a dated inventory and a well-organized freezer to rescue frozen treasures from petrification.

John Clancy, a noted chef and teacher of pastry making, was once asked, "Will this recipe freeze indefinitely?" His answer, though a little unsubtle, applies here: "Why are you making it?"

Use these soup recipes to fill your kitchen with wonderful flavors and smells this winter!

Alice Opler's Lamb Shank Soup

Makes at least 8 hearty servings

"Experiencing a wonderful meal can be as great as the magic of a tender moment. You have to be prepared and know how to savor it."

DORIS HÜLSMANN, PROPRIETOR LINDENHOF, TAVERNE, MEERBUSCH, BUDEREICH, GERMANY

Ingredients

4 meaty lamb shanks, tied inside cheesecloth or a non-terry towel
Cold water
4 sprigs fresh parsley
4 sprigs fresh thyme, or 1 1/2 teaspoons dried leaf thyme
10 black peppercorns
1 whole head celery, washed and cut into 1-inch pieces, plus leaves of 4 stalks
1 whole head garlic, cloves separated and peeled but not crushed
4 carrots, scrubbed, cut in half lengthwise and then into 1-inch pieces (peeling is optional)
3 leeks (white and light green parts only*), carefully cleaned and cut into 1-inch pieces
1 pound cultivated mushrooms, washed and cut into quarters
1 ounce powdered dried mushrooms
1/4 cup barley, rinsed
Salt and freshly ground black pepper to taste

Procedures

1. Place the wrapped lamb in a large soup pot. Cover with cold water.

2. Bring water to boil. Boil 5 minutes, skimming the scum from the surface of the soup. Add 1 cup cold water and repeat the boiling and skimming. Repeat the process 2 more times.

3. Tie herbs and peppercorns in cheesecloth and add to the pot.

4. Add remaining ingredients (except salt and pepper) to the pot, adding water, if necessary, to cover them.

5. Bring the soup to a boil, then lower the heat, cover and simmer for several hours, until meat is very tender and barley is cooked.

6. Remove the parcels of lamb and herbs.

7. Taste broth. If it's necessary to intensify the flavors, boil to evaporate excess liquids.

8. When cool enough, remove meat from bones. Add meaty pieces back into the soup.

Season with salt and pepper, if desired.

*Freeze the heavier, darker green part of leek for later use, or include it in the bundle with herbs in step 3.

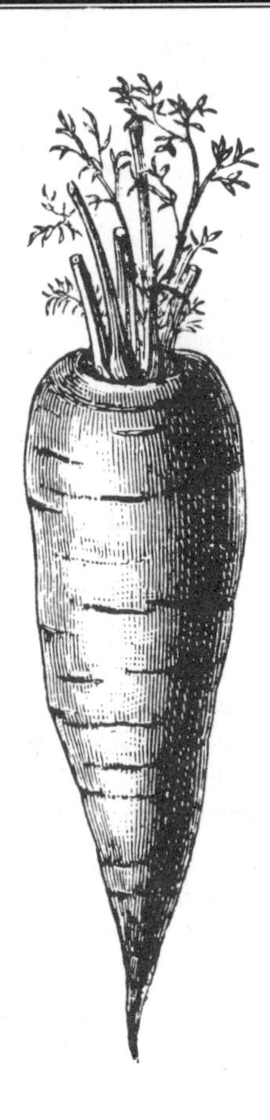

Busy First Lady's Soup

From Jane Sullivan, wife of Wyoming governor Mike Sullivan

Serves 4

Ingredients

1 pound ground beef
Dash Worcestershire sauce
Dash A.1 steak sauce
1/2 package dry onion soup mix
1 handful boxed stuffing cubes
1 large egg
1 large can vegetable juice, or 1 large can tomato juice
1 10-ounce package frozen mixed vegetables
2 carrots, shredded, optional

Procedures

1. Mix the first 6 ingredients, as for a meat loaf.

2. Form this meat mixture into 1-inch meatballs.

3. Pour juice into a large saucepan and bring to a boil.

4. Reduce heat and add meatballs and vegetables.

5. Simmer the soup until the meatballs are cooked, about 20 minutes.

Serve very hot.

SOUP-MAKING TIPS

❦ Never add salt to soup before it is completed. If reduction of liquids is necessary to intensify soup flavor, saltiness will magnify.

❦ A richer broth color can be obtained by roasting bones in a 500°F oven until dark, but not charred, before use in the soup. Unpeeled yellow onions will add nutrients and color to stocks. They must be strained out before completing soup recipe.

❦ The flavor of fat is water soluble. Clear soup stocks may be chilled, allowing fats to rise to the surface. Once solid, fats are easily lifted off.

❦ Never store hot soup tightly covered—it may sour. Cool first, then cover tightly.

❦ Connective tissues, gristle and bones can more efficiently be kept from the finished soup if meaty bones are contained in a cloth bag or cheesecloth before cooking. (Fabric stores usually sell cheesecloth by the yard. Buy the finer weaves.) The bag is easily removed; when cooled, chunks of meat can be taken off bones and then added back into soup.

❦ When peeking into the cooking pot is necessary, avoid a burned nose by lifting the soup pot lid in the direction away from your face.

Roquefort Soup

Serves 4 to 6

Ingredients

2 cups whole milk
4 green onions, cut into 1/2-inch pieces
8 ounces Roquefort or good quality Blue cheese
1/3 bunch parsley, washed and coarsely chopped
Salt and ground white pepper to taste
2 large egg yolks, beaten with 4 tablespoons heavy cream
Additional green onions, slivered
Croutons

Procedures

1. Bring milk and onions to a boil.

2. Crumble cheese into a blender or food processor and pour in the hot milk. Blend until creamy.

3. Return mixture to the saucepan and add parsley and seasonings.

4. Do not boil. Keep hot (or at room temperature for later reheating).

5. Stir 1 cup hot soup into beaten egg yolks.

6. Return egg mixture to the soup pot and reheat WITHOUT boiling.

7. If you want to make your own croutons: Cut French bread into 1/2-inch thick rounds. Rub with garlic, if desired. Grill, sauté in olive oil or bake in a 400°F oven until golden.

To make this soup in advance, I suggest not beating the eggs with hot soup until reheating. Then begin at step 5.

Serve soup garnished with slivered green onions and croutons.

Chicken Vegetable Soup

Serves 12

Ingredients

For Chicken Stock:

6 tablespoons vegetable oil
2 1/2 pounds chicken wings
2 large yellow onions, quartered
1 clove garlic, quartered
2 stalks celery, cut into 2-inch chunks
3 carrots, cut into 2-inch chunks
1 large tomato, quartered
1 leek, cut in half lengthwise, washed very well, then cut into 1-inch pieces
2 springs thyme
1 handful parsley
1 bay leaf
10 peppercorns

For Soup:

8 zucchinis, grated, tossed with 1 tablespoon salt and allowed to drain on a sieve 30 minutes
4 tablespoons butter
2 tablespoons fresh tarragon leaves
1 cup frozen green peas, defrosted
3 scallions, sliced thinly on the diagonal
3 chicken breast-halves, halved
1/2 cup crème fraîche
1 cup whipping cream
1 large egg yolk

Procedures

1. In a 450°F oven, brown chicken wings, onions, and garlic in a large roasting pan with the vegetable oil.

2. When oven mixture is well-browned, transfer it to a 4 to 7 quart stockpot.

3. Add vegetables, herbs, bay leaf, and peppercorns.

4. Cover with cold water.

5. Bring stock to a boil. Remove scum with a skimming tool. Add 1 cup cold water.

6. Bring to a boil again. Skim any more scum.

7. Cook all together, simmering, loosely covered.

8. Remove stock from stove and carefully strain the liquids through dampened cheesecloth.

9. Bring stock to room temperature before chilling, uncovered.

10. When chilled, remove solidified fat from top of stock with a metal spoon.

11. Bring chilled defatted stock to a boil and boil to reduce liquids and concentrate flavors as desired. Use this stock to make any chicken stock based soup.

To Make Chicken Vegetable Soup:

1. In a 400°F oven bake chicken breast pieces, boned, lightly coated in crème fraîche for 20 minutes.

2. Melt unsalted butter in a large saucepan.

3. Squeeze zucchini in a dampened non-terry towel to expel excess liquids.

4. Toss zucchini with melted butter.

5. Cook quickly until limp. Add taragon.

6. Cook 5 minutes on low heat, covered.

7. Cut chicken breast meat into 1- to 1 1/2-inch pieces. Reserve.

8. Place zucchini mixture, peas and scallions in a 4 quart saucepan. Add 2 to 3 quarts stock.

9. Bring soup to a boil, reduce heat to simmer.

10. Simmer 15 minutes.

11. Add chicken breast pieces and heat gently just before serving.

12. Beat egg yolk with whipping cream.

13. Add tablespoons of hot broth to the yolk/cream mixture until 1 cup volume is reached.

14. Stir egg mixture into simmering soup.

15. Do Not Boil.

Cream of Mixed Mushroom Soup

Serves 6 to 8

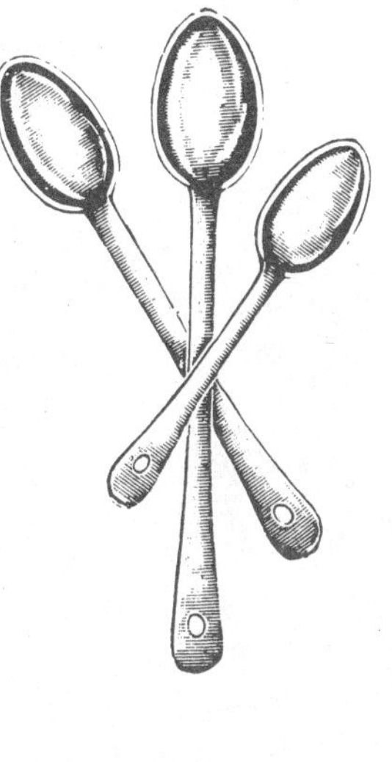

Ingredients

1 ounce dried wild mushrooms
1 pound domestic mushrooms, washed and trimmed to retain some stem
2 sprigs fresh thyme
2 small shallots, finely minced
juice of 1/2 lemon
4 tablespoons unsalted butter
6 cups chicken broth
1/2 cup whipping cream
2 large egg yolks
salt to taste
freshly ground pepper to taste

Procedures

1. In a two cup liquid measure, place dried wild mushrooms with water to cover.

2. Cover the measuring cup with plastic film and microwave on full power for 3 minutes. Allow them to stand covered while continuing.

3. Slice domestic mushrooms in 1/8-inch slices.

4. Melt butter in a large skillet until bubbly.

5. Place sliced mushrooms, thyme and shallots in the skillet. Squeeze lemon juice over.

6. Toss all together, cover skillet and sauté mixture until mushrooms are limp and have exuded juices.

7. Strain wild mushroom juices into a cup.

8. Chop wild mushrooms coarsely. Add to skillet.

9. Toss all skillet ingredients, then add strained juices. Heat to a simmer, stirring.

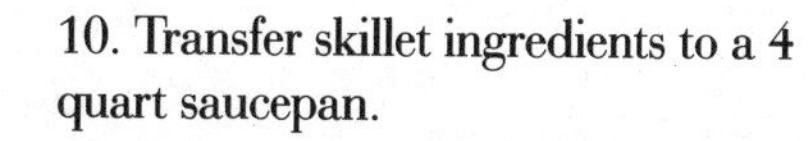

10. Transfer skillet ingredients to a 4 quart saucepan.

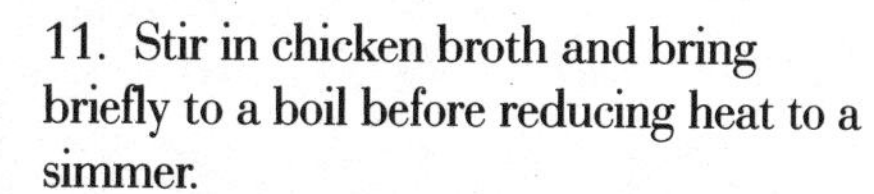

11. Stir in chicken broth and bring briefly to a boil before reducing heat to a simmer.

12. Simmer, covered, for 30 minutes.

13. Remove thyme branch.

To Serve:

14. Beat yolk with cream.

15. Stir spoonfuls of hot soup into yolk mixture until 1 cup volume is reached.

16. Return to saucepan. Heat through. Do Not Boil.

Turn Over a New Turnover

Turnovers make the ideal packable, hand-held lunch. Nearly all cultures have a turnover of some variety. Traditionally, the term *turnover* has meant a piece of pastry, filled and then folded or turned over, which is then baked or fried. Tastes in pastry crust vary. For some cooks, a crisp crust is the desired goal. Others specifically wrap their hot, freshly baked pastries in towels to entice the flavorful juices back into the crust.

While traveling, one discovers turnovers made in all sizes and called by many names. Large individual sizes may be served as a first course before dinner, a backpack lunch or, nicely garnished, as a luncheon dish. Cornish miners carry their pastries in their lunch buckets. Filled with a savory mixture of potatoes, carrots and onions, a small corner of the pastry may be reserved for a sweet surprise. Turnovers are popular worldwide as *chaussons* in France, *empanadas* in Latin America, Spain and Portugal, *chapatis* in India, *wontons* in China, *calzoni* in Italy, *pierogi* in Russia, *karjalan piirakat* in Finland and *paszteciki* in Poland.

Polish Turnovers

From Anna Moscicki

Makes 1 dozen 4-inch pastries

Ingredients

For Dough

1/2 cup milk
4 tablespoons butter or margarine, melted
2 large eggs
2 tablespoons granulated sugar
3 to 3 1/2 cups all-purpose flour
1 teaspoon salt, optional
2 1/2 teaspoons yeast, proofed in 1/4 cup water

For Meatless Filling

1 onion, chopped
1/4 pound mushrooms, chopped
1 to 2 tablespoons olive oil
1/2 pound spinach, steamed, or 1 box frozen spinach, defrosted (squeeze spinach lightly in a damp towel to remove excess moisture)
1/4 cup walnuts, chopped
1/4 teaspoon (approximately) nutmeg, freshly grated
Salt and freshly ground black pepper to taste

For Meat Filling

1 onion, chopped
1/4 pound mushrooms, chopped
1 to 2 tablespoons olive oil
1/2 pound leftover roast—venison, beef, lamb, pork, chicken or turkey, minced
Favorite spices and seasonings, for example, garlic, thyme, rosemary, basil, oregano, parsley
Salt and freshly ground black pepper to taste

For Glaze

large egg
2 tablespoons milk

PROCEDURES

For Dough

1. Scald the milk, then add melted butter.

2. In a bowl, beat the eggs with sugar until foamy.

3. Alternately add flour and milk to the eggs. Add salt, if desired.

4. Add the yeast and water to the flour mixture.

5. Add flour until the dough becomes kneadable. If you are unsure, remove the dough from the bowl and knead on the counter, adding small amounts of flour until consistency is elastic and satiny, not dry.

6. Place dough in a lightly oiled bowl and allow to rise until doubled, about 1 to 1 1/4 hours.

7. Turn raised dough out of the bowl onto a lightly floured surface and roll into a thick 12-inch square. Cover and allow to rise 15 to 20 minutes.

8. Roll out the raised square until it becomes a 1/4 inch-thick rectangle.

9. Cut shapes (2 1/2 inches by 4 inches or 3 inches by 3 inches) and roll slightly thinner before filling.

To Complete Turnovers

10. Prepare a filling (see procedures below).

11. Place 1 to 2 tablespoons filling onto each pastry piece and moisten the edges before sealing.

12. Prepare glaze: Beat the egg and milk together.

13. Glaze the pastries.

14. In a preheated 350°F oven, bake on greased baking sheets for 15 to 20 minutes, until golden.

For Meatless Filling

1. Sauté onion and mushrooms in olive oil until cooked; stir until excess moisture has evaporated.

2. Place the sautéed mixture and remaining ingredients (except salt and pepper) into a food processor fitted with a steel blade and chop until the consistency is that of a pâté (fine but not mushy).

3. Season to taste.

For Meat Filling

1. Sauté onion and mushrooms in olive oil until cooked.

2. Add the meat and heat through, making sure excess moisture is evaporated.

3. Process the mixture in a food processor bowl until the consistency is fine but not mushy.

4. Spice and season to taste.

Great served with a pot of soup and a salad.

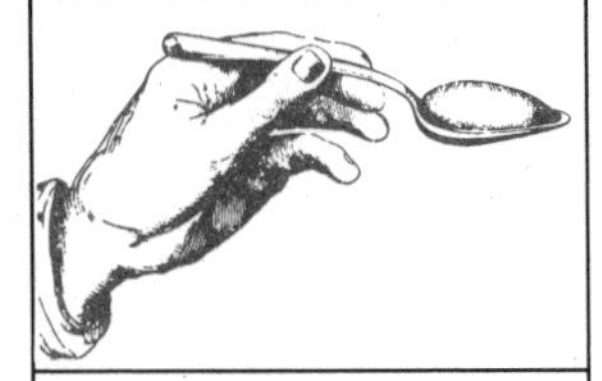

FILLING TIPS

❦ If the filling seems too dry, add an egg white.

❦ Fillings may be made ahead and refrigerated.

❦ Don't use cold fillings on warm dough. Bring filling to room temperature before using.

❦ A favorite canned pâté may be used, but be sure it is at room temperature.

Salmon or Tuna Turnovers

Makes 4–6 individual meal-sized turnovers

Ingredients

1 recipe turnover pastry (see preceeding recipe)
1 tablespoon green pepper, finely chopped
2 tablespoons mushrooms, finely chopped
1 hard-cooked egg, grated
1/3 cup heavy cream
1 teaspoon snipped dillweed
1 teaspoon fresh lemon juice
Salt and pepper to taste
1/2 cup cooked rice, cooled
6 ounces flaked salmon or tuna
1 beaten egg for glaze

Procedures

1. Roll dough into 6-inch circles, 1/8 inch thick.
2. Mix filling ingredients together thoroughly.
3. Fill turnovers by placing filling on lower half of the pastry circle, leaving a 1-inch edge.
4. Glaze edges of pastry with egg wash.
5. Fold top of pastry over filling.
6. Seal edges, pressing to seal securely. Crimp with fork or fingers to assure seal.
7. Bake about 20–30 minutes in a 400°F oven.

Veggie Turnovers

Serves 4–6

Ingredients

1 recipe turnover pastry (see recipe on p. 198-99)
1 cup broccoli, cooked, chopped, drained and cooled.
1 cup spinach, cooked, chopped, drained and cooled.
1 cup sliced mushrooms, sautéed, drained and cooled.
1 1/2 cups Swiss cheese, grated
1 cup jalapeño-pepper-flavored cheese
1 cup cooked wild or white rice, cooled
1 beaten egg for glaze

Procedures

1. Roll pastry to 1/2-inch thickness and cut into 6-inch circles.

2. Mix filling ingredients together.

3. Fill turnovers by placing filling on lower half of the pastry circle, leaving a 1-inch edge.

4. Glaze edges of pastry with egg wash.

5. Fold top of pastry over filling.

6. Seal edges, pressing to seal securely. Crimp with fork or fingers to assure seal.

7. Bake about 20–30 minutes in a 400°F oven.

Seeds: The Gift of the Opium Poppy

Poppy seeds convey a special color, texture and flavor whenever they are used. The poppy seed is a favored ingredient in the cooking of both Eastern and Western Europe. I am awaiting the revelations to come from the Balkan cuisines—a fringe benefit of our changing world order, I hope, that will surely expand our appreciation for poppy seeds.

The Cook's Encyclopedia: Ingredients and Processes (Harper and Row, 1981) tells us that poppy seeds come from the opium poppy (*Papaser omniferum*) cultivated in Asia Minor. Used as a drug in India and China since A.D. 800, the gray-blue seeds we can purchase in the store are apparently, botanically speaking, from the same species. The drug is obtained from the latex which oozes from the poppy pod. Food chemistry authority Harold McGee (*On Food and Cooking*, Scribners, 1984) assures us, however, that this latex never reaches the seeds. When the seeds are ripe, all traces of opium alkaloids are gone.

Today most commercial poppy seeds are exported from Holland. They are sometimes pressed for an edible oil I have yet to experience, and, when roasted, they are used in some curries.

I hope you will try some of my favorite ways to experience poppy seeds. Don't miss the recipe for Poppy Seed Coffeecake on page 84.

Poppy Seed Cookies

Makes 5 dozen

Ingredients

1 cup unsalted butter at room temperature
1 cup granulated sugar
1 egg yolk
1/2 teaspoon cinnamon
1/2 teaspoon ground ginger
1/2 teaspoon salt
1 teaspoon vanilla extract
1 1/2 cups all-purpose flour
1/2 cup poppy seeds
1 1/2 cups ground pecans

Procedures

1. Mix above ingredients together to form a fairly stiff dough. Add a few teaspoons of water if dough doesn't mass immediately.

2. Form into rolls 2 inches in diameter.

3. Chill the rolls, wrapped tightly.

4. Slice 1/4-inch to 3/8-inch cookies. Place onto an zungreased cookie sheet.

5. Bake in a preheated 350°F oven about 10 minutes, until edges are golden.

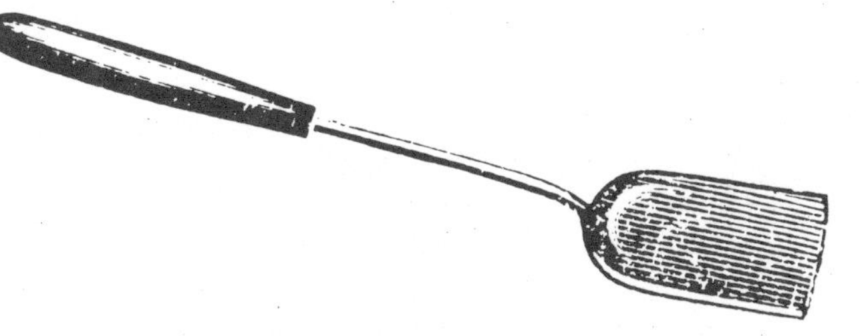

Poppy Seed Pancakes

Makes 2 dozen 4-inch pancakes

Ingredients

2 cups whole-wheat flour
2 cups all-purpose flour
1/2 cup brown sugar
1/4 cup poppy seeds
4 teaspoons baking powder
2 teaspoons salt
3 1/2 to 4 cups milk
1 1/2 cups corn or canola oil
6 large eggs
4 teaspoons vanilla extract

Procedures

1. Mix dry ingredients together well.

2. Beat eggs together with liquids and extract.

3. Beat liquids into dry ingredients until smooth.

4. Heat griddle or cast-iron skillet until medium hot.

5. Test heat of griddle with small drops of batter before beginning to make pancakes.

6. Serve pancakes with jam or syrup.

Karen True's Poppy Seed Coffee Bread

Makes 1 loaf

Ingredients

For Bread

3 large eggs
1 1/3 cups vegetable oil
1 1/2 teaspoons unsalted butter, melted
2 1/4 cups granulated sugar
3 cups all-purpose flour
1 1/4 teaspoons salt
1 1/2 teaspoons baking powder
1 1/2 cups whole milk
1 1/2 teaspoons almond extract
1 1/2 teaspoons vanilla extract
1 1/2 tablespoons poppy seeds

For Glaze

3/4 cup powdered sugar
1 teaspoon unsalted butter, melted and warm
1/4 cup orange juice
1/2 teaspoon almond extract
1/2 teaspoon vanilla extract

Procedures

For Bread

1. Beat eggs, oil, melted butter and sugar together thoroughly.

2. Sift dry ingredients together.

3. Mix milk, extracts and poppy seeds together.

4. Stir mixtures together just until moistened.

5. Grease a bread-loaf pan thoroughly. Fill loaf pan with batter.

6. Bake loaf in a preheated 350°F oven for 1 hour.

7. Cool 1/2 to 1 hour before unmolding.

For Glaze

8. Mix all ingredients and stir until smooth.

9. Pour glaze over unmolded loaf. Bread is most easily sliced when thoroughly cooled, 1 to 2 hours.

INDEX

A

Accompaniments
- chive and mussel sauce, 166
- *crème fraîche,* 68
- crunchy hazelnut wedges, 151
- horseradish sauce, 164
- Jansson's Temptation, 143
- kiwifruit jam, 191
- microwave polenta, 127
- quick provençal tomato sauce, 107
- polenta tart, 128
- Porcini cream sauce, 148
- potatoes fried with wild and domestic mushrooms, 146
- risotto Milanese, 172
- sun-dried tomatoes, 111
- toasted pumpkin seeds, 135
- twice-baked Idaho potatoes, 139
- wild rice with raisins and almonds, 155
- vinaigrette dressing, variations, 108

Almond: apple tart, 104
- coffeecake, 59
- *kugelhopf,* 156
- macaroons, 186
- pear tart, 104
- *tortoni,* 160
- wild rice and raisins, 155

Anchovies, in Jansson's Temptation, 143

Appetizers (*see also* pâté; terrine; pasta)
- crispy Brie or Camembert wedges, 30
- Finnish baked mushrooms, 145
- *fromage du jardin,* 65
- garlic potato madeleines, 143
- marinated trout seviche, 163
- ruffed grouse and partridge with artichoke hearts, 123
- smoked trout pâté, 165

Apple:*en papillote,* 27
- tart with almond, 104
- tart, French, 103

Artichoke: hearts with game birds, 125
- with risotto, 174

Asparagus and potato soup, 140

B

Baguettes, French-style whole-wheat, 180

Basics
- bread: baking, 177
  - leftovers, 28-29
- *crème fraîche,* 68
- croissant, 182-83
- edible flowers, 62
- *en papillote* cooking, 26-27
- ice cream, 72
- pasta, 32-33
- pastry for pies and tarts, 109
- pâté and terrine, 76-77
- quiche, 40-41
- risotto, 171
- scones, 191
- sourdough, 89-90
- vinaigrette dressing, 98, 108

Beef: parslied cube steaks, 44

Beverages
- lemonade, 48
- raspberry liqueur, 70

Blueberry muffins with lemon, 83

Brazilian coffee custard, 85

Bread
- baguettes, French-style whole-wheat, 180
- baking, 177
- *brioche,* 189
- cracked wheat, 181
- croissants, 182-83
- crumbs, making, 30
- *focaccia,* 178
- *kugelhopf,* 156
- leftover, 29
- *limpa,* Scandinavian, 25
- muffins: lemon blueberry, 83
  - pumpkin spice, 136
- one-rise Italian-style, 179
- *panzanella* (salad), 31
- poppy seed coffee bread, 205
- rolls, Swedish cardamom, 57
- scones, 191
- sour rye flat, Finnish *(hapanleipä),* 24
- sourdough: French bread, 91
  - corn bread, 92
  - starter, 90
- tips, 176

Brie wedges, crispy, 30

Brioche à tête, 189

Butter, herbed, 35

C

Cakes
- chocolate sheet, 132
- hazelnut sponge, 152
- lemon madeleine, 47
- strawberry whipped cream roll, 22
- tips, 132

Camembert wedges, crispy, 30

Celeriac salad, 100

Celery tian, 97

Cheese
- Brie or Camembert wedges, 30
- fondue with *risotto,* 173
- *fromage du jardin,* 65
- *risotto* Parmesan, 172
- Stilton and pear salad, 117
- strudel, 53
- Swiss, in veggie turnover, 201
- *tiramisù,* 87
- *torta dí ricotta,* 55

Cheesecake: Opler's, 51
- 15-minute, 52

Chicken: with hazelnuts and mushrooms, 149
- *en papillote,* 27
- soup with vegetables, 196
- terrine with vegetables, 80

Chive and mussel sauce, 166

Chocolate: mousse, Italian, 86
- mousse torte, 131
- pie, 130
- sheet cake, 132
- tart with pear, 119
- tipped oatmeal crescents, 187
- *tiramisù,* 87

Chowder, fish, 167

Coffee cake: almond, 59
- poppy seed, 84

Coffee custard, Brazilian, 85

Cookies
- almond macaroons, 186
- chocolate-tipped oatmeal crescents, 187
- Danish butter, 58
- frozen *kolackys,* 54
- hazelnut, 153
- ladyfingers, 88
- Moravian gingersnaps, 186

poppy seed, 203
Swedish cream wafers, 185
Corn bread, sourdough, 92
Crème fraîche, 68
Croissant, 182-83
Currants, 156
Custard: Brazilian coffee, 85
orange zabaglione, 161
tortoni, 160

D

Danish butter cookies, 58
Desserts. *See* cake; cheese; chocolate; coffee cake;cookies; custard; fruit; ice cream; pie; tart
Doves with Italian sausage, 122
Dressing, vinaigrette, 108

F

First course: fish chowder, 167
gnocchi, 36
pasta: with garlic and chilies, 37
herb, 35
spinach, 34
risotto: with artichokes, 174
basic, 171
with cheese fondue, 173
variations, 172
Finnish baked mushrooms, 145
Fish: chowder, 167
salmon, *en papillote*, 27
salmon or tuna turnovers, 200
trout: molds with shrimp, 166-67
en papillote, 27
pâté, smoked, 165
seviche, marinated, 163
smoked, in pastry, 164
Flowers, edible, 62
fromage du jardin, 65
herbed cream soups, 66
rice salad in tulips, 64
rose petals with peaches, 63
tips, 64
French: apple tart, 103
baguettes, whole wheat, 180
bread, sourdough, 91
onion tart, 106
Fromage du jardin, 65
Fruit
apple: *en papillote*, 27
tart with almond, 104
tart, French, 103
blueberry lemon muffins, 83
kiwifruit jam, 191
lemon tart, 49
macedonia, 159
peaches with rose petals, 63
pear: mousse, 120
en papillote, 27
salad with Stilton cheese, 117
tart with chocolate, 119
tart with hazelnut cream filling, 118
quiche, 42
raisin: *kugelhopf*, 156
sugar tart, 157
tips, 155
with wild rice, 155
raspberry: liqueur, 70
pie, 71
pudding, German, 69
strawberries: gratinéed, 21
Romanoff, 21
whipped cream roll, 22
Focaccia, 178
Fondue, cheese with risotto, 173

G

Game, wild
dove or quail with sausage, 122
goose breast, smoked, 125
partridge breasts, sautéed, 124
ruffed grouse or partridge with artichoke, 125
Garlic potato madeleines, 143
German raspberry pudding, 69
Gingersnaps, Moravian, 186
Gnocchi, 36
Goose breast, smoked, 125
Grouse, ruffed, with artichoke, 125

H

Ham: pasta with cognac, 38
terrine with aspic, 81
Hazelnut: with chicken and mushrooms, 149
cookies, 153
crunchy wedges, 151
filling with pear tart, 118
sponge cake, 152
tips, 151
Herbed cream soups, 66
Herbs (*see also* flowers, edible)
with pork and veal, 78

I

Ice cream: rhubarb, 74
tips, 74-75
vanilla nutmeg, 73
Italian: breads, 178-79
chocolate mousse, 86
macedonia of fruits, 159
risotto, 170-75
sausage, 122, 123
tomatoes, 110-13
tortoni, 160

J

Jam, kiwifruit, 191
Jansson's Temptation, 143

K

Kiwifruit jam, 191
Kolackys, frozen, 54
Kugelhopf, 156

L

Ladyfingers, 88
Lamb shank soup, 193
Leek salad, braised, 100
Leftovers: bread, 29
polenta tart, 128
Lemon: blueberry muffins, 83
lemonade, 48
madeleine cakes, 47
tart, 49
Limpa bread, Scandinavian, 25
Liqueur, raspberry, 70
Lorraine, quiche, 41
Low-fat skillet soup, 140

M

Macaroons, almond, 186
Madeleine cakes, lemon, 47
Meaty dishes (*see also* chicken; fish)
braised veal shanks, 175
ham terrine, 81
Italian sausage, 123

lamb shank soup, 193
parslied cube steaks, 44
pork and veal pâté with herbs, 78
pork tenderloins with mushrooms, 148
Moravian gingersnaps, 186
Mousse: chocolate, torte, 131
Italian chocolate, 86
pear, 120
Muffins: lemon blueberry, 83
pumpkin spice, 136
Mushrooms: cream of, soup, 197
with chicken and hazelnuts, 149
Finnish baked, 145
with fried potatoes, 146
Porcini cream sauce with pork tenderloins, 148
salad, 99
soufflé, 147
Mussel and chive sauce, 166

N

Niçoise, salad, 108
Nuts (*see also* almonds; hazelnuts)
Pecan pumpkin pie, 135
Sugar tart, 157

O

Oatmeal crescents, chocolate-tipped, 187
Orange zabaglione, 161

P

Pancakes, poppy seed, 203
Panzanella, 31
en Papillote: apples and pears, 27
chicken, 27
salmon and trout, 27
Parsley: with cube steaks, 44
using, 43
Partridge breast: with artichoke hearts, 125
sautéed, 124
Pasta: basic, 33
garlic and chilies, 37
gnocchi, 36
ham and cognac, 38
herb, 35
spinach, 34
tomatoes: with olives and capers, 39
sundried, 113
with tuna fish, 112
tips, 33
Pastry (*see also* pie; tart; turnover)
basic, 109
baking shells, 109
brioche à tête, 189
crunchy hazelnut wedges, 151
smoked trout in filo, 164
scones, 190
tips, 107
Pâté: basic, 76-77
pork and veal with herbs, 78-79
smoked trout, 165
Peaches with rose petals, 63
Pears: mousse, 120
en papillote, 27
salad with Stilton cheese, 117
tart with chocolate, 119
tart with hazelnut filling, 118
Peas potage, 44
Pecan pumpkin pie, 135
Peppers, tian of sweet roasted, 95
Pie (*see also* tart)
chocolate, 130
pumpkin chiffon, 134
pecan pumpkin, 135
raspberry, 71
torta di ricotta, 55
Polenta: microwave, 127
tart, 128
Polish turnover, 198-99
Poppy seed: coffee bread, 204
coffee cake, 84
cookies, 203
pancakes, 203
Pork: Italian sausage, 122, 123
tenderloins in Porcini cream sauce, 148
and veal pâté, 78-79
Potato: fried with wild and domestic mushrooms, 146
garlic madeleines, 143
gnocchi, 36
Jansson's Temptation, 143
low-fat skillet soup, 140
soup with asparagus, 140
soup with sorrel, 141
soup with tomato and basil, 142
tips, 139
twice-baked Idaho, 139
Poultry. *See* chicken; game, wild
Provençal cooking, 105-8
Pudding, German, raspberry, 69
Pumpkin: cooking, 133
creamy curried soup, 137
pecan pie, 135
chiffon pie, 134
spice muffins, 136
toasted seeds, 135

Q

Quail with Italian sausage, 122
Quiche: crustless, 41
fruit, 42
Lorraine, 41
tips, 42

R

Radish salad, 101
Raisins: *kugelhopf*, 156
sugar tart, 157
tips, 155
with wild rice and almonds, 155
Raspberry: liqueur, 70
pie, 71
pudding, German, 69
Rhubarb ice cream, 74
Rice (*see also risotto*)
salad in tulips, 64
wild, with raisins and almonds, 155
Risotto: with artichokes, 174
barolo, 172
basic, 171
with cheese fondue, 173
Milanese, 172
Parmesan, 172
primavera, 172
Rolls, Swedish cardamom, 57
Roquefort soup, 195
Rose petals with peaches, 63
Russian Garden soup, 44
Rye: Finnish sour, flat bread, 24
Scandinavian *limpa* bread, 25

S

Salad
braised leek, 100
celeriac, 100

dressing, 98
mushroom, 99
niçoise, 108
panzanella, 31
pear and Stilton cheese, 117
radish, 100
rice with tulips, 64
spinach, 99
Salmon: *en papillote*, 27
turnover, 200
Sauce
chive and mussel, 166
ham and cognac, 38
horseradish, 164
Porcini cream, 148
tomato, quick provençal, 107
tomatoes, olives and capers, 39
Sausage, Italian, 122, 123
Scandinavian cooking
almond coffee cake, 59
Danish butter cookies, 58
Finnish baked mushrooms, 145
Jansson's Temptation, 143
Swedish cardamom rolls, 57
Swedish cream wafers, 185
Scones, basic, 191
Seviche, marinated trout, 163
Shrimp with trout molds, 166
Skillet soup, low-fat, 140
Sorrel and potato soup, 141
Soufflé, mushroom, 147
Soup
busy first lady's, 194
chicken vegetable, 196
cream of mixed mushroom, 197
creamy curried pumpkin, 137
fish chowder, 167
herbed cream, 66
lamb shank, 193
low-fat skillet, 140
peas potage, 44
potato: with asparagus, 140
with sorrel, 140
with tomato and basil, 142
roquefort, 195
Russian garden, 45
Sourdough: basics, 89
corn bread, 92
French bread, 91
starter, 89
tips, 93
Spinach: pasta, 34
salad, 99
Stilton cheese and pear salad, 117
Strudel, cheese, 53
Sundried tomatoes, 110-11
with pasta, 113
with pasta and tuna, 112
Swedish: cardamom rolls, 57
cream wafers, 185
Swiss chard *tian*, 97
Strawberries: gratinéed, 21
Romanoff, 21
whipped cream roll, 22

T

Tart: almond pear, 104
chocolate mousse torte, 131
French apple, 103
French onion, 106
lemon, 49
pastry, 109
pear with chocolate, 119
pear with hazelnut filling, 118
polenta, 128
sugar, 157
torta di ricotta, 55
vegetable, 105
Terrine: chicken vegetable, 80
ham with aspic, 81
Tian: roasted sweet peppers, 95
Swiss chard or celery, 97
zucchini, 96
Tips: bread: baking, 176
crumbs, making, 30
freshening, 29
cakes, removing from pans, 132
croissants, 183
edible flowers, 64
hazelnuts, 151
ice cream, 74-75
en papillote, 27
parsley, 43
pasta, 33
pastry, 107
potatoes, baking, 139
soup making, 194
sourdough, 93
tarts, 103
turnover fillings, 200
Tiramisù, 87
Tomato: Italian with pasta and tuna fish, 112
sauce, quick provençal, 107
soup with potato and basil, 112
sundried, 111
sundried with pasta, 113
Trout: molds with shrimp, steamed, 166-67
en papillote, 27
pâté, smoked, 165
seviche, marinated, 163
smoked, in pastry, 164
Tulips, rice salad in, 64
Tuna fish: with pasta and tomato, 112
turnover, 200
Turnover: Polish, 198-99
Salmon or tuna, 200
Veggie, 201

V

Veal: braised shanks, 175
and pork pâté, 78-79
Vegetable dishes (*see also* mushroom; pasta; potato; salad; sauce; soup; *tian*; tomato)
chicken terrine, 80
French onion tart, 106
polenta tart, 128
Polish turnover, 198
risotto: with artichokes, 174
primavera, 172
veggie turnover, 201
Vinaigrette dressing, 98
variations, 108

W

Wheat: cracked, bread, 181
whole, baguettes, 180

Z

Zabaglione, orange, 161
Zucchini *tian*, 96